THE MEXICAN SHOCK

Other Works in English by Jorge G. Castañeda

UTOPIA UNARMED:
The Latin American Left After the Cold War

LIMITS TO FRIENDSHIP:
The U.S. and Mexico (with Robert Pastor)

THE MEXICAN SHOCK

ITS MEANING FOR THE UNITED STATES

JORGE G. CASTAÑEDA

THE NEW PRESS

NEW YORK

Part II translated by Marina Castañeda.

"The Mexican Difference" was originally published as
"Ferocious Differences" in *The Atlantic Monthly,* July 1995.

A slightly modified version of "Can NAFTA Change Mexico:
The Risk of Free Trade" appeared originally
in the September/October 1993 issue of *Foreign Affairs.*

"Democracy and Inequality in Latin America: A Tension of the Times"
was originally written for and with the support
of the Inter-America Dialogue and is published with its permission.

LIBRARY OF CONGRESS
CATALOGING-IN-PUBLICATION DATA

Castañeda, Jorge G., 1953-
    The Mexican shock: its meaning for the United States/
Jorge G. Castañeda.
    p.   cm.
    Includes bibliographical references.
    ISBN 1-56584-311-8 (hardcover)
        1. United States—Relations—Mexico. 2. Mexico—Relations—
        United States. 3. Mexico—Politics and government—1988-
        4. Mexico—Emigration and immigration. 5. Mexico—
        Economic conditions—1982-   . I. Title.
    E183.8.M6C27   1995
    303.48'272073'09049—dc20

95-23330
CIP

PUBLISHED IN THE UNITED STATES BY THE NEW PRESS, NEW YORK
DISTRIBUTED BY W.W. NORTON & COMPANY, INC., NEW YORK

Established in 1990 as a major alternative to the large,
commercial publishing houses, The New Press is the first full-scale
nonprofit American book publisher outside of the university presses.

The Press is operated editorially in the public interest,
rather than for private gain; it is committed to publishing
in innovative ways works of educational, cultural,
and community value that, despite their intellectual merits,
might not normally be commercially viable.

The New Press's editorial offices are located
at the City University of New York.

BOOK DESIGN BY HALL SMYTH
PRODUCTION MANAGEMENT BY KIM WAYMER

PRINTED IN THE UNITED STATES OF AMERICA

95 96 97 98   9 8 7 6 5 4 3 2

FOR MIRIAM, AS ALWAYS.

CONTENTS

CONTENTS

ACKNOWLEDGMENTS

The author is grateful to MARINA CASTAÑEDA
for her splendid and speedy translation,
the MONTGOMERY ENDOWMENT AT DARTMOUTH COLLEGE for its support,
the DEPARTMENT OF POLITICAL AND SOCIAL SCIENCES
at the NATIONAL AUTONOMOUS UNIVERSITY OF MEXICO for its cooperation,
and ABRAHAM LOWENTHAL for his comments
regarding three of the essays.

INTRODUCTION

RARELY HAS A COUNTRY COME UNDER SUCH INTENSE AND sudden scrutiny as Mexico in the past few years. Strictly for specialists, writers, and the romantic until the mideighties, the nation became, overnight, a perennial subject of analysis by neophytes, of endless reporting by a multitude of journalists, and of weighty investment decisions by countless merchant banks, mutual funds, and mom-and-pop investors. After years of being perceived largely as a problem for Washington, Mexico now became part of the solution: an apparently growing, dynamic, "emerging" market for U.S. goods and services—especially those unable to penetrate other markets and appeal to other tastes. Every detail of Mexican life, from the universities its leaders attended to the traditions and calamities of every one of its indigenous cultures, became an object of attention from abroad, particularly from the United States. The reason was obvious: as the debate over the North American Free Trade Agreement (NAFTA) and the fallout from the Mexican collapse in early 1995 proved, Mexico had suddenly become terribly important for the U.S. Unlike so many other countries in the post–Cold War world, what occurred in Mexico actually affected Americans in all walks of life, whatever their awareness of this relationship may have been.

There was no single, clear vision of Mexico behind this fascination. The view of the U.S. establishment—that what counted above all was Mexico's rush to modernity under President Carlos Salinas de Gortari, and its newly found addiction to free markets and the United States—was dominant, but by no means did it exclude other perspectives. The absence of representative democracy in Mexico, the egregious violations of human rights, the discrimination against the indigenous communities, and the overwhelming injustice of Mexican society were all detected and pointed out by groups

[1]

and individuals north of the border who, for different reasons, did not share the cheerleading optimism of the Bush and Clinton administrations.

The U.S. press reflected both facets of this new and rigorous examination, although by and large it tended to adopt the views of the friends and allies of the Salinas regime. Even before the NAFTA debate, the media, academia, and the subscribers to the so-called Washington consensus all lavished praise on Mexico's "new" English-speaking, U.S.-trained, market-oriented, and "reform-minded" leaders. Once a direct and immediate American interest emerged through the free trade agreement, this "tilt" became more pronounced. True, it never banished other approaches, and more critical opinions were never silenced.

Nonetheless, it scarcely prepared the American public, or policy- and decision-makers in Washington and New York, for that matter, for what came later: the shock of discovering that for whatever reasons, the Mexican house of cards could come crumbling down once again, as it had in 1976, 1982, and 1988. The crisis of late 1994 and early 1995 generated a double shock: one, that the situation in Mexico was so serious; two, that the press, the "Mexico-experts," and the financial community had been so mistaken. The way many of the members of these communities rapidly proceeded to make the same mistakes in relation to the new Mexican administration, insured that future shocks could not be far removed.

Despite these limitations, however, the discussion in the United States did take place, and involved—restrictions notwithstanding—all segments of the political spectrum.

This was not generally the case in Mexico, nor, with regard to dissonant Mexican voices, in the United States. The great debate about Mexico's end-of-the-century course, about the present and future nature of its relationship with the Unites States, its authoritarian past, and its dramatically deteriorating inequality, never really took place in Mexico. Nor did expressions of Mexican dissent truly figure in the mainstream U.S. debate over NAFTA, other than through the writings and commentaries of isolated critics of the Salinas government (myself among them). This monochrome landscape did not do service to the complexity and ambivalence of Mexico's attitudes toward the changes it was undergoing, and the lopsided reportage failed to capture the country's skepticism and deep reservations about many of the decisions made both at the presidential palace of Los Pinos and at the White House and on Capitol Hill.

This book attempts to fill those blank spaces for the American reader. It is written in an unmistakable tense: the systematic, virtually across-the-board criticism of the Salinas administration's program and of the authoritarian political system upon which it rested. The ideas, the narrative of events, the reflections and suggestions contained in the following chapters all spring from—are reactions to or outright rejections of—a number of basic premises that were outlined and incessantly repeated during the Salinas years, both in Mexico and the United States. Among my ideas that ran counter to the received wisdom of the day were the conclusion that the absence of democracy in Mexico was not just a political drawback but one of the principal causes of the glaring social inequities that plague Mexico; that cold-turkey, free-market policies would not solve Mexico's economic dilemmas; that only a combination of state and market, trade liberalization and protectionism, redistribution and integration with the United States could place Mexico back on the path of economic growth; and that a better and more constructive relationship with the United States could not be based on doing whatever Washington desired or on mistaking Mexico's interests for those of its northern neighbor. These were all seemingly counterintuitive views during those years; worse still, they contradicted the trend that seemed to be engulfing all of Latin America, not just Mexico.

The crisis that struck Mexico in December 1994, when the currency was devalued, the bottom fell out of the exchange and stock markets, and the Salinas-NAFTA bubble was punctured, vindicated some of these points of view, but not all. The crisis—which lasted well into 1995 and quickly spread to the political arena, as the former president himself was exiled and his brother jailed on charges of master-minding the murder of the secretary-general of the PRI, José Francisco Ruiz Massieu, in September of 1994—did succeed in rekindling the debate on the causes of and solutions to Mexico's travails.

After the fact, there seemed to be no shortage of experts explaining what went wrong. What a pity they did not raise their voices when the United States, Wall Street, the international press, the World Bank, the IMF, and the OECD were noisily celebrating Mexico's imminent entry into the First World. Hindsight and all, there are still plenty of questions that need answering. A handful come immediately to mind: Why were so many surprised by the collapse of the Mexican economy? Who was to blame for the disaster and how can similar debacles be avoided in the future? What can the United States do?

The international community should not have been surprised by the economic crisis that struck on December 20, when, just three weeks after his inauguration, President Ernesto Zedillo devalued the peso. Mexico had overvalued its currency before (in 1976 and 1982) and had paid an astronomical price for doing so. Moreover, most of what had happened leading up to the December 20 devaluation was warned of, written about, and clearly visible early on in the Salinas years. But no one, it seems, was willing to analyze the overwhelming evidence of abuses and financial mismanagement in Mexico since 1988. The Mexican economy began to run a huge current-account deficit with disappointingly low levels of growth from 1992 (nearly $25 billion of deficit and only 2.5 percent growth). The Mexican "miracle" was quite special: bountiful imports and no significant expansion of the economy. In 1993—well before the political turmoil of Carlos Salinas's last year in office, when the peso should have been devalued, according to those in the U.S. who were supposedly (though only in private) counseling Mexico in that direction—Mexico experienced negative per capita growth.

The country still required more than $20 billion in short-term speculative capital flows to finance its yawning external gap, and volatile portfolio investment accounted for more than two-thirds of those flows. It was also not difficult to spot the glaring signs of corruption in Mexico under Carlos Salinas de Gortari. The revelations of abuses and sheer delinquency in which the outgoing administration engaged should have surprised no one. Credible reports about the corruption and excesses of several members of the Salinas family were widespread in Mexico City, as were the growing strength and ubiquity of the nation's drug lords. Those surprised by the economic collapse and the stench of it all had simply neglected to open their eyes.

The blame for the debacle itself, however, lies elsewhere. It must first of all be placed squarely on the lack of democratic reform in Mexico under Salinas. Economic mistakes, political abuses, and the dramatic increase of inequality in what was already one of the world's most unjust societies might not have been entirely avoided through democratic rule and authentic accountability, but they were absolutely inevitable in the absence of representative democracy. Without it, overcoming the weight of tradition, corruption, and triumphalism (often fanned from abroad) was simply impossible. It was not just a pity, however, that Salinas did not practice *glasnost* along with his supposed—and failed—*perestroika*; the lack of the former condemned the latter to dogmatic zeal and ultimate failure. The restraints that democratic politics would have imposed on Salinas's "modernization" drive and economic reforms would have allowed Mexico to achieve the right mix of change and stability, modernity and tradition, competitiveness and justice.

But the Salinas cheerleaders abroad must also share part of the responsibility for the crash of '95. The whiz-kid brokers and venerable investment firms, like the bankers in the late seventies, simply poured money into Mexico. They did not bother with niceties such as learning something about the "emerging market" they were hawking and benefiting from. The Bush and Clinton administrations also reinvented Mexico as a "modern, outward-looking, reform-minded country" in order to sell NAFTA to a reluctant Congress and a skeptical American public.

Washington deliberately overlooked or downplayed the social effects of the economic model in Mexico. The latter contributed to—though they did not cause—widespread unemployment, the Chiapas insurrection, the political assassinations of 1994, gross official corruption, and the growth of the drug trade. These effects in turn affected the economy. How did U.S. officials want their protégés in the PRI to win the 1994 elections, if not through massive spending, pump-priming, and statistical deceit, given that electoral fraud was no longer tolerable? Would they really have accepted a devaluation of the Mexican currency during the NAFTA debate in 1993, or before Mexico's elections in the summer of 1994, or on the eve of the U.S. midterm elections in November?

For over eighty years, traditional U.S. policy toward Mexico helped the two nations live peacefully and for the most part harmoniously. The two premises of that policy were that Washington sought to maintain stability in Mexico over and beyond immediate business, sectoral, or short-term domestic political concerns. Secondly, U.S. policy acted on the conviction that, whatever our peculiarities or problems, we Mexicans were best able to guarantee that stability. By imposing on Mexico one of the most draconian austerity programs in memory, Washington violated the first tenet; the United States placed the protection of Wall Street investors ahead of safeguarding long-term stability in Mexico. And by seeking to micro-manage the Mexican economy from the U.S. Treasury Department, the United States disregarded the second tenet.

Mexico's famed stability is not eternal and must not be taken for granted. Few nations in the world would have accepted the loan conditions Washington demanded of Mexico—and for good reason; those conditions led to the most drastic recession and to the most serious social crisis in Mexico in decades. The United States has been able to avoid instability on its borders since the

Mexican Revolution, almost a century ago. But the authoritarian stability that Mexico enjoyed for sixty-five years is over; the transition to democratic governance will continue to be painful and turbulent. It will also, in all likelihood, be costly. The Clinton administration would have done well to acknowledge these facts and stop hoping matters would improve overnight thanks to a couple of speeches, an injection of money, and wishing the problem away.

Washington should stop applauding the Mexican strongmen: before and after Carlos Salinas, Mexico's presidents have been a principal cause of Mexico's corruption and collapse. For too long, everyone postponed democracy in Mexico and then expected that a burst of economic reform and enlightened despotism would fix everything. That recipe failed spectacularly. The only way forward is profound political and social reform to balance the economic blows that have devastated Mexico over the past couple of years.

The book is organized in a sequence that unifies segments that, in their initial version, were written at separate times and for different audiences. It begins with a reflection on the single most important reason why Mexico should matter to Americans: immigration. It then seeks to lay out the broader, more abstract differences between the two nations, partly as an explanation for the way in which Mexico always surprises the Americans, partly as an attempt to understand why there is a deeper reaction in the United States to immigration from Mexico, partly as a commentary on the themes the NAFTA debate in the United States glossed over in regard to Mexico.

The next chapter—written in the heat of the NAFTA debate—was originally intended to address several of the main Mexican issues in that debate, and to warn against some of the negative consequences the free-trade agreement might have if it was not accompanied by fundamental changes in the way in which Mexico was governed. It leads directly to the following section: a detailed scrutiny of the series of events which occurred in Mexico throughout 1994 and in early 1995, with special emphasis on the (missed) electoral opportunity of August 1994. The premise of that long section, and the reason why the pre- and post-election issues are examined in it in extenso, is that Mexico had an opportunity to truly change in 1994 and, for many reasons, did not.

The consequences of that failed transition are reviewed in the last two installments of that section, as they are dedicated to the reemergence of violence, assassination, and the drug barons in Mexico, and to the devaluation and subsequent economic debacle that began on December 20, 1994. The last chapter seeks to place the Mexican conundrum in a broader Latin American context. It contends that the tension existing throughout the region between inequality and representative democracy is real, lasting, and pervasive; that the Mexican dilemma, while perhaps more acute and present today than that of other nations in the hemisphere, is part of a broader problem, whose origins are historical and social. While no solution exists to the problem in itself, there are better (and worse) ways to manage it.

This book, then, purports to explain what happened in Mexico since late 1993, as well as why the events that have shaken the country since then matter—and should matter—to Americans. It also revisits the differences between Mexico and the United States, emphasizing the difficulties involved in the marriage of two such contrasting societies. These pages should be read as the ropes and slats of a bridge between two worlds: a bridge that may never be completed, but whose construction should never cease.

PART I

THE UNITED STATES AND MEXICO

CHAPTER 1

*Mexico and California: The Paradox of Toleration
and Democratization*

NEVER AS IN RECENT YEARS HAS MEXICO MADE LIFE SO DIF-
ferent—difficult, some would say—for the United States. One issue
after another—NAFTA, Proposition 187 in California and immigration in general, the $50 billion bailout of 1995—has kept this
complex and confounding relationship on the front page, on the
White House agenda, and on the congressional floor. However
much one should warn against neophyte Mexicanists "discovering"
a country and a cluster of problems that have in fact existed for
decades, the process of economic integration has changed matters:
Mexico affects the United States in ways and intensities that are qual-
itatively distinct from those of years gone by.

The differences between these many impacts are multifold, but
perhaps the central distinction lies in their varying localization and
intensity. Mexico's economic implications for the United States
involve, to one degree or another, all Americans. At the same time,
the import of the economic sphere is relative: the sizes of the two
economies are too asymmetrical for Mexico really to make much
of a mark on the U.S. on a macroeconomic scale. Conversely, though
immigration entails tremendously significant consequences viewed
positively and negatively—for those Americans touched by it, those
Americans are still few and far between. It is always worth recalling that fully half of the Mexican immigrants in the United States
—documented or not—remain in California and that a substantial proportion of the other half is concentrated in Texas, Illinois,
and, more recently, in Florida and New York. Indeed, Mexican
immigration to the United States, and the immigration issue in the
U.S., is essentially a California matter—which explains why
Proposition 187 sprang forth on the West Coast and why the
Mexico-California connection is worth dwelling on at all.

As the lines below suggest, over and beyond the traditional

[13]

arguments regarding the pluses and minuses of immigration in general, there are political connotations to the migratory flows that have led Mexicans to California for nearly a century now. These connotations do not erase the classical arguments. Mexicans head north because the U.S. offers them (relatively) good jobs at (relatively) decent wages (that is, there is a sustained demand for their labor) and because of the absence of the same attraction at home (that is, there is a surplus of labor in Mexico). If the two conditions had not coincided continually over the years, immigration from Mexico to the U.S.—legal or not—would have ceased years ago. How much insistence there is in the north on the legality of the flow and how much persistence there is in the south to overcome new impediments to immigration are all secondary matters, determined by circumstantial factors such as the business cycle of the two economies, the swing of the ideological pendulum in the United States, and regional politics in Mexico.

Each country has benefited from this long-standing arrangement, both from the substance and the form. For those sectors of agriculture and industry in California that have traditionally exploited cheap, unprotected Mexican labor, the presence of an almost infinite supply of *mojados* has permitted higher profits, greater competitiveness, and, in many cases, simple survival: without Mexicans to harvest the produce, it would rot in the fields. There was no other way of employing Mexicans except without documents. Fully complying with the law would have entailed higher wages and fringe benefits, a political backlash from other economic sectors, and an enticement to emigrate for many more Mexicans than those who could find employment in the California valleys, fertile as they are. For Mexico, emigration has also served several purposes, some of them undeniably perverse: it has opened job slots in an economy incapable of generating employment for all; it has brought sustained remittances to Mexican families that have relatives working across the border and this influx of dollars has become a significant source of income for depressed regions, on occasion contributing to reduce the imbalance of Mexico's foreign accounts; it has provided an "exit" for those who could have a "voice" (following Albert O. Hirschman's trade-offs), thus helping to perpetuate the authoritarian nature of the Mexican political system.

There were—and still are—other downsides for both nations. For Mexico, as is often the case with emigrant nations, the "best and the brightest" in each family, in each town, in each region, tend to leave, or so it is generally thought, although there is little evidence to substantiate this conviction. And for the United States, two important drawbacks are implicit in the immigration *quid pro quo*. Firstly, the undocumented or illegal nature of much of the flow runs counter to the legalistic nature of a society that has little else to hold it together beyond the belief in and devotion to the rule of law. The only sustainable and useful flow has been partly illegal; deterring it or doing without it—were this a viable option—would have been worse than the alternative. But the very idea of countenancing an ongoing, widespread, and flagrant violation of legality contradicts the myths and needs of American ideology.

Secondly, as Manuel García y Griego and others have emphasized, broad-scale undocumented immigration in California functioned as a progressive income tax, precisely at a time when Californians—and Americans in general—were rebelling against taxation, particularly against progressive taxation. Because migrant workers incomes are lower than those of virtually the entire rest of society, Mexicans in California pay less tax in relation to their income than others; that is the principle of progressive taxation. They do pay taxes: income and social security taxes are deducted from their paychecks; property taxes are assessed indirectly through their rents; sales tax and indirect taxes on cigarettes, liquor, and so on are levied against them whenever they buy things. There is nothing as false as the idea that undocumented immigrants do not pay taxes. But they do pay less than others, not because they are immigrants, but because they are poor.

Mexicans in California also use many of the services financed by taxes—such as public schools, and public transportation and housing (when it exists)—more than most other segments of society. That is the redistributive logic of progressive taxation: the poor pay less and receive more. The problem is not economic or even political; it is psychological. At a time when so few Americans still subscribe to the principle of the redistribution of wealth and the need to actively reduce inequality in society, the very fact that the white, suburban, middle-aged middle class should be paying taxes to provide services to Mexicans—that is, to the brown, Catholic, Spanish-speaking poor—became anathema. Pile on the California recession of the early nineties and the undeniable growth in the sheer numbers involved, and Proposition 187 becomes explainable, if not understandable.

The proposition on the 1994 California ballot sought, effectively, to bring to an end the tacit arrangement that had governed Mexican immigration to California for decades. By denying basic services to immigrants without papers, by weeding their children out of public schools, by ostracizing and intimidating them as much as possible, the initiative sought to upset the previous balance and to square the circle: Let there be less immigration and let it be legal—all of this at a cost paid by someone else: the federal government. The effects of Proposition 13, which passed nearly twenty years earlier and, the recession that began in 1991, hitting California (chiefly its southern regions) harder than any other area of the country, together with the effects of nearly a decade of a "double immigration whammy," all converged in November 1994 to bring forth perhaps the single most conflictful change in the U.S.-Mexican status quo since the mass deportations of "Operation Wetback" in 1954.

The premise for the "double whammy" was probably initially identified by Mexican scholar Jorge Bustamante, but just about every immigration expert on either side of the border has long known about it. The "push-pull" effect is truly the decisive determinant of the intensity, size, and evolution of migratory flows. Not until the 1980s had this effect operated in a context that was doubly favorable to high immigration from Mexico to the United States. From 1982 onward, the Mexican economy found itself, at least through 1990, in a state of utter prostration: zero growth in absolute terms, negative expansion per capita. Simultaneously, the U.S. economy was experiencing the Reagan "boom": artificial, doomed from the start, and pregnant with countless vices for the future, but unquestionably dynamic. Moreover, the kind of labor that the American economy was demanding in greater and greater volumes during those years was exactly the type Mexico was generating in untold quantities: cheap, unskilled, unstable. Mexico's working-age population was growing at a faster rate than ever before, even if the fertility rate of the entire population was finally beginning to drop. And Mexico was providing fewer jobs than ever for these exploding cohorts, whose talents and specifications were more sought-after than ever in the United States. The result was certainly not difficult to forecast: more immigrants than ever before, mostly undocumented, since legal quotas did not rise during the 1980s.

This trend is neatly illustrated by the fact that New York became a Mexican immigrant town in the space of just ten years. In the early 1980s, Mexican-accented Spanish was virtually unspoken in the Big Apple: the norm was Puerto Rican, Dominican, some Colombian, perhaps a bit of Cuban Spanish left over from the sixties or spilled over from New Jersey. There were fewer than twenty-five thousand Mexicans in the entire New York area, most of them living in New Rochelle and Yonkers, north of the city. By 1990, the Mexican consulate was estimating—based on registrations, documents issued, and work load—that approximately 250,000 Mexicans lived in the metropolitan area: a tenfold increase in ten years. Every flower shop on the sidewalks of the urban canyons, every backroom of a restaurant, every Korean grocery store with a helper—there one will find young men, and some women, from Puebla (nearly all), Oaxaca, and Guerrero.

If the same thing was happening on the other side of the continent and California was still receiving half of all expatriates from Mexico, no wonder, then, that a majority of the Golden State's voters—though well under half its inhabitants—decided that enough was enough. They were wrong, and the damage they may eventually do to themselves with simplistic recourses such as Proposition 187 could be disproportional to the possible benefits they expected, but their attitude was logical enough. Its limitations lay in not comprehending or studying the real nature of Mexico's effect on California, and in the absence of leadership in adjusting policy to reality.

BROADWAY IN DOWNTOWN LOS ANGELES IS A MEXICO CITY shopping street, what San Juan de Letrán was in days gone by: crowded, noisy, boisterous, and overwhelming. Los Angeles is in a time warp: its Mexican neighborhoods resemble Mexico City's years ago, before they were either bulldozed for *ejes viales* (high-speed multilane avenues) or intolerably overpopulated by the explosion of the informal economy. It reminds any *chilango* of his home town —or, in any case, of what it used to be. Long ago, the workers and women of the job-holding-poor sectors of Mexican society would shop downtown on weekends, where shopping was dignified: in cheap but well-supplied stores, on the main streets but off the sidewalks: Broadway. Today their choice is between a poor man's version of a California mall and the Lima-like *tianguis* sprawling over and across the streets of the inner city: a part of Mexico City's past has moved north.

Mexico's effect on California is of course much more than this, but it starts in the sights, sounds, fragrances, and memories evoked by two cities that have more in common than either appreciates. The influence Mexico is bringing to bear on the society of its northwestern neighbor lies here: urban and different, unassimilable and obtrusive. Mexico's presence is still felt in the orchards and fields of the Central Valley, but it is more prevalent in the parking lots, restaurants, and gardens of Los Angeles, and in the twenty-first-century manufacturing plants of Silicon Valley.

Mexico acts on California society directly, through the millions of expatriates who bring their lives and families, language and food, music and mores to a foreign land that can scarcely handle the resulting cultural and political explosion. Its impact is immediate and apparently cultural, but below the surface it is political. Mexico helps establish what Mike Davis, in *City of Quartz,* called the basic Californian distinction between "those who work and those who vote."[1] The massive numbers of Mexican (and Central American) undocumented immigrants who swell the bottom tier of an increasingly two-tier society are not only excluded socially and economically and disenfranchised politically, they are barred from even formal national belonging. Thus, immigration from Mexico in its undocumented, politically maimed form is directly linked to the "dedemocratization" of California society.

Mexican immigration to the United States differs from previous migratory waves by virtue of the twin phenomena of contiguity and continuity. Emigrating from next door produces sharply different effects on the mind-set and lifestyle of the migrant than does embarking on a long, once-in-a-lifetime voyage with no return. Modern technology has enhanced this distinction: the modern-day "*mojado* red-eye*" daily, nonstop flights from León, Guadalajara, or Zacatecas packed with migrants—some legal, some not—are a far cry from the ships that brought millions of Europeans ashore on Ellis Island. Continuity also makes a difference. Previous waves of immigration were of fixed duration; they came to a halt after a certain period. Mexican emigration to the United States will soon enter its hundredth year, according to accounts from the sending communities of Guanajuato and Los Altos de Jalisco and the reports of Mexican immigrants used to break strikes at steel mills in Gary, Indiana, before the turn of the century. This emigration shows no signs of stopping; every demographic, economic, or social projection minimally rooted in reality foresees it lasting well beyond the year 2000.

Contiguity and continuity mean that the impact of Mexican emigration on the home country is very different from that of its precursors—or even contemporary flows from Asia and Central and South America. In contrast to other eras, countries, and contexts, Mexican immigration to California has a "blow-back" cultural effect on Mexico. It is not a one-shot deal, a once-and-for-all event with no return, halfway measures, or shades of consummation. On the contrary, study after study has shown that Mexicans, be they from rural communities or urban centers, come and go for a sustained period of time before—in many cases but not all—they finalize their departure from Mexico. In the coming and going process, Mexicans take back with them many of California's darker facets, but also its most positive ones: tolerance, a significant degree of democratization, familiarity with "the other side." At a time when so many detrimental influences are flowing from the United States to Mexico, California's democratizing impact is beneficial. Mexico should seek even greater access to this democratic, open, plural, and tolerant side of American life, which the migrants do not encounter often enough, but which they cannot help but contrast with the many closed, archaic, and narrow-minded facets of Mexican society. Notwithstanding the bitterness, deceit, and even absurdity of some returning migrants' claims of success and glory "*del otro lado,*" these expatriates bring back much of what the rest of the world admires in the United States and California. The flow of people to and from Mexico, despite the resistance in both countries to giving this part of the bilateral relationship its due importance, is contributing far more to Mexico's *aggiornamento* than massive microwave imports or free-trade hyperbole.

Unfortunately, Mexico's influence on California is not so positive or beneficial. Through no fault of its own, undocumented Mexican immigration is contributing to the "dedemocratization" of California society. In an increasingly polarized environment, these illegal migratory flows are depoliticizing, denationalizing, and depriving of security and protection a significant sector of the so-called California underclass. Mexico's most lasting effect on California is thus political: by the end of the twentieth century, the richest state in the world will have a terribly skewed political system, with a foreign plurality that works, consumes, and pays taxes but does not vote, run for office, organize, or carry much political clout.

This outcome is linked, not to the migrants themselves, but to the specific conditions of Mexican immigration to California, and to the evolving character of Californian society and politics. Together with other regions of the United States, California is becoming what many have called a two-tier society. Structural change and adjustment have been accompanied by a dramatic growth in economic inequality and social polarization. Homelessness, unemployment, urban blight, drugs, delinquency, and ostentatious (often insulting) disparities in wealth and living standards: the symptoms of underdevelopment in the United States and California are too striking to be ignored.

Mexican immigrants are particularly vulnerable to the negative effects of the two-tier society. In California today, the upward mobility achieved by previous migrants may no longer be possible. As Mike Davis writes in his book on Los Angeles: "In the absence of any movement toward social justice, the most explosive social contradiction may become the blocked mobility of these children of the new immigrants. As a 1989 UCLA study revealed, poverty is increasing faster amongst Los Angeles Latinos, especially youth, than among any other urban group in the United States."[2]

According to Jackie Goldberg, former president of the Los Angeles school board, one-fourth of the children in Los Angeles, a large number of whom are Latino, live below the poverty line. One-seventh can be classified as being in "dire poverty," which Goldberg describes as those who "pay rent or have health care, but not both; choose between food, clothing or transportation, but not any two together; and whose only food is the free breakfast and lunch they receive in school."[3] Mexican immigrants are disproportionately represented in the bottom tier of society; and because their numbers are constantly replenished from abroad, even upward mobility does not reduce the size of the poor, Mexican-born share of California's population.

Economic and social polarization are exacerbated by the fact that the number of people who actually vote in California represents a sharply decreasing percentage of the total population. Kevin Phillips documents this trend at the national level: "Seventy-five percent of the citizenry voted in Pacific Palisades, 25 percent in the South Bronx. Election analysts could not be quite sure, but persons in the top quintile conceivably cast almost 30 percent of the total presidential vote ballots in Ronald Reagan's 1984 landslide, and people in the two top quintiles together probably accounted for over 50 percent of turnout."[4]

California statistics convey a similar impression at the state level. Of California's 30 million residents, only 7.5 million vote; indeed this figure has remained stable for several years despite substantial increases in the total population. Seventy-five percent of the voting population is white, compared to only 60 percent of the total population, and half of those who vote are over fifty years of age. By contrast, the state's younger ethnic groups are seriously underrepresented. Asians, who account for 10 percent of the population, cast only 4 percent of the votes; Latinos, who make up 26 percent of the population, cast only 10 percent. Thus, only a minority participates in elections, and that minority is white, Anglo, middle or upper-middle class, and elderly. Most important, from the perspective of this essay, the voting minority is American: foreigners do not vote.

This dilemma cannot be reduced to the shortcomings of Mexican political culture. It is true that Mexicans have been far more reluctant to seek naturalization than previous immigrants to the United States: "Overall, fewer Mexican than other immigrants become citizens, and when they do, they take an average of four more years to do so (11 versus 7)."[5] Moreover, Mexicans who acquire U.S. citizenship continue to be informed by their own political traditions:

elections and other political endeavors are viewed with a complete sense of futility. But apathy among immigrants eligible to participate politically is only part of a much larger problem. As long as undocumented immigration is a fixture of California life, dedemocratization will remain one of the central ways in which Mexico and other nations affect the state.

The emergence of what has been called "electoral apartheid" in California is related to the fact that a significant and growing portion of its population is of foreign nationality. According to the Current Population Survey, 55 percent of California's six million Latinos do not have citizenship; in Los Angeles, the figure rises to 62 percent.[6] This means that more than three million people, or one-tenth of the state's population, are politically disenfranchised. Mike Davis's distinction between those who vote and those who work is beginning to overlap with the distinction between Americans and foreigners, those with documents and those living outside legality.

These overlapping distinctions have dire implications for California society. In effect, a small, privileged minority is determining the fate of a largely poor, nonvoting majority. This minority uses fewer and fewer of the social programs its taxes are financing. According to Jackie Goldberg, 75 percent of registered voters and 88 percent of the people who actually go to the polls in California *have no children in public schools*. Sixty-three percent of the students in the Los Angeles school district are Latino; of these, two hundred thousand are not proficient in English. Faced with a choice between funding programs of little direct benefit to themselves and paying lower taxes, the response of the electorate should come as no surprise. California, which is the richest state in the union, ranks last both in class size and in the share of personal income spent on education.[7]

Today, in many cases, those who vote, run for office, get elected, legislate, and rule are less and less a reflection of society as a whole, although they are an increasingly faithful image of the electorate. This could be named the Richard Riordan syndrome: How did the most cosmopolitan, tension-ridden, socially and racially diverse city in the United States elect a white male Republican millionaire over the age of fifty as its mayor in 1993? It didn't: the people of Los Angeles did not elect Riordan, the voters did, and the people and the voters are not the same thing. According to the *Los Angeles Times* exit polls, 85 percent of voters who cast ballots for Riordan were Anglo; although his opponent, Michael Woo, captured 86 percent of the black vote, blacks accounted for only 12 percent of the turnout. Riordan did do better than expected among Latinos, but again, only a small fraction of Latinos voted; in Los Angeles, of all cities, only 10 percent of the voters were Latino.[8] Not that Los Angeles had a black, Asian, or female mayor before Tom Bradley; nonetheless, the contrast between the social configuration of the city and the elected officials that have governed it is much more striking today than it was years ago. And this purely electoral bias or breakdown in the democratic system soon began to churn out economic and social effects, basically through its influence on the country's fiscal situation.

The sad dynamic that this process unleashes is well-known. Since more and more the poor, the nonwhite, the young, and strictly urban citizens do not vote or participate in politics in any meaningful fashion and they are by definition able to shoulder only an exceedingly light tax burden, there is an ever greater overlap between those who vote and those who pay taxes. Yet the people who vote and bear the tax burden are also those who least use or consume the goods and services funded by taxes: public education, public health care, public transportation, government-funded job training, and so on. They are older, more affluent, tend to be white and Anglo-Saxon. They either have no children, send them to private school, or have already put them through school. They do not use public transportation or public health services and, have little use for welfare or other forms of public assistance, or for that matter, for parks, playgrounds, child-care centers, and public sports facilities. So they are not ecstatic over shouldering a high tax burden to pay for the services that they do not consume. Inevitably, these taxpayers want to pay less in taxes for things of little direct use to them, while those who do use them, pay little tax and don't vote in sufficient numbers to force the others to pay more tax. This voting pattern serves to further exclude from the system the nonvoting or low-turn-out groups: minorities, the poor, and residents of the inner city.

In a more traditional democratic system, such as in Europe, where the redistributive aspects of taxation, equal representation, and political inclusion are all more or less taken for granted, this American dilemma would not be a problem. Where it is widely accepted that societies are made up of different classes and regions, and where the principle that the richer sectors have a social obligation to transfer income to the poorer and less blessed is respected, paying taxes for services one does not directly consume is not the end of the world. There are other perfectly decent reasons for carrying a heavy tax burden: a more equal and livable society, fewer social tensions, a cleaner environment, and so on. But where society is considered uniform and homogeneous to begin with—that is, where class cleavages and gender, racial, and regional disparities are not truly acknowledged, and in any case, the role of the state in diminishing them is not contemplated—the principle of redistribution cannot be validated and paying taxes to finance goods or services one does not consume seems absurd.

This bias in favor of the top tier and against the bottom tier is aggravated by a proliferation of user and impact fees to pay for schools, roads, mass transit, hospitals, and other "public facilities." In contrast to taxes, these fees are levied on those who consume (or are affected by) a given service or project. Only those projects funded by fees can be carried out, and only those projects that provide a service to a paying community of users can be funded. Because these fees severely dilute the redistributive effects of taxation and the democratic process, they are the fiscal equivalent of dedemocratization. Those who least need public services receive them, while those who need them the most do not, since they lack the means to pay for them. When coupled with the transfer of fiscal responsibilities from the federal level to local communities, these fees have the following effect: "These voters (suburban, affluent, white, Anglo) can satisfy their need for government services through increased local expenditures, guaranteeing the highest possible return to themselves on their tax dollars, while continuing to demand austerity at the federal level. Suburbanization has permitted whites to satisfy liberal ideas revolving around activist government while keeping to a minimum the number of blacks and poor people who share in government largesse."9

Under these circumstances, it is virtually impossible for a democratic system to function. California's "top-tier" electorate is being asked to vote for higher taxes to finance public schools for blacks and Latinos in the bottom tier. A system based on universal suffrage should work the opposite way. Blacks and Latinos should vote for higher taxes, levied progressively on everyone, to finance public services. But, in California, universal suffrage is quickly becoming de facto restricted suffrage as the poor and the foreign do not vote. And since the large majority of California's foreign population is and will continue to be Mexican, part of the problem, and certainly part of the solution, is also Mexican.

Immigration from Mexico is likely to continue regardless of what enthusiasts of free trade, peace in Central America, or the closing of the border may say or do. The only realistic way to alter the negative effect of Mexican influence on California, then, is to change the nature of its origin by legalizing immigration and giving foreigners the right to vote in state and local elections. The relevance of this idea is highlighted in Jack Miles's article devoted to it in the May 1994 issue of *The Atlantic Monthly*, coupling it with the unacceptable, but unfortunately not unlikely, proposal to shut down the border.

Legalization is much less out of the question than many tend to believe. The Immigration Reform and Control Act (IRCA) itself was a mass legalization venture, regularizing the status of over three million undocumented foreigners. Recent Justice Department rulings on asylum and refugee status for Central Americans also constitute the equivalent of generalized legalization, as do family reunification and semi-"green-card" marriages. In Europe, following a long period when legal immigration was virtually halted and illegal migratory flows took its place, the trend is once again toward "regularization," as the consequences of maintaining a large, highly concentrated, and illegal population are deemed greater than the disadvantages of legalization.

There is no dispute that legalization poses costs and perils. The main danger lies in providing a powerful additional incentive for future immigration and in the increased migratory flows that would undoubtedly result in the short term. But these costs are clearly no greater than the costs of the status quo, which threatens to tear Californian society apart. The real stumbling block is that the decision to legalize immigration will not be made by those who would most benefit from it most—the bottom tier—but rather by a white, Anglo, middle-class, and elderly electorate. The only way to change the nature of Californian politics is through legalization, but the only way to achieve legalization is to change the nature of Californian politics. Not an easy circle to square.

Giving foreigners the right to vote is also a complex task, but it, too, represents a growing trend elsewhere in the world. As one study concludes, "The main reason Hispanics have not yet fully translated their increasing numbers into proportional increases in political representation and power is because most are not eligible to vote because of their age or lack of citizenship."[10] It would be naive to expect that simply by granting Mexicans in the United States the right to vote they would immediately jettison the remnants of their political and cultural baggage and turn out at the polls like Scandinavians or Italians. But if Mexicans were placed on an equal legal footing with their peers in the United States, the process of eliminating the vestiges of Mexican political culture would be swifter and less painful.

In 1975, Sweden became the first European nation to grant foreigners the right to vote in elections for municipal and state legislators. Denmark, Norway, and Finland all followed suit in the early 1980s; the Netherlands, Ireland, and Switzerland proceeded in the same fashion later. In France, the Socialist Party's 1981 platform advocated granting foreigners the right to vote in municipal elections, although President François Mitterand did not carry out his promise. This cross-national trend reflects the spectacular increase in the numbers of foreigners, either refugees or working immigrants, flocking to Scandinavia from Greece, Turkey, and Yugoslavia, and to other parts of Europe from western Asia, the Caribbean, the Maghreb, and sub-Saharan Africa.

In the United States, city council members in Santa Monica, Chicago, and New York have raised the possibility of granting foreigners the right to vote, but until now the idea has met with indifference or outrage. The tradition in the United States has always been that foreigners should become U.S. citizens if they want to stay in the country and should not be granted political rights if they are only passing through. But qualitative and perhaps even quantitative changes in recent migratory flows to the United States show that this tradition is no longer appropriate. Many people from Mexico and Central America have simply not made up their mind as to the length or nature of their stay. Moreover, since the flows are ongoing, there is always a large cohort of nonnaturalized foreigners in the United States. As this number grows and the proportion of naturalized citizens relative to all foreign-born individuals in the United States diminishes, enfranchising foreigners only through naturalization becomes increasingly ineffective.

The choice, then, lies between enfranchising foreigners along European lines or continuing to deny foreigners political rights and relegating them to the bottom tier of Californian society. The fact that the problem is so strongly concentrated in California should serve as an incentive to finding a state or municipal solution. What happens in California, or in Los Angeles and San Jose, need not be a federal policy applicable throughout the country. Although most Californians are likely to balk at the idea of giving foreigners the vote, regardless of what may be happening in other countries, the short-term feasibility of the idea should not detract from its intrinsic merits. Simply initiating a debate on this issue could push Californians to question long-held assumptions about political rights and responsibilities that no longer work in the face of new social and economic realities.

Legalization and foreigner enfranchisement will not solve California's democratic crisis, nor will it automatically lead millions of Mexican and other Latin American immigrants to the polls. But without such changes in firmly entrenched American customs, the dedemocratization of Californian society will only get worse. Mexico's influence will become more pernicious, not because it is Mexican, but because any massive, ongoing migratory flow that is illegal cannot but harm a society that is already as polarized and unequal as California's. There are no easy solutions to California's plight, which foreshadows that of the rest of the country. In the long term, however, all Californians will lose more by letting dedemocratization continue than by giving foreigners the right to vote. Enfranchising the bottom tier is not a panacea, it is not a sufficient condition for rolling back the two-tier economy, but it is a necessary step in the right direction.

The complex, convoluted, and endlessly changing Mexican-Californian interface expresses itself today in a paradox. California's influence on Mexico has never been healthier, as mass migration and reflows bring change to the mentalities of Mexican communities that would otherwise remain fixed in time and custom. As Mexico is ever so slowly and painfully forced to reject its past, the new identity it forges—if any at all—will inevitably have Californian, Chicano features. The more the Chicano experience reaches Mexico, the stronger the country's refurbished nationalism will be, if it ever emerges from the ruins of the last decade and the havoc wrought by the headlong rush to economic integration with the United States.

Mexico, for its part, solves many of California's economic problems by exporting part of its country's labor force, but the undocumented, disenfranchised, and massive nature of the immigration piles onto the state's existing problems, aggravating them by denationalizing the poorest, most excluded and oppressed sector of Californian society. The intensifying rivalries between blacks, Mexicans, and Central Americans in areas where they coexist is nothing more than a violent, tragic, and foreseeable outgrowth of this situation. In the very long run, the problems it generates may simply fade away, as emigration from Mexico and Central America starts to wind down and American society begins to tackle the disparities and dramas it has created and continues to ignore. The problem is the meantime, as it generally tends to be in matters of human endeavor.

CHAPTER 2

The Mexican Difference

AS MEXICO SINKS INTO ECONOMIC AND COLLECTIVE DEPRESSION, it may be time to dwell on some of the lessons of this new Mexican meltdown, for the country itself and for its neighbors to the north, now so dramatically affected by the fourth major economic debacle in Mexico in less than two decades. It might be particularly worthwhile to wonder why foreigners in general, and Americans in particular, seem so often caught by surprise by what happens in Mexico: they should know by now, given proximity, import, and history.

The United States—meaning, essentially, the American press, academia, business, and at least two branches of government— cannot be blamed for the disaster that befell Mexico late in 1994. But the U.S. establishment should not have been surprised by the economic crisis that struck on December 20, when just-inaugurated President Ernesto Zedillo devalued the currency, sending it into an ever-downward spiral. Nor should Washington, Wall Street, and Los Angeles have been caught off guard by the political and psychological turmoil springing from the revelations of the corruption, abuses, and sheer delinquency in which the outgoing administration of former president Carlos Salinas de Gortari had engaged. All of what happened in the course of the first few months of the year was warned of, written about, and clearly visible early on in the Salinas years: no one was watching, listening, or willing to read the writing on the thick white walls that crisscross Mexico City.

Since 1992, the economy had been running up a huge current-account deficit and registering disappointingly low levels of growth: nearly $25 billion of deficit, only 2.5 percent expansion. By 1993, a full year before the Chiapas uprising and the moment when the currency should have been devalued according to Monday-*mañana* quarterbacks, Mexico grew negatively in per capita terms, and still required $22 billion in short-term speculative capital. From the outset, this huge deficit was being financed by portfolio invest-ment, the drawbacks of which were self-evident: volatility, depen-dency on high yield differentials with the rest of the world, and exchange-rate stability. The NAFTA debate in the United States obscured a crucial trade-off: in order for Mexico to become a dynamic market for American exports—thus providing "good jobs at good wages" for U.S. workers—it had to maintain an overval-ued currency that would eventually drive *Mexican* firms out of business, and *Mexican* workers out of *their* jobs. All of this was cal-culated, stated, and denounced by countless Mexican and Latin American economists and pundits; it simply was not paid atten-tion to north of the border, except by a few Bush, Salinas, or Clinton administration critics whose views were dismissed as partisan, resentful, or simply out to lunch.

Nor were the telltale signs of corruption and abuse noticed in the United States. The violence inherent in Mexican society, magnified by more than a decade of economic stagnation and several years of economic policies that even further concentrated income and wealth, was pointed to by many, yet not acknowledged by those with money to invest, axes to grind, or treaties to ratify. The woeful lack of political reform and the autocratic fashion in which Carlos Salinas was implementing his economic modernization program were repeatedly underlined in Mexico—and even fre-quently in the U.S.—but the link between politics and economic policy in the south was not established in the north: the nonsi-multaneity of *glasnost* and presumed *perestroika* in Mexico was lamented, but it was not singled out as a decisive predictor of future disaster. As alien as the idea might appear if it were to be advo-cated in the U.S., enlightened despotism was deemed perfectly natural for Mexico: What a pity Salinas, who was doing the right things, was doing them the wrong way. The very notion that it might not be possible to pursue this self-contradictory course indefinitely was rarely considered, let alone identified as a source of major, upcoming predicaments.

So what made Mexico once again so opaque to the beholder from abroad? What rendered the foreign—mainly American—*regard* so distorted, so blind, so mistaken? Clearly an initial answer must single out the incestuous relationship that soon developed among the brokerage firms and investment banks peddling Mexican paper, the self-styled experts on Mexico often advising the financial institutions, and the Bush and Clinton administration officials who at all costs sought to avoid embarrassing, then weakening, their new-found Mexican friends in the Salinas regime, particularly when the latter embarked on the NAFTA adventure. Even correspondents for the U.S. press in Mexico fell for the combination of Salinas's charm and urbanity and their editors' discreet but persistent suggestions that Mexico's modernization be reported on "fairly." Everyone had a stake in Mexico succeeding in its effort to achieve what "everyone" wanted: a more market-oriented, more pro-American, more compliant Mexico, and, if possible, a more democratic Mexico, too.

But this explanation, while necessary, is obviously not sufficient. A series of deeper, more abstract, factors contributed this time around, as so often in the past, to make Mexico mysterious, even to the most trained or sympathetic eye. The key to that series, the single element that explains the opacity of Mexican society and politics to so many, is difference: the simple but critical fact that Mexico is radically, substantively, ferociously different from the United States and will remain so for the foreseeable future. The mistake many outside Mexico made was to believe that the highly perceptible differences of the past were superficial enough to be swept away by a modernizing leader and an apparently acquiescent population. The mistake so many inside Mexico committed was to convince themselves (ourselves) that those differences would surface automatically, almost immediately, and work their magic directly in the streets and villages and at the polls. From abroad, the absence of reaction to change was interpreted as support, enthusiastic at best, resigned at worst. Domestically, opposition was

reduced to waiting for the children of Sánchez to rise up in arms
or protest over the destruction of their myths, if not their world.
Both views missed the point: the Mexican difference is everything
a difference should be; no more, no less. This essay purports to
delve into that difference.

A REVEALING ITEM OPENED THE BUSINESS PAGES OF A MEXICAN
daily at the height of the Salinas glory years. According to Hyde
and Associates, an American consulting firm working in Mexico,
99 percent of the prospective alliances attempted by U.S. firms in
Mexico never get off the ground. The reason: so-called cultural differences between the two nations, ranging from "lunchtime hours"
to tax systems and including stereotypes, language, and business
culture. The onslaught of events in Mexico since New Year's Day
1994, when the peasants of the Chiapas highlands took the city of
San Cristóbal and CNN by storm, cannot but have surprised the
authors of *Newsweek's* 1993 year-end "Conventional Wisdom"
section, which hailed Mexico's NAFTA-inspired transformation into
a "U.S. sunbelt state." A guerrilla uprising, the unsolved kidnapping of one of the nation's premier financiers, the successful conspiracy to assassinate the ruling party's presidential candidate and,
subsequently, of its secretary general, and the complete collapse of
an economy supposedly on the verge of an Asian-style boom are
exactly not what one would expect in Arizona, or even Dade County.

Such difficulties and surprises are inevitable when it comes to
U.S. perceptions of Mexico. The now distant but still tedious debate
over NAFTA was not about Mexico nor about what the United States'
relations with its neighbor were and should be. The debate became
a proxy discussion of other issues: jobs in the United States, protectionism versus free trade as an economic theory, the power and
authority of the president to pursue foreign policy, the kind of
"New Democrat" Bill Clinton would like to be. With the NAFTA
debate well behind them, Americans might want to ponder what
makes Mexicans and Americans different from each other.

Over the years, journalists, anthropologists, historians, and writers have, of course, suggested answers, emphasizing differences in background, religion, history, economic development, language, and ethnic origin; all are valid. But these differences were overshadowed in recent times by a presumed commonality of purpose, enlightenment, and economic doctrine. The advent of a "modern" Mexico—business-oriented, outward-looking, and sympathetic to most things American—blurred the contours of a different Mexico: one that, despite convergences of ideas among the elite of both nations, remained profoundly different from the United States and proved capable of generating the surprises that have cropped up in the past year and a half.

THREE ESSENTIAL DIVERGENCES COME TO MIND WHICH CON-tribute as much as any other factors to our being two different peoples and cultures. One is economic and social, the other two are cultural.

First, the United States is fundamentally a middle-class society in which, although inequalities have undoubtedly sharpened over the past decade or two, a large majority of the population (in the vicinity of 70 percent) is bunched around the middle of the income, opportunity, and employment scales. Mexico's scales are nowhere near as balanced: although great progress was achieved between 1940 and 1980 in building a middle class, Mexico is still (or, as recent data indicate, more than ever) a polarized society with enormous gaps between rich and poor, town and country, north and south, white and brown (or *criollos* and *mestizos*).

There is, of course, a middle class in Mexico, Ross Perot notwithstanding, but it constitutes a minority: somewhere between a quarter and a third of the population. The majority—poor, urban, brown, and often excluded from the characteristics of modern life in the United States and other industrialized countries (public education, decent health care and housing, formal employment, social security, the right to vote, hold public office, and serve on a jury, and so on)—mingles with itself. It lives, works, sleeps, and worships separately from the small group of the very wealthy and the larger but still restricted middle class. The United States is the proverbial mass society (though less so than ever before), where a white, middle-class, suburban majority coexists with various minorities who are undeniably though unevenly segregated and discriminated against. Mexico is a society terribly riven by class, race, gender, age, region, and future, where a middle- and upper-class minority segregates and discriminates against the vast majority of the population. It is one of the most unequal societies around, though certainly not one of the poorest.

In 1992, the richest 10 percent of Mexicans received 38 percent of the country's total income, the poorest half only 18 percent, and the trend in recent decades has been worsening, not improving. Some countries are worse yet: in Brazil, the richest 10 percent receive 42 percent of total income, whereas the poorest half receives only 15 percent. On the other hand, India, not exactly the epitome of equality, has a much fairer structure, and in the United States, the most unequal of the industrialized nations, the numbers are quite different from those in Mexico. Until the polarization of family incomes took hold in the Reagan years, the top decile in the United States garnered approximately 30 percent of total income, while the poorest half of the population received around 25 percent. Another contrast between the two societies can be found in the middle class. In the United States, before the shrinking effects on the middle class of the "Reagan Revolution," the second and third quintiles received 15 percent and 22 percent of total income respectively. In Mexico in 1992, the second and third quintiles received 10 percent and 16 percent respectively.[11]

Herein lay, probably, the main mistake committed by NAFTA's opponents in the United States. They systematically emphasized and sometimes exaggerated Mexico's poverty, which is real enough, often confusing it with Mexico's inequality. Alexander von Humboldt, the great German writer and traveler, and perhaps the world's first Latin Americanist, made the point as early as 1802: "Mexico is the country of inequality," he wrote. "Perhaps nowhere in the world is there a more horrendous distribution of wealth, civilization, cultivation of land, and population." Foreign writers, from Bruno Traven to Ambrose Bierce, photographers, anthropologists, and observers from all walks of life have reached the same conclusion over the years. The contrast between rich and poor in Mexico and the extremes reached by both are almost unheard of elsewhere.

According to the 1994 *Forbes* count of the world's wealthiest individuals, the country with the largest number of people on the list, after the United States, Japan, and Germany, was Mexico, with twenty-four. Their declared fortunes combined would represent nearly 10 percent of Mexico's annual gross national product. Yet outside city limits or where the broad avenues and glittering stores within the cities end—San Bernabé in Monterrey, or just behind the Mexico City airport—tens or hundreds of thousands of people live in squalor with no running water or sewer lines and only rudimentary electricity. They travel three to four hours daily to work —when they have work.

But the inequality is not simply economic; it is also social. In 1994, a government undersecretary (one level down from the top echelon of public service) made approximately $180,000 after taxes, excluding health insurance and perks but including all sorts of bonuses, premiums and expense accounts—almost twice what his U.S. counterpart earns *before* taxes. His chauffeur (provided by the government, of course) makes $7,500 a year. That difference enables the official to address the employee with the familiar "*tu*," while the latter must speak to the former with the respectful "*usted.*" The official and his peers in the business or intellectual elites of the nation tend to be white (there are still exceptions, but they are becoming more scarce with the years), well educated, and well traveled abroad. They send their children to private schools, remote from the world of the employee. The employee and his peers tend to be *mestizo,* rarely read a newspaper, and have several children, most of whom will attend school only through the sixth grade.

The equalizing institutions that reduced injustice and segregation in the United States for many years, before they ran into nation-wide resistance, have never really existed in Mexico. Nominally there is a draft; in fact no son of even a middle-class family will ever serve in the military. The public school system did play a certain equalizing role in the past, and still does to an extent. Every president of Mexico through Ernesto Zedillo has attended public schools and the National University or the Polytechnical Institute. But odds are that no children of sitting cabinet members, leading business-men, opinion makers, artists, or civil servants are enrolled in a public institution below the university level. The decades after the Mexican Revolution—through the 1950s, perhaps—provided some upward mobility, some mingling, certainly the advent of a new business elite and an emerging middle class. But the impetus was soon lost. By the 1980s, Mexico was once again a country of three nations: the *criollo* minority of elites and the upper-middle class, living in style and affluence; the huge, poor, *mestizo* majority; and the utterly destitute minority of what in colonial times was called the Republic of Indians—the indigenous peoples of Chiapas, Oaxaca, Tabasco, Michoacán, Guerrero, Puebla, Chihuahua, and Sonora, all known today as *el México profundo*: deep Mexico.

These divisions partly explain why Mexico is as violent and unruly, as surprising and unfathomable as it has always prided itself on being. It is a nation stricken by violence from birth. The perva-siveness of the violence was obfuscated for years by the fact that much of it was generally directed by the state and the elites against society and the masses, not the other way around. The current rash of violence by society against the state and elites is not a symptom of a new trend. It is simply a retargeting.

And Mexico is unpredictable. The dictator Porfirio Díaz is reputed to have said, as he sailed for exile in France in 1911, "In Mexico nothing ever happens until it happens." The country erupts sporadically and regionally because the inequities from which it suffers become at some point intolerable, worse than any conceivable consequence of attempting to redress them by other means. But the very inequality and segregation from which those eruptions spring make it impossible to foresee them. Mexican politicians, intellectuals, and businessmen were too estranged from the indigenous peoples in Chiapas early in 1994, from university students in 1968, and from the peasants in Morelos in 1910 to sense when tolerance had been stretched too far. The "leading indicators" available to scholars, pundits, and technocrats in the United States and elsewhere do not operate in Mexico.

A second difference is cultural, and it often drives Americans and other foreigners in Mexico to distraction, largely because they refuse to understand it. It has to do with time: stereotypically and arrogantly, the *mañana* syndrome or, as the T-shirts have it: "I'm on Mexican Time." As Octavio Paz wrote in his memorable "Reflections: Mexico and the United States," published in *The New Yorker* in 1979, the two societies differ dramatically in their attitudes toward, even conception of, time. And it is no coincidence that Mexico's greatest living novelist has entitled the sum of his life's work *The Age of Time*: Carlos Fuentes's obsession with time, by his own admission, covers half his narrative creation.

It is not merely a question of punctuality, formality, or responsibility, but rather a different conception of time, its role in life, and its social function. The expression of these differences can undoubtedly be found in the stereotypes: Mexicans are, in most of the country, less punctual, quick, and hurried than Americans (or Germans or the British, for that matter). But to reduce deep differences in culture and tradition to one of their most superficial manifestations is to miss an essential characteristic of Mexican life and customs. Time is not just a question of time. Mexico's definition of time is not "premodern," soon to be "modern" like everyone else's.

It is not that Mexicans are "still" plagued by a lack of attachment to time; they are simply different. Nor is the difference inexplicable or mysterious; it has its explanations and origins. The nonexistence of a mass society in Mexico begins to explain it. Because of the abysses separating different sectors of Mexican society, Mexicans can behave differently from one another, according to varying sets of rules.

Millions of Mexicans consume, work, rest, and drive the same way, of course, but many more do not. Some Mexicans attach great importance to time; others may choose to act differently, without prejudice to themselves. Certain Mexicans may subscribe to a series of rules, from traffic regulations to work discipline and punctuality; others may decide, consciously or otherwise, that they prefer not to. The absence of an authentic mass society allows for these mass exceptions.

There is a sociological explanation, too. Because so many Mexicans work, live, and even love informally, time is not of the essence. Letting and watching time go by, being late (an hour, a day, a week) are not grievous offenses. They simply indicate a lower rung on the ladder of priorities. It is more important to see a friend or the family than to keep an appointment or make it to work, especially when work consists of hawking wares on street corners. An economic explanation is also available: there is a severe lack of incentives for being on time, delivering on time, or working overtime. Since most people are paid so little for what they do, the prize for punctuality and formality can be meaningless: time is often *not* money in Mexico. The choice between making a few pesos more and having a good time is easy and as rational as any other. Everything is slow in Mexico, but not because Mexicans cannot do things quickly. Everything is slow because the passage of time is less noticeable. Time is flat: too frequently nothing changes with time, and the sense of its going by—the reason for putting a premium on it—is absent. From the simple and obvious explanation—much of Mexico is a region with no seasons, except when it rains and when it doesn't, and in the countryside the dry season is basically devoted to waiting for rain—to the more complex, time in Mexico is not what it is in the United States. Time divides our two countries, as much as any other single factor.

One of the most obvious implications of this difference—which actually pertains to much of Latin America, particularly in those nations with a strong pre-Columbian heritage—is that immediate responses, rapid cause-and-effect relationships, are rare. Time lags, delayed reactions, an often incomprehensible patience, tend to be much more common. Quick causes are not always matched by equally quick effects. On many occasions, the effect is simply slow in coming: it will happen, in time.

This expression of the difference is somewhat unsettling to foreigners, especially Americans. When "nothing happens" in Mexico right after a special event, such as trade liberalization, recognition of the church by the state, the decision to enter into a free-trade agreement with the United States, the privatization of the traditional *ejido* land-tenure system, an armed uprising in the countryside, the assassination of a presidential candidate, the stealing of an election, or the advent of an economic crisis, external observers or students of Mexico tend to assume that "nothing" will continue to happen. But the time lag between cause and effect is simply greater. The Chiapas rebellion, to review a recent example, was largely motivated by a series of convergent trends that had been in the making for several years in Mexico: the fall in world prices for coffee (the main crop in the Chiapas highlands), the dismantling of the old price-support system, the consciousness-raising effort carried out by priests and lay workers in the area, the organizational work undertaken by agrarian semi-Maoist activists from the north, the eviction of indigenous communities from their land by cattle grazers and timber companies. None of these trends was recent; they were all set in motion some time ago. Why they came together on January 1, 1994, is anybody's guess, but the absence of any perceptible expression of their existence before that date did not mean that they were not operating. It just took time for them to come to fruition.

A third difference between Mexico and the United States is directly related to the question of time: the role and weight of history in the two cultures. One of the reasons time so divides Mexico and the United States is that, on a broader scale, time seems to be more immobile south of the border. Historical time is slower, fewer blips appear on the historical screen, permanence and immobility much more than change are perceived as the main features of history. Mexican history appears to be one long continuum, with great and long constants and underlying continuities and only sporadic bursts of compressed, highly intense events. From the great pre-Columbian civilizations to the conquest there is perceived continuity; from the conquest to independence is a three-hundred-year period of apparent colonial continuity; from independence through the American invasion, the reform, and the French intervention, on to the Porfiriato and up to the revolution is an additional century of nation-building continuity; from the revolution through the oil expropriation and the student movement of 1968 and all the way up to the current crisis is the continuity of the "system." The bursts of events become more frequent, perhaps more intense, but still, long-term continuity reigns supreme.

In this conception of history, what little change there is acquires inordinate importance. Each cluster of events becomes crucial. The rest of the time, not much occurs, but whatever does is overloaded with meaning and import for the future. Although the difference in the significance attached to history by Mexicans and Americans has often been emphasized—leading to clichés such as "The United States is oriented toward the future; Mexico's orientation is just the opposite"; "Mexicans are obsessed with history, Americans with the future"—the deep gap it opens between two nations and cultures makes it far more than a matter of temperament. For the Americans, history is folklore plus the recent past; for Mexicans, it is the historicist essence of the present.

There are many good reasons for this difference. To begin with, history has played a different role in nation building in the two countries. In the United States, history has barely served to forge the ties that bind a nation together. How could it, if the past is not shared? Many other factors fill the void history leaves: the rule of law, the frontier, an ideological attachment to a unique form of government, and so forth. Mexico, on the other hand, to the (dubious) extent that it is a fully consummated nation, is so because of a common origin, from which everything else stems: territory, *la raza*, language, religion. They all stem from the conquest and the successive episodes of Mexico's subsequent transformation: independence, the reform and Juárez, the revolution. In a country as deeply divided as Mexico, as segregated socially and splintered regionally and ethnically, one of the few unifying themes is precisely a shared history, even if an official version of it has to be invented in order for it to be common to all.

This is why debates over school history texts, historical figures, favorite periods, and past moments of national shame are so impassioned. The way history is taught, read, and written is a fundamental part of political debates, of ideological discourse, and even of policy options. The two national debates that took place in 1992 and 1993 over the rewriting of the nation's single elementary school history manual were both revealing and foreseeable, although they obviously surprised the government of former president Salinas. It was not just the textbook that was being rewritten, of course; the country's history underwent excruciating revision. Political passions and nationalist emotions were unexpectedly ignited by seemingly arcane or obsolete discussions of the colonial period; of the way in which Mexico lost more than half its territory to the United States; of what was or was not a balanced assessment of the Porfiriato period of foreign-dominated, authoritarian, but undeniably successful economic development at the turn of the century; of the 1968 student massacre in Tlatelolco, and of the final verdict on the administrations of Presidents Luis Echeverría and José López Portillo. The surprise was all the greater because this outburst of national introspection occurred at a time when it seemed that

Mexico had, as many American commentators surmised, put its demons and obsessions behind it. It had not, needless to say, because these are not demons or obsessions: they are all that tie an unfinished and polarized nation together.

Mexicans harp on past tensions and conflicts with the United States, not because of anti-Americanism, but because of the significance of history. It's the history that counts, not the Americans' specific part in it. The United States is just one slice of Mexican history, whereas the idea of history cuts across every alley of Mexican political and cultural life: its literature and archaeology, its education and art, its identity or lack of it. If the American dream is the archetypal bond in the United States, the Mexican memory unites Mexico. Without it, the country simply might not exist as we know it.

Again, the Chiapas episode neatly illustrates the weight of history. The peasants and organizers in Chiapas rose up in arms under the banner of possibly the most revered hero of the Mexican Revolution, Emiliano Zapata, a visionary village leader from the central state of Morelos. As every Marlon Brando fan knows, Zapata was betrayed and assassinated in the hacienda of Chinameca, on the orders of his revolutionary rival and president, Venustiano Carranza. In a country where treason abounds and loyalties are short-lived, the sensitivity to betrayal is always high. It rose to a boiling point a few days after the Chiapas rebellion exploded, as President Salinas de Gortari, either out of insensitivity or with deliberate symbolism, issued his proclamation of amnesty for the Chiapas insurgents in the Carranza Room of the presidential palace. He addressed the nation with a portrait of the white-haired, bearded coauthor of Mexico's constitution behind him. Zapata's self-styled heirs were being forgiven under the watchful gaze of the idol's murderer: a message not particularly comforting or subliminal. The rebels' leader, *subcomandante* Marcos, promptly stated his mistrust of Salinas's amnesty, and pundits and historians rapidly seized on the historical irony. Was the Carranza-sponsored amnesty for the

Zapatistas a replay of the tragedy at Chinameca? Other, deeper questions were less insistently asked: Where else could such a discussion of the value and relevance of historical symbols take place? What meaning did it hold for Mexican modernity? How was it that a name like Zapata continued to possess such a grip on Mexicans' memories and motivation for struggle and sacrifice?

One answer is that the recourse to history as an instrument of political debate and contention, and the need to refer to it constantly for electoral or insurrectional purposes, is in all likelihood a deeply ingrained, possibly permanent feature of Mexican life. Like the perception of time, it is not a lagging indicator, part of the ballast from Mexico's premodern past that must and will be shed as the country ventures forth into modernity.

Inequality, time, and history, are not soluble in water or free trade. If anything, the true test of partnership lies in acknowledging and mastering these differences, without pretending that they are either subsidiary or passing. The ones addressed here are neither: they are essential, and lasting.

From 1940 to 1980, the Mexican economy grew at an average rate of 6 percent a year; that is how the existing middle class was created. It will take at least that many years, with similar rates of growth, or twice as long at half the pace, to expand that middle class to the magnitude it has acquired in the United States. Mexico's social configuration will begin to look like the United States' sometime in the middle of the next century, if all goes well. We in Mexico will live on "Mexican time" at least until then, and probably until much later. Were this a problem obstructing a better and closer relationship, it would have no solution—a terribly un-American situation. But it is just a reality—one whose joys and promise Mexicans and Americans, as well as those millions that are both, should all revel and indulge in.

Mexico will continue to surprise Americans, as it should. All the more reason, perhaps, to heed warnings when they do surface, to avoid surprises when they are fully forecast. The wake of Mexico's current economic debacle is obviously one such occasion, and one present call of alarm should be listened to in particular.

During the NAFTA debate, at the height of his credibility in the U.S., Carlos Salinas argued that failure to ratify the treaty would bring about an economic collapse in Mexico, which in turn would unleash a wave of undocumented immigration to the north. The economic collapse came anyway, but the wave looks more like a steadily rising tide. Were the Clinton administration, in its obsession with reelection politics, to try to stem that tide, it would threaten the only true deterrent to the proverbial wave: Mexican stability. Any attempt to clamp down on immigration from the south by sealing the border—militarily, by forcing Mexico to deter migratory outflows, or through some federal version of California's Proposition 187—would make social peace untenable in the *barrios* and *pueblos* of Mexico. The United States should count its blessings: it has dodged instability on its borders since the Mexican Revolution, now nearly a century ago. The warnings from Mexico are loud and clear: This time, it might be a good idea to heed them.

CHAPTER 3

Can NAFTA *Change Mexico?*
The Risk of Free Trade

INFORMED MEXICAN POLITICANS, COMMENTATORS AND BUSI-
nessmen all knew, early on, that President Carlos Salinas de Gortari
had bet the store on NAFTA. It was the keystone of his administration, the achievement or failure that would determine the fate of
his government, and his own. If approved on time by the U.S.
Congress, it would allow the Mexican economy to grow again, in
time for the 1994 presidential elections, which then the PRI could
win cleanly; if rejected on Capitol Hill, disaster would follow: capital
flight, a devaluation of the currency, disenchantment with the
free-market reforms, possible institutional breakdown.

Yet some in Mexico refused to cast the debate in those terms.
The issue was not whether NAFTA, as it stood, was indispensable
for the country or not, but rather, under what conditions could
the United States and Mexico negotiate a process of economic
integration that would truly serve Mexico's interest, and not just
the White House's and Carlos Salinas's. What type of NAFTA, with
what contents and philosophical underpinnings, were the issues
raised by many north of the border, and by some from below. The
following essay, originally published weeks before the vote in the
U.S. Congress, attempted to address these questions, while at the
same time seeking to establish common ground with those sectors
in the United States that were approaching the NAFTA debate from
a similar perspective.

Many Mexicans have welcomed NAFTA as an undisguised blessing, whatever its effects on the United States. In the government
and among the general population, the agreement is seen as a ready
course to modernization. President Carlos Salinas de Gortari's policies have consciously supported this impression. His administration has determinedly pursued NAFTA as part of a dual strategy.
Economically, the trade agreement was to provide Mexico's ailing

economy with the foreign capital injections it has long required for sustainable growth. Politically, an expanding Mexican economy—one linked to the United States—would help lay the foundations for an eventual and controlled democratic transition.

Overlooked, however, has been the fact that NAFTA itself entails great risks. No country has ever attempted to develop an export manufacturing base by opening its borders so quickly and indiscriminately to more efficient and lower-cost producers. No nation today, not even the United States, has so willingly sacrificed an industrial policy or an equivalent form of managed trade. By unilaterally renouncing these advantages, Mexico will lose far more jobs in the next few years than it will create. Old industries and agricultural producers will die, be swallowed up, or join with foreign ventures, long before the new jobs arrive.

Mexico is not a modern country. True, over the past half-century it has witnessed dramatic change. An inward-looking, illiterate, and agrarian land has become an urban, partly industrialized nation with a growing middle class and a nascent civil society. But Mexico's underlying problems persist. It retains a largely corrupt and unchallenged state that possesses only the merest trappings of the rule of law. The enduring obstacles to Mexico's modernization—its repeated failure to transfer power democratically or to remedy the ancestral injustice of its society—remain and will require Mexico to continue to change itself, with or without a trade accord.

Any Mexican government's performance, as well as the virtues of a new relationship with the United States, must be measured against this background. Under certain conditions, NAFTA provides an opportunity to build a more prosperous, democratic, and equitable nation. But NAFTA alone will not modernize Mexico. In the short term especially, the accord as it stands may only exacerbate the country's already stark disparities and dislocations. Rather than speeding and facilitating Mexico's long-awaited and much-hoped-for democratic transition, the near-term effect may be to slow the momentum for political reform. This must not happen.

WAITING FOR DEMOCRACY

Whatever political advances may have occurred under President Salinas, Mexico has yet to devise a system to transfer power democratically. The 1994 presidential succession promises to be as traditional a ritual as ever. The outgoing president will choose his successor, and then do everything necessary at the polls to secure his election. This system worked adequately for more than half a century. But it dealt only with half the problem of modern government—order—leaving the other half—democratic representation—unresolved.

This quasi-magical procedure functioned properly only so long as everyone accepted its rules. But by the mid-1980s parts of the political establishment began to wonder whether they might not do better outside the system. In the 1988 election, former governor Cuauhtémoc Cárdenas, the son of Mexico's most revered president this century, and former Institutional Revolutionary Party Chairman Porfirio Muñoz Ledo broke with the PRI and ran for office on their own, faring much better than they would have otherwise. Muñoz Ledo was elected senator for Mexico City, and Cárdenas, in the opinion of many Mexicans, won the presidency.

Since then, despite two electoral reform laws under Salinas, Mexico's democratic transition has not come to pass. The opposition and Mexicans generally, according to polls, believe that the 1994 elections will again be a sham. The umbilical cord between party and government has not been severed. This was demonstrated by the "shakedown dinner" at which the PRI, in the presence of President Salinas, attempted to extract campaign contributions of $25 million each from thirty of Mexico's richest business leaders. But this time, the PRI's central problem of appointing a candidate and securing the election and accession of a new president will be further aggravated by Mexico's economic doldrums and social deterioration. Salinas seems unable to satisfy either of the two desires of his middle-class constituency: a democratic and orderly transfer of power and a growing economy with low inflation and a stable exchange rate. The only solution, as Carlos Ramírez, the most widely read columnist in Mexico, has put it, lies in the de facto exclusion of the presidency from the electoral arena, ensuring that, come what may, the next president will be the PRI candidate.

Part of the problem is that Mexico's opposition has yet to become a viable alternative to the status quo. The National Action Party (PAN) lacks strong national leadership and a nationwide presence; Cárdenas and his Party of the Democratic Revolution (PRD) are still perceived as too radical, divided, and inexperienced to take office. Yet both probably maintain sufficient strength to prevent the PRI from tampering with next year's election without incurring exorbitant costs. Thus, in addition to winning the election more or less cleanly, the PRI candidate will also have to convince his rivals of their defeat and his victory. Mexican politicians and pundits across the spectrum believe that the 1988 crisis must not be repeated. It would be terribly costly to carry into office another PRI candidate whose victory at the polls was disputed by adversaries representing half the electorate.

The need to manage a difficult succession makes a political solution more likely. Instead of emphasizing continuity in economic policy, Salinas will more likely choose a successor who can both win and persuade the opposition he won. Manuel Camacho, the mayor of Mexico City, and Luis Donaldo Colosio, the minister of social development, look best placed to accomplish this task, although Finance Minister Ernesto Zedillo cannot be overlooked. The appointment of either Camacho or Colosio would enhance the possibility of what many are calling for privately: a pact among the PRI, the PAN, and Cárdenas to set ground rules for the campaign, the election itself, and some sort of postelection national reconciliation. Camacho best understands the need for such an arrangement, but has aroused suspicions among the business community that he is a closet populist who places negotiation above a firm hand. Colosio, meanwhile, is experiencing difficulties in gaining national support.

While the PAN seems to pose no serious challenge in the presidential race, Cárdenas's situation is more complex. Conventional wisdom holds that he has squandered the popular support garnered in 1988 but that he will still fare better than the 9 percent his party obtained in the 1991 midterm elections. Polls give him strong recognition ratings—over 60 percent—higher than any other contender, but he also has high negatives. A poll for the daily *Excelsior* showed 35 percent of those questioned felt Cárdenas should run again, while 44 percent said he should not.

Cárdenas's fate will ultimately be determined by the state of the economy, the extent of social inequities, and the eventual divisions within the PRI. Also critical will be his ability to focus the campaign on his strong suits—democratization, social justice, and the fight against corruption—and at least to neutralize his weaknesses —the lack of a detailed economic alternative and the fear that he represents instability.

MEXICO'S FLAGGING ECONOMY

Mexico's lacerating social and economic inequality stems partly from the antidemocratic nature of its politics. High levels of postwar economic growth, progress in education and health, and the emergence of a significant middle class have not remedied Mexico's atrociously lopsided income distribution. If forty years of growth did not help, then a decade of economic stagnation in the 1980s only made matters worse. A recently published survey found that the richest 10 percent of Mexicans, those who earned 32.8 percent of national income in 1984, saw their share jump to 37.9 percent by 1989. Conversely, the share of the poorest 40 percent shrank from 14.3 percent to 12.9 percent. The 1990 census, moreover, revealed that 63.2 percent of the nation's inhabitants made no more than twice the minimum wage—$200 per month—while price levels approached those in the United States. The long absence of free elections, of an emancipated labor movement, and of the rule of law has helped keep the fruits of any economic expansion in the hands of a minority.

Much of the problem has been Mexico's inability to hurdle an apparently immovable obstacle to its economic growth: the need for substantial foreign capital injections. Since 1972, Mexico has been unable to overcome this external constraint on growth, except during the ephemeral convergence of exceptional circumstances—high oil prices, cheap and abundant lending, wholesale privatization, or high yields in the stock market. The costs of attracting foreign capital—higher interest rates and reduced domestic spending—have become a severe burden and have engendered boom-bust cycles in the economy. Either the economy does not grow or, if it does, immense current-account deficits spring up, requiring equivalent magnitudes of capital to finance them. The outcome of each cycle has been a currency devaluation, like those in 1976, 1982, and 1987, or an economic downturn with equally devastating consequences.

The Salinas administration sought to break these frustrating cycles and to achieve high growth—5 to 6 percent a year—with a moderate external imbalance. Trade liberalization, privatization, and reduced restrictions on foreign investment were means to this end. After an initial, prudent economic expansion, however, the trade balance began to deteriorate drastically, rising from $4.3 billion in 1990 to more than $20 billion in 1992. Imports have risen by approximately 25 percent annually since 1988. At the same time, exports have stagnated, growing less than one percent in 1991 and 1.5 percent in 1992. This imbalance was made largely inevitable by the rapid opening to foreign trade, an appreciating real exchange rate, and the remarkable propensity of the Mexican middle class to consume imported goods. By 1992, the overall current-account deficit had reached $23 billion, or 7 percent of GDP—Mexico's highest level ever.

Consequently, the Salinas administration was forced to throw the economy into a virtual recession, as the foreign capital imbalance prevented faster growth. After expanding in 1990 at 4.5 percent, economic growth slowed to 3.5 percent in 1991 and 2.6 percent in 1992. Government figures forecast slightly lower levels for both 1993 and 1994. Mexico's per capita growth has thus once again fallen dangerously close to zero.

Moreover, Salinas was forced to make a series of bold moves to attract enough foreign capital to finance even these reduced and more realistic growth rates. He thus pursued a free-trade agreement with the United States, the privatization of the Mexican banking system, and a policy of encouraging powerful local investors to transform the Mexico City stock exchange, or Bolsa, into a magnet for money from abroad. These steps paid off. There has not yet been, and probably will not be, a major devaluation of the currency, and Mexico has built up an unprecedented $20 billion of reserves.

But there were costs. Yields on the Bolsa had to stay astronomically high (over 60 percent, in dollars, in 1991), and when they declined or stagnated, as they have since mid-1992, interest-rate differentials between the United States and Mexico had to rise to stabilize portfolio or speculative investment (estimated at approximately 70 percent of the total). Direct foreign investment remains dismally low, as in the 1980s, ranging from 1.5 percent to 1.8 percent of GDP. And overall investment, despite the unprecedented flow of funds, has not budged, remaining at a disappointing 19 percent of GDP. The dire need for foreign capital drove domestic real interest rates to nearly 15 percent in dollars by mid-1993; lending rates reached 30 percent. Besides, the capital these moves attracted was not ideal. Two-thirds was speculative, and the rest was concentrated not in the creation of new wealth but in services, largely tourism, and in foreign purchases of existing Mexican assets.

In the end, the course Salinas set is more responsible than that of his predecessors, but it still has not achieved the long-sought goal of high growth combined with manageable external accounts. The economic downturn, together with the effects of the previous decade of stagnation, has contributed to rising unemployment and social decay. Manufacturing employment, flat even while the economy was growing, has now fallen: in an index in which the year 1980 equaled 100, it never rose above 87 under Salinas, and by early 1993 it was down to nearly 80. By 1993, tens of thousands of factory workers, bank employees, and retail-store clerks had lost their jobs. Although a number of new jobs have been created, many more have been lost as a result of the economic downturn and the growing, and so far irresistible, competition from abroad.

Many in the United States nonetheless believe that economic integration and NAFTA have moved jobs on a "fast track" to a modernizing Mexico. In fact, the country's disparities are deepening. Ever more dispossessed accompany the growing number of Mexican "yuppies." The loud "sucking noise" of American jobs going south that U.S. presidential candidate Ross Perot ominously announced last fall is, from the Mexican side of the border, singularly difficult to hear.

IS NAFTA THE ANSWER?

The Salinas regime's strategy in the face of these myriad economic and political difficulties was simple and single-minded: free trade with the United States. To hold a clean election and at the same time to secure the victory of Salinas's hand-picked candidate, the economy had to deliver high growth and create near the million jobs per year necessary to absorb population increases and facilitate social spending.

The only way to attract the foreign capital necessary to stabilize the exchange rate and to fund the ensuing current-account deficit was to provide hesitant potential investors with guarantees of continuity of economic policy and access to the U.S. market through an ironclad agreement with Washington. NAFTA, it was hoped, would satisfy both requirements. The sustained economic growth generated by NAFTA would narrow income differentials by creating jobs. President Salinas's antipoverty program, known as Solidaridad, would ease the transition from past stagnation to NAFTA-fueled high growth. As the fruits of growth trickled down and discontent no longer threatened economic policy, Mexico would gradually evolve into a democracy.

More than a complement to the modernization policies embarked upon since 1985, NAFTA was seen as a silver bullet to neutralize the obstacles those policies engendered. When more capital than expected was needed and greater reluctance to invest was encountered, NAFTA would make up the difference. It would also relieve pressure from abroad to accelerate political reform, as U.S. supporters of NAFTA toned down their criticisms of human rights violations and electoral fraud in Mexico to avoid imperiling free trade. Investment from abroad would enable the economy to grow, while introducing new technology and greater efficiency and modernizing Mexican society. Most Mexicans' traditional identification of modernity with the United States would be reinforced; their traditional resentment of the United States over past injuries and present asymmetries would be softened.

While it was hoped that NAFTA would address many of these problems, it has not defused the end-of-term crisis that Mexico's succession process has traditionally generated. Granted, the government's expectations, however inaccurate or overblown, touched a receptive chord among large sectors of the population. Polls repeatedly indicate strong support for NAFTA, as well as unfounded reasons for it: a recent survey found that 45.8 percent of those interviewed believed NAFTA would make it easier for Mexicans to get jobs in the United States. Similarly, it has created illusions in the United States that it would help stem Mexican immigration. Most immigration scholars in both countries expect NAFTA and the economic policies it will encourage in Mexico to stimulate migratory flows in the short run, as displaced peasants and laid-off employees take advantage of large wage differentials and head north.

But the dichotomy between the short and long term runs through the debate on NAFTA's advantages and drawbacks. Economic integration between the United States and Mexico, already under way for years, is surely better served by a legal framework to rationalize and administer it. And Mexican economic development and living standards—if not national autonomy or cultural identity—will benefit in the long run from more invest-ment and trade with the United States. The problem lies in the interim: How will the adjustment costs of NAFTA be distributed among the three partners and among different regions and sectors of the population within each country? How should the agree-ment address these questions?

NAFTA either ignores these problems or leaves their solution to the market. The trade pact presupposes that the amount of money needed to bring together economies and societies as distinct as Mexico, the United States, and Canada is not overwhelming and that market forces alone will provide it. In fact the United States will have to retrain tens of thousands of workers and cushion the shock to innumerable communities and factories. Canada is already losing jobs and markets, while Mexico confronts its balance-of-payments difficulties. The three countries will also have to tackle environmental problems and infrastructure deficiencies, along the border and inside Mexico, together with major regional disrup-tions and a costly process of harmonization.

NAFTA'S HIDDEN COSTS

As the European's have learned, bringing together advanced and backward economies is an expensive proposition. Since the dispar-ities between Mexico and its neighbors are greater that any com-parable differences in western Europe, odds are that the North American experience will be more costly. The three governments hope whatever must be done will be accomplished by private invest-ment: low wages and solid business opportunities will attract private capital to Mexico, paying for infrastructure, environmental cleanup, the trade gap, and debt service. But private money is unlikely to prove sufficient; nor will it flow to Mexico as freely as expected. For now, NAFTA incorporates no contingency provision—no special funds and no special taxes.

Moreover, Mexico's regulatory situation was largely excluded from NAFTA, with the exception of those areas where strong

American interests are involved: foreign investment, intellectual property, and the textile industry. But if Mexico profoundly differs from its neighbors in any way besides overall wealth, it is in the absence of the rule of law and the regulatory framework that characterize developed market economics. The Mexican judicial branch is totally subservient to the executive; regulatory agencies have no independence whatsoever; corruption is egregious. By omitting both supranational mechanisms for enforcement of norms and rights— on the environment, labor, consumer protection, due process— and any demand for the overhaul of Mexico's political and legal system, NAFTA's signatories ignored a fundamental facet of the Mexican reality.

Finally, NAFTA does not address the issue of whether Mexico has —or should have—the same type of market economy as that espoused by the United States. Is Mexico more like the United States, where nearly everything is left to the private sector and the relatively free workings of the market? Or are Mexican traditions closer to those of the European social-market-economy model, with greater emphasis on state involvement and more stringent regulations and constraints on the market? Will NAFTA be an association of like-minded partners, like Europe before Britain joined, or will Mexico always play the role of former British prime minister Margaret Thatcher, defending seemingly eccentric customs and preferences? In the initial euphoria of negotiations, these matters were all shunted aside, dismissed as irrelevant, or to be taken up at a later time. That time may have suddenly arrived.

NAFTA NEEDS REFORM

In the same way that the Clinton administration decided that a series of so-called supplemental agreements would serve U.S. interests, a number of changes would render NAFTA far more beneficial to Mexico as well. Various proposals have been placed on the table to transfer resources from NAFTA-winners to NAFTA-losers: border-transaction taxes, a windfall-profit tax, a North American development bank, a European-style regional fund scheme, and a deeper reduction in Mexico's debt, among others.

These proposals are viable because their proponents come from the two wealthier nations, who would have to foot most of the bill. Moving forward with NAFTA without provisions along these lines would mean missing an excellent opportunity to attack the key obstacle to Mexico's development. A long-term program, including social conditionality and accountability—whereby local authorities and nongovernmental organizations receive and supervise part of the funding—would work wonders for Mexico's balance of payments, the reconstruction of infrastructure, and the redistribution of resources.

NAFTA should also be designed to contribute to political change in Mexico. It should only go into effect with a preamble like that issued in 1978 by the European Community at the start of negotiations to include Spain, Portugal, and Greece: "The heads of state and government solemnly declare that respect for and maintenance of representative democracy and human rights in each member state are essential elements of the European communities." The application of the European precedent would entail a crucial test: submitting Mexico's August 1994 presidential elections to international monitoring by the United Nations and the Organization of American States. U.S. or Canadian congressional certification of the elections should be explicitly excluded; the multilateral nature of the exercise should be firmly proclaimed.

Support exists in Mexico for the idea. The PAN has often called for international observers, and grassroots groups have invited contingents from abroad. Cárdenas met with former president Jimmy Carter in May to explore the possibility of Carter's participation in monitoring the Mexican elections. Ratification of NAFTA and its entry into law could be postponed until the elections, as may occur anyway. Or NAFTA could be ratified, but its entry into law conditioned on free, fair, and internationally monitored elections in 1994.

Finally, there is a necessary social facet to the new U.S.-Mexican relationship. Money of the right sort will not flow to Mexico in adequate volumes, nor can it be put to good use, unless a series of deep changes are carried out in social policy and structure. These policy changes must extend to unions and the environment and include efforts to reduce income disparities through tax reform and higher social spending, as well as measures to strengthen civil society. These are the famously debated labor and environmental chapters of NAFTA—side agreements with teeth, that is, commissions independent from the three governments with the resources and power to impose sanctions.

Beyond the side agreements, though, the bilateral relationship must empower Mexican society to achieve its own aims and fight its own battles. Mexico's social inequities can only be redressed through major efforts in education, health, housing, and combating poverty. This enterprise, in turn, can only be achieved through significant tax reform. Other than improvements in collection, little has been achieved on this score; the adjustment in Mexican public finances over the past decade occurred entirely on the spending side. According to the Organization for Economic Cooperation and Development, total tax revenues over GDP stagnated from 1980 (17 percent) through 1991 (16.8 percent), remaining at a level well below not only that of Europe and the United States but also that of most successful developing nations.

There are, of course, other additions to the trade pact that would be beneficial to Mexico, such as beginning immigration negotiations on temporary domestic-service workers. And there are issues of concern to the United States—and to many Mexicans—that can be partially approached through democratization: the authentic establishment of the rule of law, improved drug enforcement, and an end to corruption.

CHANGE WITH OR WITHOUT NAFTA

The question in the final analysis is whether a free-trade agreement without these improvements is still in both countries' interests and, conversely, what consequences NAFTA's rejection or postponement would have for Mexico. As with the rest of the NAFTA debate, hyperbole has contaminated the discussion of what these options would imply: a collapse of the Mexican economy, a reversal of the structural reforms, a run on the currency, a dramatic drying up of investment, a deep-rooted nationalist backlash.

Except for short-term pressure on the peso—manageable in many ways, including the Federal Reserve's intervention in exchange markets—should the agreement not be approved by the U.S. Congress by January 1, 1994, these catastrophic scenarios are unlikely. They are mainly a scare tactic to expedite passage. The Mexican economy is already in recession. Adopting NAFTA on time might set off a rush of short-term financing, but raising the long-term volume of direct foreign investment is an arduous task, especially given the global economic slowdown. The economic reforms undertaken in Mexico over the past few years were largely inevitable; with logical, and necessary, rectifications and adjustments, they are here to stay.

NAFTA's rejection would lead to a nationalist backlash only if the Mexican people felt strongly enough about it. But while polls show they support NAFTA, Mexicans are increasingly skeptical and vastly uninformed about the accord. Undoubtedly, some would engage in "gringo-bashing," but outside the immediate circle surrounding Salinas and the largest Mexican conglomerates, NAFTA's postponement may either be regretted or hailed but would not mean the end of the world.

Indeed, the more severe consequences of postponement may well be political. President Salinas bet the store on NAFTA, and if passage is his triumph, rejection or delay is his defeat. There was no need to frame the issue in those terms, but now that Salinas has, damage to his prestige and power may be unavoidable. That this complicates the succession is beyond dispute, although it is already clear that Salinas will have to choose the PRI candidate without knowing the outcome of the NAFTA debate. It is equally evident that quick approval of NAFTA would strengthen Salinas's hand in the succession; its postponement or rejection would weaken him. But whether it would weaken Mexico is highly dubious.

The broader issue is which process for transferring power will help to address Mexico's deep-rooted dilemmas. The case has been made that the most desirable outcome can, under present conditions, only be secured through the traditional authoritarian process; a NAFTA-induced crisis would favor supposed "nationalist-populist" options, either within the PRI itself or in the Cárdenas camp. But others argue, more persuasively, that if postponement of NAFTA forced an opening of the political system and a clean election in 1994, the process itself would guarantee the outcome: whoever was elected —even a closet populist from the PRI, Cárdenas, or an inexperienced PAN candidate—would have to govern in the center, because that is where the votes are. Instead of the perfect outcome resulting from an increasingly unstable process, a reformed democratic process would ensure an acceptable outcome for everyone.

In the end, this is the central issue Mexicans and their neighbors to the north must face. The country has enjoyed unparalleled stability for more than seventy years, but the levers and gears that maintained it are worn out. There are two risks to choose from: sticking with the old system until it breaks down, seriously and irreparably; or taking the leap into a new system, knowing full well that both the transition period and the new order itself will not be free of dangers. Had everything neatly fallen into place—the economy buzzing along at 6 percent, jobs and social spending up, corruption and drugs under control, NAFTA approved on time and with minimal damage—a painless and risk-free, gradual and perfectly managed transition might have been feasible. But in the real world, everything does not always break the right way; many of the things that could have gone wrong did. In view of the options, the best choice for Mexico is evident: change at last. It is not without perils, but it offers the chance of finally making Mexico the country its people have always deserved, and never possessed.

PART II

WHEN MEXICO LOST ITS CHARM: A MEMOIR OF 1994

CHAPTER 4

NAFTA *and the Succession*

THE LAST YEAR OF CARLOS SALINAS DE GORTARI'S TERM DID NOT actually begin on December 1, 1993, three hundred and sixty-five days before he would transfer the presidential sash to his successor. Nor did it start in early January 1994, with the indige-nous uprising in the state of Chiapas. It really began on the night of November 17, 1993, when the much vaunted North American Free Trade Agreement was passed by the United States House of Representatives. Thus commenced an era that was to abolish forever the eternal Mexican habit of leaving things unfinished, or badly finished in the best of cases. Thanks to NAFTA, and despite the eventual cost of its passage, there was finally, some hoped, a chance for Mexico to overcome the six-year jinx—at least this time around.

It is worse than a Greek tragedy, more cruel than a Sicilian *gettatura*. Few things in the world are as persistent and disheartening as the impossibility for presidential terms to end well in Mexico. Díaz Ordaz, Echeverría, López Portillo, De la Madrid and now Salinas: it is for the reader to decide which ending was the most unfortunate and did the most harm, but none will say that any of those fateful finales was worthy of celebration, beyond the mere fact of its coming to an end. Nor can one believe that those leaders —intelligent, informed, and undoubtedly vain—did not try to avoid the infamous destiny allotted them by Mexico's newest mythology. Our past presidents spent their entire six-year terms struggling in vain to avoid the fate of their predecessors. The blame, then, does not lie in the personality of these very different leaders. Rather, it is to be found in the mechanism of succession: the source of our stability, our disorderliness, and our shame.

Doubtless, part of the problem is in the rhythm of things. The outgoing president loses power at dizzying speed; his successor does not gain it at the same pace. During that transitional sharing of power, all the political snipers, speculators, poor losers, and other assorted enemies have a field day. The more vulnerable the system, the weaker its guardians; the lesser the power of the presidency—the only power that counts—the greater the temptation to strike a blow. To have maintained this mechanism for the transmission of power—erratic, vulnerable, and obsolete—has been the height of folly for over twenty years. But each president would rather be the last to have used it than the first to relinquish it. By dint of fear and sheer doggedness, every six years Mexico begins anew: Sisyphus scaling, yet again, the slopes of Popocatépetl.

Thus the autumnal wager of Carlos Salinas: if NAFTA passed—no matter the cost—his chances of making it through the last year of his term successfully would increase exponentially. When U.S. representative number 218 voted for the treaty, a new cycle in Mexican politics began in Washington and on CNN. The presidential term would come to a happy end. And that would be the basis for everything else: a presidential succession as God meant it to be, a strong and healthy reactivation of the economy, elections acceptable to the international community and, one hoped, to most Mexicans, and finally, the president making a calm and contented exit into the realm of history.

A former president (with whom we discussed these matters a few days after the elections of August 1994) predicted the sequence of events to a group of friends: we would have the treaty, or *tratado*, and then the *tapado* (the chosen successor, carefully kept under wraps until his dramatic unveiling). If the first came off well, there would be a broad margin for the second. It was obvious to many that, if the trade treaty was ratified in time and without too much trouble, Salinas would be able to choose whomever he wanted to succeed him, without any difficulty. In that case, said our discerning interlocutor and the man on the street as well, the candidate of the Institutional Revolutionary Party, or PRI, would be Luis Donaldo Colosio, the minister of social development. Only if things got complicated would Mexico City Mayor Manuel Camacho come out ahead. The key to the unveiling was thus to be found in Washington, in the halls of the Capitol and Bill Clinton's give-and-take with the congressmen of Florida, Illinois, Louisiana, or wherever, who were reluctant but might still be persuaded or bought.

I acknowledge now that many of us expected, rather innocently, that NAFTA would be rejected by the U.S. Congress. Until the famous televised debate between vice president Al Gore and Ross Perot, everything indicated that the neoliberal Mexican team, which had bet so heavily on NAFTA, would lose the only round that counts: the final one. On November 4, Democratic majority leader Richard Gephardt confided to Carlos Heredia and me that he suspected NAFTA would lose. However, to think so was to ignore or underestimate the magnitude of what really was at stake: Mexican stability and the United States succeeding in one of its oldest and most persistent aspirations—Mexico's full incorporation into the American economic sphere and the subsequent political and international alignment of Mexico with Washington.

Only later would everyone perceive the decisive nature of NAFTA's ratification, once it became clear how many blows and attacks the regime was able to withstand in the course of 1994. Without NAFTA, any one of the devastating events of that year—the Chiapas uprising, Manuel Camacho's challenge to the system, the assassination of Colosio, the Harp and Losada kidnappings, economic stagnation, the murder of the PRI leader Ruiz Massieu—would have been enough to bring down the government. All of them together would very probably have demolished the political system that has governed Mexico since 1929. Clearly, Salinas could not foresee what was coming—but he surely imagined something. NAFTA was his lucky charm, or in any case his antidote, against Mexico's six-year jinx.

For his part, Clinton was overly disingenuous—or perhaps too statesmanlike. Now we know that his defeat in the most pressing issue facing his administration (and for which he was elected, in large part: to reform the U.S. health care system) was partly due to his obstinacy in pushing through the trade agreement with Mexico and Canada. He squandered his political capital and the legislative calendar to achieve a goal that wasn't even his own: free trade with Mexico was a Republican objective, handed down to him by his predecessor, George Bush. Clinton's voters were either indifferent or frankly hostile to NAFTA. Instead of a universal and accessible health care system, Clinton gave them the Mexican market—with the blessings of Henry Kissinger. He put foreign policy and national security concerns above the imperatives of domestic policy and his voters' aspirations. And, as was to be expected, they made him pay for it as soon as they could. In November of 1994, the president's party was handed one of the worst defeats ever in congressional midterm elections.

Ever since Carlos Salinas's government made public its decision to secure a free trade agreement with the United States, in February 1990, many Mexicans—though not enough of us—tried to modify the nature of the treaty while it was still being drafted. When the negotiations concluded and the agreement could no longer be amended, the only choice left was either to support it or oppose it in its definitive form. With no further options, many decided to oppose it, along with citizens from the two other signatory countries. We did so in the hope of achieving our ends, but also with the conviction that, if we were to lose—an outcome that seemed very likely, then doubtful, and finally unavoidable—it would be better to lose than share in a victory that was not ours.

Those of us who fought for "another NAFTA" believe that the agreement, as finally approved, is harmful to Mexico's national interest. It was negotiated for circumstantial reasons (related to the balance of payments) as quickly as possible and at any cost: this placed Mexico, from the outset, in a position of weakness from which it never recovered. Similarly, Mexico unilaterally excluded a series of goals and topics, such as labor mobility, needed in order to legalize and promote our major export, which is people; compensatory financial mechanisms, to ensure an affordable and adequate flow of resources for infrastructure and industrial reconversion; and supranational democratic institutions, in order to begin to bridge the overwhelming asymmetry between Mexico and the United States —these were all left out in order to expedite ratification. But this meant renouncing the possibility of forging a true instrument for equity and growth in Mexico. In addition, the entire exercise was permeated by a conservative and simpleminded veneration for the market's "invisible hand." Nothing would be left in the hands of the state, but instead would fall to market forces. Furthermore, thanks to the government's insistence on excluding any consideration of internal democracy, NAFTA became a powerful means to consolidate Mexico's authoritarian system, at least in the short and medium terms. The Mexican government, along with the Bush administration until 1992 and the Clinton administration since then, drew up an accord among magnates and potentates: an agreement for the rich and powerful in the United States, Mexico, and Canada, and agreement effectively excluding ordinary people in all three societies. That's why the elites of the three nations joined together on behalf of NAFTA as never before; and that is why public opinion everywhere in North America became increasingly skeptical.

Despite the good intentions of many government officials whose honesty and dedication are above suspicion, many doubted that any agreement negotiated as this one had been could open an era of economic expansion for Mexico. The government's strategy did not leave any room for the deeper issues raised by the agreement: Where will Mexico secure the funds to finance the growing gaps in the current account? What will we export in order to pay for all the imports that NAFTA proponents in the United States encourage us to consume? What instruments for the redistribution of income and wealth will Mexico use to strengthen the domestic market and establish a minimal level of social justice? On the contrary, NAFTA could well lead to a genuine disindustrialization, greater social inequality, and a lengthy period of low growth rates.

It was only fair to acknowledge the good faith in the argument repeated most frequently in the weeks before ratification: at that stage, a defeat would have been disastrous. Thus said many Mexicans who harbored strong reservations about the viability of the entire scheme. Too bad they didn't express them when there was still time to modify or stop the agreement without further harm. Today there is nothing left but the hope that all those unspoken doubts and reservations will eventually come forth.

The agreement brought certain advantages. For the first time in the history of Mexico, a matter of vital importance to the country's future was the object of democratic debate and exchange. There had been historic decisions in the past—the oil expropriation of 1938, the signing of the Bucareli agreements with the U.S. in 1924, the successive devaluations of the currency in 1976, 1982, and 1987—but none had given rise to a great debate, both open and pluralistic, substantive and political, with forces clearly aligned for and against it. Unfortunately, all of this happened not in Mexico, but in the United States. The future of the nation had never been democratically discussed in Mexico; the actual discussion finally involved not our countrymen, but our neighbors.

Clearly, however, the country did learn something. Millions of Mexicans perceived that important decisions are open and can go either way—with pressure from all sides, insults and arguments, and changing votes, resources, and positions. This is typical of a process whose outcome is unknown: wagers cross and interests line up against each other, but nobody can say beforehand what the result will be. For a country accustomed to "presidentialism," to arbitrariness, and the inscrutable motives of the *tlatoani* of Aztec rulers, this could only be beneficial. It is only unfortunate that it did not take place in Mexico, either before the final approval of NAFTA or during the 1994 electoral campaign.

For some it was neither possible nor desirable to jump onto the system's "new look" bandwagon, with or without the indirect or long-term virtues of NAFTA. One does not adopt a position because it wins or loses, but because one believes in it. Nothing that happened during those days or since has led Mexican opponents of

NAFTA to modify their position. Only those without convictions can suddenly change them. But one must be a good loser, as the saying goes. Above all, we opponents of NAFTA had to adjust our stance to fit the new situation, which has arisen precisely because of our defeat. Today, NAFTA is part of the landscape. Whether we like it or not—and I happen not to like it—it is the instrument that governs Mexico's foreign relations and much of our domestic economic policy. To continue fighting for its repeal would have been sterile, unrealistic, and somewhat insincere: a process of this type has never been reverted, even when parties or leaders promising to do so have been elected. It was imperative that we avoid the mistake made by the European left, which for years had opposed the European Economic Community instead of accepting its parameters and realities so as to transform it and, above all, make it democratic. This last goal was embraced by most NAFTA opponents in Mexico. It was also adopted, tacitly and wisely, by Cuauhtémoc Cárdenas during his 1994 presidential campaign.

Today, the best path for Mexico is to try and change NAFTA, molding it into an instrument for growth with justice, for democracy within the rule of law, to help consolidate whatever sovereignty we have left, and to struggle against the intolerable corruption that plagues the country more than ever. Until November 17, 1993, our task was to oppose the ratification of a bad agreement; now, however, we must aim not at its repeal, but at its transformation. Again, this will be a solitary struggle: those who made an act of betrayal of any dissonance in the chorus of approval and adulation will continue to string up whoever does not believe that NAFTA is the best possible agreement of all times and all possible worlds. But this is the only path uniting principle and opportunity, conviction and realism.

The magnitude of our defeat must not be underestimated. Some process of economic integration between Mexico and the United States was inevitable; but the agreement achieved by the Salinas regime was perfectly avoidable. Indeed, it was almost defeated despite the very unequal terms of the struggle. But all things come to those who wait; one must *prendre date*, as the French say, and wait for reality itself to prove who was right. The Mexican people have countless reasons to harbor great expectations from integration with the United States: centuries of hardship and injustice are behind them. The lack of debate, and of channels for the discussion that should have taken place when it would still have been useful—and possible—explains why there is now no other option to bridge differences and undo enigmas than time itself. Illusions are rarely dissolved by argument; they dissipate only (and not always) before the obdurateness of fact.

THE DECISIVE NATURE OF NAFTA'S PASSAGE SOON BECAME apparent in a most important arena—the Mexican presidential succession, which followed on the heels of the Washington vote. Independent of any psychological or affective considerations— important but, by definition, unfathomable—there are reasons to suspect that at least two potential contenders for the presidency rejected the possibility of making an unorthodox run, due to Salinas's success with NAFTA. Jesús Silva Herzog—who, though he never committed himself to an extra-PRI candidacy did not categorically reject it, either—accepted a post as minister of tourism within two weeks of the Washington vote. Would he have done the same if he had known what was to happen in Chiapas, in Lomas Taurinas (where Colosio was killed), in the Mexico City mayor's office occupied by Manuel Camacho? If the decisive reasons for his reluctance to break with the system and seek an independent candidacy rest in the depths of his psyche, then NAFTA had little to do with it. But if his decision was a political one—at least in part— then the free-trade agreement clearly played some role in it.

As it doubtless did in Camacho's decision, when he abandoned his job as mayor of Mexico City after being a finalist for the PRI nomination, only to lose it to Luis Donaldo Colosio. He resigned his post, refused to support Colosio, and finally accepted the Foreign Ministry in a surprising about-face. For Camacho as well, NAFTA must have counted in the cost-benefit analysis of a break with the PRI. His strongest suit as a potential candidate was always the supposed inability of anyone else to defeat Cuauhtémoc Cárdenas, of the Party of the Democratic Revolution (PRD), under conditions of economic hardship: inflation, devaluation, economic stagnation. With NAFTA in place, the two phenomena expected for 1994 faded away: there would be no devaluation or inflationary surge before the elections. So why take any risks in a battle already lost?

The unveiling of the candidate and its aftermath confirmed many suspicions and a few certainties that many observers still denied—some out of innocence, and others, bad faith. If anyone still had any doubts that the PRI was not a party like any other party, that its candidate was not a candidate like any other, and that the umbilical and incestuous link (not an easy metaphor to combine) between party and state was anything but distant, the sundry somersaults that followed the nomination of Luis Donaldo Colosio as PRI candidate to the presidency, in November 1993, made things abundantly clear. Five cabinet members, ten under-secretaries, countless budget officers, chiefs of staff, directors-general, and public relations officials were shifted around, fired, or replaced. The unveiling was thus much more than the simple nomination of a party candidate; it was actually an extensive government and cabinet shuffle.

From that point on, a question arose which that remains unanswered: Under such conditions, how could the country achieve an electoral competition that would be at least minimally fair and meaningful? The basic premise of any fair contest—that all participants should be on a more or less equal footing—has never been fulfilled in Mexico. That candidate who disposes freely of the entire state apparatus to recruit his team, shape alliances, meet his payroll, and conduct his campaign is simply not a candidate like any other. He is the successor kept carefully under wraps, the product of an authoritarian system. There are many reasons to defend or maintain a system such as Mexico's, but its supposedly democratic nature is not one of them.

From the time of Colosio's designation, an eternal and profound truth about Mexico became evident: Mexicans do not vote for one contender or another, but rather for or against a system that has not shown itself able to survive without its worst defects—among them, the notorious unveiling, the president's magic finger pointing at his chosen successor. It is the president's greatest prerogative, executed at the height of his power. The unveiling would be neither conceivable nor possible without the enormous presidential power offered by Mexico's political system. In November 1993, this power was made manifest as never before. Carlos Salinas nominated the PRI candidate without any attempt at dissimulation; he convinced and shuffled ministers of state, committed his protégé to his own policies, and then surrounded him with his own lieutenants.

Another weak point in the system—the traditional fear of a schism—was fully confirmed and justified. If he had broken with the regime and gone over to the opposition, Manuel Camacho would have unleashed a major commotion, even if he had merely gone home and proclaimed himself "on reserve for the republic," as De Gaulle did in Colombey-les-Deux-Eglises. Neither the unveiling, nor the system, nor the spanking-new candidate would have emerged unscathed from a Camacho break. In this sense, the system's enormous strength resides partly in its weakness. The strongest political argument on behalf of party discipline rests upon the incalculable danger of dissidence. To stifle it has a large and unquestionable opportunity cost for the country, though the losers' reasons for accepting their defeat are understandable. However, the complete refusal of almost all Camacho's or the other presidential hopefuls' followers to express publicly their disagreement with the president's decision, the form it took, and the ensuing adulation of the new candidate was more than disheartening. How could everybody agree, or not dare to say that they didn't?

Between November 17, 1993, and January 1, 1994, when the Chiapas rebellion upset the nachos table, a window of opportunity opened briefly: the possibility of inducing the regime, at its moment of greatest strength, to undertake substantive negotiations (at least regarding the elections) and perhaps even initiate a gradual transition toward democracy. Several facts suggest that this window of opportunity did, indeed, exist: some signs of flexibility on the part of Salinas and Colosio and an apparent willingness to negotiate on the part of PRD leaders Cárdenas and Porfirio Muñoz Ledo. However, this was not to be.

On December 23, during a lunch for three that began early in the afternoon and lasted until ten at night, the novelist and host Carlos Fuentes (and to a much lesser extent this author) convinced Carlos Salinas of something he had thus far apparently rejected: inviting international election observers through the United Nations so as to inspire in the opposition greater trust in the elections, thus making them more credible at home and abroad. When Salinas perceived that Fuentes, long opposed to international observers, was now in favor of them, he resigned himself to the possibility and understood that it might even benefit him—though preferably without involving Jimmy Carter or other U.S. public figures. At the height of his power and success, it seemed logical for Salinas to accept an idea that in his view no longer implied any risks, but only advantages.

That very night, Fuentes invited his friend and neighbor, PRD leader Muñoz Ledo, over for a drink. They discussed that afternoon's conversation with the president, especially the part about the observers. Muñoz Ledo was still convinced that in a clean election his party's candidate, Cárdenas, would win. If Salinas also thought that his candidate, Colosio, would win in a clean, closely monitored election, then he should be taken at his word.

Muñoz Ledo recommended that instead of Salinas being the go-between for possible meetings, Fuentes himself should promote an encounter between Colosio and Cárdenas, to discuss international observers and other electoral issues. In sum, Muñoz Ledo suggested, and Fuentes agreed, that the writer should draw up an agenda covering points of dispute between the opposition and the

PRI and then promote meetings and negotiations to bring the two sides closer together.

Cárdenas and Colosio accepted promptly, within one day of each other. Despite an unfortunate meeting with Cárdenas three years earlier, the PRI candidate said that their relationship was not tarnished by any personal animosity. The date was set for lunchtime, January 3, at Carlos Fuentes's house. Almost immediately, however, the same problems that would beset Cárdenas until the very day of the election began to surface. In discussing the idea with some of his followers, the PRD candidate found that it generated disagreement rather than approval. And he began to entertain doubts: Would the meeting be useful? How could it be kept secret? What would his followers say if it became public? What compromises might be required if he undertook negotiations with Colosio or Salinas, or both? Cárdenas changed his mind about attending the lunch and asked Fuentes to promote instead a series of meetings including the two candidates, Fuentes himself, and other guests, in order to pave the way for a possible later meeting. Cárdenas's reluctance and the Chiapas uprising a few days later effectively canceled the first of many attempts throughout 1994—all futile—to mediate between Cárdenas and the system.

Those attempts were doomed to failure for many reasons. The terms of the debate were relatively simple. In favor of negotiations, there was the logic of Pascal's wager concerning the existence of God: if we believe he exists, we have everything to gain if he does; and if he doesn't, we lose nothing. To bet on the government's need or willingness to negotiate was a low-risk, high-profit strategy. The worst that could happen was that God should not exist and that the negotiations should not prosper—and nobody would die of that. The regime's reasons to negotiate at that moment were, if not obvious, at least discernible. To reach an agreement then—before the inevitable surveys, rallies, and gossip, and other unexpected elements, could reflect the situation's true complexities—was neither foolish nor far-fetched. For the government, it was the best time to negotiate. The advantage of securing in December a series of agreements to prevent chaos in August was clear to see. The cost of incorporating Cárdenas into a democratic electoral system that would both give him a real chance and commit him to the process was indeed high. But it was affordable, certainly less costly than it might be later.

These were, more or less, the ideas held by the writer Héctor Aguilar Camín, who, along with this author, attended the two meetings organized by Fuentes. Salinas's government was the richest in many years "in fiscal and political capital"; it could thus look forward to a "clean" election, or at least one without visible fraud. Thanks to NAFTA and its attendant expectations, the economic recovery supposedly just around the corner, the apparent popularity of Carlos Salinas, the divisions among the opposition, the unity within the PRI achieved by the unveiling, there were no foreseeable complications for the regime.

But this reasoning, such as it was, did not take into account the mood or the political motivations of Cuauhtémoc Cárdenas. A strategy of this type was completely unacceptable to him. He would never adopt it: not in December, nor in January, nor after Colosio's death in March, nor in July, when Salinas and several of his own closest advisers urged him to meet with the president. First of all, the argument cited above assumed that negotiations would not cost Cárdenas anything, unless they failed; the worst that could happen was that the government would not fulfill its promises. But this was a false premise, from Cárdenas's perspective. The cost to him of any contact with the government was twofold. In the short term, it implied the risk of alienating his followers: within the ranks of the Cardenista faithful, resentment against the regime and fears of betrayal were both virulent and widespread. To negotiate with the government, even under the most advantageous conditions, was a form of surrender. Cárdenas's mistake was to assume that this sentiment—authentic and legitimate though it may have been—prevailed throughout his real and potential electorate and not just among his most zealous militants.

The second cost, though less immediate, was heavier to bear. There could be no negotiation with the regime without offering something in exchange. Cárdenas was far too serious and experienced a politician to ignore that basic fact of life. What could he give, aside from a historic "photo op" of himself and Salinas shaking hands? The only card he could play was a commitment to accept the election results, even if he lost. But to accept the results beforehand meant foregoing the equivalent of a runoff election in the streets: the postelectoral mobilization. It meant having his hands tied without any certainty or guarantee that the elections would indeed be clean. Cárdenas's entirely understandable mistrust of the regime, the lack of any means to ensure that agreements would be kept, and his belief that he could stop a "gigantic fraud" by dint of massive protests, made any pact with Salinas untenable. And if there were to be no pact, why meet with him or Colosio at all? The reasoning was watertight—but mistaken.

Those who tried to convince the opposition candidate of the benefits of negotiation understood that the Cardenista movement was painting itself into a corner. Intransigence at this early stage of the campaign meant reducing the options to a simplistic heads-or-tails: if people voted for the PRD and there was no fraud, then Cárdenas would win. If there was fraud, it would be defeated in the streets thanks to mobilizations prepared by a massive voter turnout. No margin was left for a different hypothesis, even then the most plausible: that many people would indeed vote for Cárdenas, but not enough to win or to feel robbed of a legitimate victory. The former analysis, which did not even contemplate the possibility of defeat in a more or less clean election, left the opposition with nowhere to turn. It condemned it, once again, to choose between total condemnation or shameful capitulation. That had been the quandary of 1988, and it would be that of 1994.

Then, while the opposition, mediators, and government were busy pondering their interests and fantasies, *subcomandante* Marcos burst upon the scene and froze all the action.

CHAPTER 5

The Chiapas Surprise

WITH A FIERCE "I TOLD YOU SO, YOU SONS OF BITCHES!" THE much-feared Mexico awoke from its apathy and subservience in the remote jungle of Chiapas, land of Indians and anthropologists, *huipil* dresses and synchronicity. The sudden appearance of a guerrilla war in Mexico unleashed a political crisis within the country, an image crisis abroad, and, for a short time, a crisis of conscience among the Mexican elites, separated by centuries from the indigenous peoples now up in arms. These were the immediate results of the surprising events that erupted in Chiapas on New Year's Day 1994.

Soon the first opinions, mostly accurate, appeared regarding the Chiapas rebels. First of all, unlike the peasant uprisings in the state of Guerrero during the early seventies, these were not just a ragtag group of aggrieved and rebellious peasants. Clearly, not all the members of the Zapatista Army of National Liberation (EZLN) carried weapons as modern and powerful as those proudly displayed on television; but the several thousand fighters were undoubtedly part of a well-defined and coordinated structure, with a single command and a consistent political discourse. Their organizational capacity and logistics in communication, public relations, and military tactics and strategy revealed a group with years of preparation, and that included well-trained cadres and instructors.

In the second place, the mere appearance of the Zapatistas denoted a problem, or else an almost incomprehensible mystery, within the workings of the Mexican state apparatus. For three years, there had been mentions of a guerrilla movement in Chiapas; in July and August of 1993, the daily *La Jornada* and the weekly magazine *Proceso* had published extensive reports on combats in the Lacandon jungle and near the town of Ocosingo. As Carlos Montemayor, the leading authority on the history of the armed struggle in Mexico put it, "In those regions the mountains have eyes."[12] Everything is known. In addition, Mexico's intelligence services, corrupt and ruthless though they might be, enjoy a well-deserved reputation for effectiveness. When they want to capture somebody, find something out, or infiltrate a group and deactivate it, they succeed in doing so. It was incomprehensible that several thousand Chiapas peasants—led by military chiefs both white and indigenous, from both Chiapas and other regions of the country—should train, accumulate supplies, and prepare a complex, incredibly ambitious operation, without anybody noticing. It was even more baffling when one recalled that Interior Minister Patrocinio González Garrido, responsible for internal security, had been governor of Chiapas until early 1993 and that he maintained political control over his state. So the very serious breach in intelligence within the government of Carlos Salinas revealed either enormous irresponsibility—that of allowing the uprising in order to achieve a political purpose—or else a series of internal divisions much greater than had been apparent. This was the first exorbitant cost of NAFTA.

Thirdly, the Chiapas uprising proved right the obstinate and much-reviled critics, opponents, and skeptics in Mexico who since 1988 had insisted that the course followed by the regime of President Salinas would one day lead to a crisis of major proportions. And this would happen, they warned, not in a nation magically propelled toward the First World by irresponsible headlines or high-level trade agreements, but in a country as firmly anchored as ever in the Third World, a country consisting of several segregated nations, plagued by injustice and inequality, authoritarianism and corruption, poverty and marginalization. The Chiapas uprising became a symbol of that crisis—which was not, however, confined to Chiapas. Nor was it just an ethnic phenomenon or one caused only by the poverty and backwardness of Chiapas, real as they were. Although Chiapas is one of Mexico's most forsaken states, it was also one of the four that most benefited, under Salinas, from the government's

Solidarity program to combat poverty. The origin of the uprising in Chiapas was not just a matter of backwardness, indigenous marginalization, and isolation; it was, above all, a political problem.

Under Salinas, the government spent money in Chiapas; but the region's authoritarian, corrupt, and oligarchical social and political structures were left intact and even strengthened. State authorities and the army itself had for years watched the indigenous communities being stripped of their land, without doing anything about it. The security forces repressed indigenous villages without mercy: they violated human rights, raped women, jailed leaders and priests, burned villages and hamlets, and failed to address the region's age-old demands. The typically economicist, enlightened-despot approach of the Salinas regime translated into a policy doomed to failure: spending money to save the furniture while the house burned. The people of Chiapas, like millions of Mexicans, did not just want a trickle of cash, but real resources; and they wanted to participate in decisions regarding how and where those resources would be spent, and by whom. And, above all, they wanted to be treated with dignity, instead of being humiliated, beaten, and repressed.

Fourthly, from the outset it was clear (and later confirmed) that the EZLN had more people than weapons. This is not always the case. At various times during the war in El Salvador, for instance, the Farabundo Marti National Liberation Front (FMLN) had to store part of the weaponry it received, though at other times it had fewer weapons than people to bear them. The Guatemalan guerrillas, who in the late seventies and until 1981 had many more fighters than arms, was obliged to bury large quantities of weapons and ammunition after the brutal, scorched-earth offensives launched by Efraín Ríos Montt in 1982 and 1983. The presence of fighters without arms carried a simple meaning. Any guerrilla movement in that situation is practically condemned to grow, if it avoids mistakes, has funds and logistical networks, and does not lose too many of its fighters or supporters. It might not grow in its place of birth, if it is surrounded by the enemy, but it will grow somewhere.

A fifth observation: the political stance of the Zapatistas is virtually a first in Latin America—and this is the rationale for a movement that might otherwise seem suicidal. As expressed in the startling communiqué of January 11, 1994:

> There is a common reason for the grave conditions of poverty among our compatriots: the lack of liberty and democracy. We believe that a genuine respect for the liberties and democratic will of the people are indispensable requisites for the improvement of social and economic conditions among our country's dispossessed. That is why, just as we brandish the banner of improvement in the Mexican people's living standards, we also demand political liberty and democracy...[and] clean elections throughout the country, at all levels of government.[13]

ONE MAY BELIEVE THE GUERRILLAS OR NOT, AND ONE MAY contrast these sentences with other statements by the EZLN concerning socialism, the defeat of the army, and other utopias, but their words were far from insignificant, based as they were on history and an acute assessment of the balance of power. The Zapatistas, for example, forged their own coherent interpretation of the armed struggle in El Salvador. In their view, the FMLN— thanks precisely to the armed struggle—achieved what nobody else had in decades: not the conquest of power, nor the socialist revolution, but in-depth political reforms, clean elections, the rule of law, an end to violence and the repression of the poor, and various social and economic reforms, including the beginnings of land redistribution and a purge of the military and security forces. According to statements attributed to the Zapatistas, the aim of their revolt was not to take power or defeat the Mexican government militarily, but to be "the armed extension of the people" and to impose that which intellectuals, political leaders, civic movements, observers, intermediaries, and extremists had not been able to achieve: real democracy.

The implications of this for the Mexican conflict, and its eventual deactivation, were contradictory. Clearly, it is easier for a government to negotiate with an armed movement of this nature: it is not asking that much. But in real life, matters were more complicated because this particular movement had an ambitious agenda of its own: democracy, human rights, clean elections, and so on. Thus, from the time negotiations began in February between the Clandestine Revolutionary Indigenous Committee and Marcos on the one hand and Peace Commissioner Manuel Camacho on the other in the cathedral of San Cristóbal, there was a tension between two possible strategies, for both the Zapatistas and the government.

One strategy focused on Chiapas first: solve the problem there, and then see about the rest. This option allowed Manuel Camacho and the government to limit the scope of discussion and not go into matters beyond the peace commissioner's mandate, such as voters' lists and electoral bodies, the role of the media, campaign finances, and national and international observers for the presidential elections of August 1994.

The other approach linked the Zapatistas demands to a national agenda for democracy. It acknowledged that without a democratic transition in Mexico there could be no solution in Chiapas. It implied a political reform in Chiapas, directly associated with genuine reform on a national scale, and suggested that Chiapas be used as a pretext and a lever to transform Mexico's political system definitively.

The two approaches coexisted, like twin shadows accompanying the country, beginning on January 1. From the revelations of *subcomandante* Marcos published in *Proceso* on August 8, 1994, we learned that the government not only attempted to limit the matter to Chiapas, but also to its strictly financial aspects: it proposed giving money and public works to the Zapatistas in return for a few symbolic weapons. But we also know that the electoral advances that did occur in 1994 were due to the government's need or awareness that Chiapas should be used to open other spaces. Finally, the conflict in the south remained at the center of national concerns until well after the August elections: indeed, negotiations on the election in Chiapas itself were closely linked to the so-called fourth electoral reform of the Salinas administration and to the national dialogue among political parties. The government never explicitly accepted Chiapas's inclusion within the national context; nor was it able, however, to dissociate Chiapas from the rest of the national agenda. There can be no better proof of the movement's importance.

Among many other consequences, the Chiapas uprising sparked several important debates in Mexico and all of Latin America. The first—perhaps the most limited to specialists—concerned the viability and relevance of the armed struggle. Few events within the region have stirred Latin American public opinion as much in recent years as the uprising in the Lacandon jungle. Due in part to the false expectations aroused by the supposed "Mexican miracle," in part to the fact that NAFTA went into effect that very day, and in part to the epiphenomenal nature of any indigenous rebellion on our continent, the feat of the Zapatistas had an extraordinary impact on Latin America's social imagination. For some, it highlighted the enduring marginalization, poverty, and discrimination suffered by the hemisphere's indigenous communities. For others, it underscored the continuing violence that permeates the Latin American landscape—always just beneath the surface, ready to explode. Finally, it revitalized the old debate on the military option and the current prospects of the revolutionary armed struggle in Latin America. One of the more marginal discussions prompted by events in Chiapas concerned an issue raised in a recent book of mine, *Utopia Unarmed.* Some concluded that the appearance of a supposed guerrilla movement in Chiapas proved that the armed revolutionary struggle was still current and that part of the analysis in *Utopia Unarmed* was not.

However, as has often been said, the strategy of a struggle does not determine its reformist or revolutionary character. One of the central arguments in *Utopia Unarmed* emphasizes the obsolescence —for now—of the very concept of revolution (democratic or of any other kind that does not corrupt the meaning of the word) in Latin America. Revolution simply ceased to be on the agenda, just as it hadn't been in the decades preceding the Cuban revolution. Nowhere in my book—except perhaps in a certain interpretation of its title—is there any emphasis on the viability of the armed struggle. As Che Guevara said in 1959, wherever there exists the reality—or even the impression—of other ways to channel the expression of discontent or popular aspirations, armed struggle is virtually impossible. Furthermore, the hardship and sacrifice required by guerrilla warfare are so great that they are hardly compatible with a reformist outlook. One does not lay down one's life for the sake of a larger education budget. Though the Latin American left does include a few examples of armed reformist movements— such as the Montoneros in Argentina and the M-19 in Colombia —they are exceptions rather than the rule. The Zapatistas are another exception.

The interesting thing about the Chiapas uprising lay precisely in the reformist character of the Zapatista Army of National Liberation and the tactical nature of its recourse to arms. In a sense, the rebellion confirms my thesis that any leftist movement in Latin America today is necessarily reformist—even if it is armed, indigenous, and encircled in that heart of darkness that is the Lacandon jungle. From their first statements in San Cristóbal, the Zapatistas, through Marcos, their mysterious masked spokesman, emphasized the reformist nature of their struggle and demands: land for the peasants, dignity for Indians, democracy and free elections for all Mexicans. Revolution was not on the agenda. Indeed, Marcos's reasoning was novel precisely because it was so reformist: the EZLN did not seek to take power or overthrow Mexico's one-party system by the strength of its arms; rather, it would use them to help those without arms achieve something like democracy in Mexico. The

justification of the Zapatista movement was to be found precisely
in the characteristics of Mexico, in the durability of an authoritarian political system, that does not allow any expression of social
discontent through meaningful elections. Marcos sought to elimi-
nate the raison d'être of his very existence—thus the clear and
undeniable link between the armed uprising, the moment of its
appearance, and the country. All of which justifies the term coined
by several others: "armed reformism."

If the Zapatista movement was not revolutionary in its goals,
neither was it strictly speaking an armed movement. It had arms,
unquestionably, but more men than guns, and those of a more rudimentary type than the weaponry displayed in the first images transmitted from San Cristóbal on New Year's day 1994. But, more
importantly, Marcos's soldiers have behaved strangely for guerrillas. They do not confront their enemy, they do not harass or attempt
to destroy him; they do not seek to take territory or positions; they
do not move beyond their strongholds. They depend for their survival on the protective mantle of a national and world public opinion
moved by the spectacle of indigenous peasants facing a modern-
day air force. At bottom, the movement is eminently political. It
was able to use the few weapons it had, together with an extraordinary dramatic flair and sense of timing, to thrust itself onto the
center stage of Mexican political life within less than seventy-two
hours of combat, without any possibility of extending its military
activity beyond that lapse or any chance of resisting a sustained
offensive by the Mexican armed forces. The Zapatista Army is not
a Mexican version of the heroic guerrillas of the Sierra Maestra. Its
members are heroic, but they are not guerrillas.

IF THE INSURRECTION IN THE SOUTH CAUSED DEBATE WITHIN
the Left, it also generated within the Mexican government doubts
and suspicions that revolved around three basic themes: the origins
of the uprising, its immediate consequences in terms of political
reform, and the possible division within the PRI caused by the

resurrection of Manuel Camacho (with or without the president's blessing), following his designation as peace commissioner.

No political regime is inoculated against an upheaval like that in Chiapas. Not even the most refined representative democracy can prevent radical outbreaks of anger or despair. All countries have known social, political, and psychological upheavals like that which erupted in Mexico on January 1, 1994: the Los Angeles riots of 1968 and 1992, the events of May 1968 in Paris, the disturbances in Santiago del Estero, Argentina, in 1993 and Caracas in 1989. The difference in Mexico has to do with the authoritarian regime in place since the twenties (or perhaps always) and its accountability. Mistakes also have a price in Mexico: the cost of the crisis could be read in the roller-coaster evolution of Mexican and other emerging financial markets; in the president's face in January, March, and September; in the fate suffered by some of his subordinates and the reappearance of others; and in the political turbulence that affected everybody. In contrast with other countries, however, in Mexico the explanations that society demands of government and receives from it are elliptical and clearly insufficient. That is why the country got bogged down in sterile, Byzantine discussions and by the old Stalinist habit of making unanswerable generalizations without addressing the real issue: what happened, and why did it happen?

At first, the government's response to the Chiapas surprise and the enigma of its origins was to stammer that the administration would change "that which hadn't worked." The president's unfortunate phrase became the catchword of his acolytes; it gradually replaced any serious analysis of one of the greatest lapses in intelligence, security, sensitivity, and statecraft in the history of Mexico's one-party system. With those or similar words, other officials repeated the same chorus: the agricultural reform did not generate investment as expected; the economy did not grow as planned; social disparities did not lessen as had been hoped; exports did not increase as projected. The presidential leitmotif was repeated up and down all the levels of government, without the slightest discernment. It began to sound like an exercise in exorcism: if the need to change "what didn't work" was emphasized and repeated enough times, then whatever it was would start working again.

What was it that didn't work? The designation of Patrocinio González Garrido as minister of the interior or the authoritarian pattern of political control? The gradual, extremely dangerous dismantling of the national security system? The eternal hope that NAFTA would be ratified or the fond wish that money from the Solidarity program and the miracles of the market would automatically neutralize the anger and discontent of a whole decade of economic stagnation, social decay, and political deadlock? The government's little tricks and electoral pseudoreforms, supported by the National Action Party (PAN), or the (innocent) conviction that even the strongest opposition could be swept aside without consequence?

The problem lies in the *retour du refoulé*, the return of the repressed, in French psychoanalytic language. Until it is resolved, an injury in the unconscious continues to generate effects, traumas, neuroses, and crises. The murders of Cardinal Posadas, Colosio, and Ruiz Massieu, the kidnapping of Harp, and the uprising in Chiapas all derived from that injury. They were indirect results, consequences indecipherable in their precise mechanism, of a problem left unresolved or buried in the national unconscious.

Ungovernability in Mexico has always arisen from two sources: the collapse of mechanisms for the peaceful settlement of disputes among elites, and the sporadic exacerbation of popular discontent compounded by the absence of channels for its expression. In recent times, especially since 1988, the governing group has devoted itself to dismantling the procedures previously used to settle differences among the powerful, without building any new ones. In addition, the government had generated greater tension among the masses by extending the economic recession for more than ten years, without opening any channels for the expression of discontent. As with the unconscious, the timing, intensity, and form of a crisis are by definition unpredictable. That is why crises always take us by surprise and why they are always unavoidable.

One effect of the outbreak in Chiapas was the agreement among the political parties drawn up by the newly appointed interior minister, Jorge Carpizo, and signed on January 27, 1994. It paved the way for negotiations and the so-called Barcelona Agreements (named after the street where the negotiations were held). The pact included various essential points, indispensable in any agreement: in particular, it acknowledged the need for consensus. The document also emphasized the need to broaden those spaces left open by the electoral law then in force, or else to amend it. This meant accepting, at least tacitly, that the existing legislation—reformed twice already under Salinas—was deficient.

The devil lay in the details of the document's eight points, as well as in two matters not mentioned but undoubtedly on the political agenda: national election observers and their international counterparts. Clearly, an external audit of the voters' roll could help clean up what was obviously a questionable list or merely serve to bleach it somewhat. Everything hinged on how the audit was conducted, by whom, and what was meant by *audit* in the first place. Beyond that, the question was what would be done to correct the deficiencies found by the audit—if any were.

As for the "impartial, honest and competent" composition of the electoral bodies, everything depended on the people involved. If the government and the PRI continued to propose PRI followers disguised as independents and the PRD continued to propose independents disguised as Cardenistas, the electoral bodies would continue to suffer from serious deficiencies. This was indeed the case for several months. As a result, the six "citizen councillors" of the Federal Electoral Institute (IFE) who were finally chosen did not assume their posts until early June, when there was hardly any time left for them to fulfill the enormous expectations raised by their designation.

The same dynamics prevailed in discussions of the media and campaign finances. Twelve and a half percent of government-owned time on television was an important gain for the political parties, but the real issue was Jacobo Zabludovsky, Mexico's only significant television newscaster, who has been on the air every evening for the last thirty years and where the overwhelming majority of Mexicans get their news. As long as the government and the PRI refused even to discuss the news programs on Televisa, the major progovernment media conglomerate, there could be no civilized elections. Once again, the essential point was hidden among the details: Who broadcasts the news, who can complain about them, to whom, and with what consequences? The seriousness of the matter would become apparent only after the fact: the least progress was made precisely in ensuring candidates' access to the mass media —perhaps the most important point.

Something similar happened with the problem of campaign spending. For the IFE to set a limit on contributions was not enough; what was missing was a commitment by the candidates not to spend more than a certain amount, no matter what the origin or sum of what they received. But retrospectively, we might say that the reform's weakest point was that concerning the international observers, for reasons we shall examine shortly. Knowing now the bitter aftertaste that the election would leave us, we should have advanced further in this area. It is worth analyzing in some detail, as it caused a great deal of confusion and not a few misunderstandings.

If international scrutiny had been well implemented, it would have been almost impossible to delegitimize or violate the right of Mexican voters to elect a president from another party. But outside observation could also be used as a smoke screen, for purely propagandistic purposes. This type of scrutiny hinged on personalities: if one or two former Latin American presidents, a couple of European social-democratic politicians, and a threesome of U.S. academic personalities were chosen as observers, the monitoring would serve little purpose. If, in addition, these personalities arrived in Mexico only a few days before the election, they would be even less of a guarantee. They would not understand the situation well enough, nor gain the necessary trust of all the parties involved throughout the process, to play any useful role on election night. In a word, the process as a whole would escape external institutional scrutiny; the voters' list, the media, and funding and electoral organs were unaffected. This "light" brand of international scrutiny is not entirely useless, but it is not worth much and can even be dangerous.

International scrutiny as it should be is entirely different. To begin with, it involves institutions, not personalities. The United Nations and the Organization of American States (OAS) have successfully observed several elections in Nicaragua, Haiti, El Salvador, and Namibia. Other institutions have observed elections in countries more similar to Mexico (Pakistan would be the best example), though perhaps with less success. When an institution is involved, electoral observings, moral weight and authority given the need of the institution to account for its performance increase substantially.

In the second place, an observation process by the United Nations or OAS implies a much larger number of observers: in principle, it can involve up to one observer per ten voting booths. Thus the large number of observers in South Africa, for example. This format makes it much more difficult to commit fraud or question the legitimacy of election results; observers know what they are talking about, because they have been present throughout the country. Thirdly, observation processes sponsored by the U.N. or OAS imply a longer stay within the country and greater involvement in the entire electoral process: voters' list, campaigns, mass media.

The presence of observers usually has several effects. In highly polarized countries, in which enormous distrust reigns among the different parties and there are no external, impartial bodies trusted by everyone, or any recent (or remote) precedents for democratic competition, observers tend to serve as a board of appeals. The opposition parties resort to them when available judicial recourse does not seem to work; and the government resorts to them when it needs an effective mediator to solve otherwise intractable problems. Opposition candidates tend to follow the observers' rulings; the opposition cannot systematically reject them without losing credibility and seriousness. Besides, most of the observers' decisions tend to favor the opposition. It is the government, almost by definition, that tends to commit the most infractions. By becoming involved in reviewing countless accusations and irregularities among parties and candidates, the observers gradually secure their confidence and that of the population.

Then the presence of an ubiquitous, highly visible, and lasting body of outside observers inspires trust in a population generally mistrustful of elections—though it may also arouse nationalistic feelings of humiliation and rejection. (The hatred or love that people eventually feel toward observers is another story.)

Finally, observers commit all the contending parties to the election process. As a result, the government and official candidate cannot resort to any last-minute ploys. They must go forward to the election with whatever they did before—good or bad, honest or dishonest. There is no chance for the computer system to "fail" (as happened on election night in the presidential election of 1988). There can be no power cuts, changed ballots, or other alchemical maneuvers. There can be an *ex ante* fraud—in the voters' list or by using duplicate voters, "group" ballots, or various types of pressure on voters. Some of these tactics, however, will be detected.

Of course, opposition candidates find themselves in the same boat. If they are able to present accusations that are duly attended to, if the process is adequately monitored, and if they do not withdraw from the race, then they can hardly question the results backed by an international authority to which they have resorted on many occasions. Accusations of fraud, run-offs in the street, and the rejection of results are no longer up to opposition candidates; they are, instead, a matter of certification by the observers.

The Mexican government handled the issue of international observers with all the cunning and subterfuge it had become famous for. Angel Gurría, then the PRI's secretary of foreign relations and subsequently Mexico's foreign minister, addressed the matter at a symposium held at Georgetown in June of 1994. According to him, when Mexican authorities tried to find out about the observation statute at the United Nations, the U.N. Secretariat in New York responded that it would be better for Mexico not even to submit an application. The reasons given were essentially bureaucratic. According to Gurría, the United Nations indicated that a Mexican application would be turned down, as Mexico did not fulfill any of the four conditions required for the U.N. to send an observers' mission: a lack of technical expertise to hold elections, a scarcity of resources, the end of a civil war, or the end of a dictatorship. If Gurría's statement is true, then the United Nations' response sinned either from ignorance or disingenuousness. Mexico's case could indeed be assimilated, *sui generis*, to an end-of-dictatorship hypothesis, but only if all the Mexican parties involved agreed to share the responsibility for that statement.

In reality, the United Nations did not want to get involved in the hornet's nest of Mexican politics—and neither did the government. That is why the government approached the U.N. only when the deadline for initiating an observation process had already passed. The opposition was also partly to blame. At the Georgetown symposium mentioned above, the regime's advisers argued that former legislation (reformed in 1993) did not permit the presence of foreign observers and that amending it would require the opposition's approval, which would be too long in coming. The officials argued that the opposition's delay had to do with its own reluctance to have international observers present at the elections.

Once again, Cárdenas's ambivalence and the PAN's opportunism exacted a heavy toll. Cárdenas had pronounced himself in favor of international observation years before. He even traveled to Atlanta in

May 1992 to discuss the matter with former president Jimmy Carter. But he never made it into a major issue. His approval of international observers was reserved, sincere but silent; he expressed it only when specifically asked. The reasons for Cárdenas's ambivalence are easy to infer: many in his party (although not Porfirio Muñoz Ledo) were against observers. Furthermore, as long as the government itself was not convinced, there was the risk that it would launch an insidious—and well-financed—campaign against the "traitor who sold out his country." Nor was Cárdenas certain of any benefits to be had from negotiating the matter with the regime in order that government and opposition submit a joint petition to the United Nations.

The PAN was the first party to launch the idea of international observers. Among other initiatives taken by the PAN since 1986, were its appeals to fora such as the OAS and the Inter-American Human Rights Commission to denounce the bias in Mexico's electoral legislation. The PAN favored observation not only in principle: National Action militants actually participated in observation missions sponsored by various U.S. organizations. Shortly before his death, the PAN leader Manuel Clouthier attended the May 1990 elections in Panama as a member of the delegation headed by Jimmy Carter. But, as the PAN negotiated electoral reforms with the Mexican regime, it lost interest in an issue—international observers—which irritated the government and might one day prove embarrassing to the PAN itself. It was not at all clear that international observers, no matter how well disposed, would accept the backroom deals made, say, in Guanajuato or more recently in Yucatán. Thus, National Action did not take up the cry for international observers, either. As a result, the government was able to do more or less as it pleased, in this as in many other areas.

The regime needed to push through some electoral reform, for three reasons. The first was Chiapas. Given the enormous difficulty—or, more likely, the impossibility—of finding a complete regional solution to the Chiapas conflict in the short term, the government's only viable response to the crisis generated by the events of January 1, 1994, lay in a nationwide political opening. Even if Peace Commissioner Manuel Camacho had been able to distribute thousands of hectares of land to the region's peasants and remove dozens of PRI mayors, the Chiapas problem would still persist for a long time. Unless a majority faction of the Zapatista forces could be disarmed quickly, the government's only other option was to neutralize their major demands—both local and national—so as to render the recourse to arms unnecessary in the eyes of society. Those demands included clean elections.

The second reason for reform lay in the risk of a political explosion. The dangers of fraud, postelectoral protests, and a second round were not the same before and after Chiapas. After January 1, weapons were involved—and the example of what could be accomplished with them. There was also great irritation, even exasperation, on the part of broad sectors of society and a greater awareness among so-called civil society.

The third reason concerned Mexico's image abroad. The Clinton administration probably would have overlooked a large-scale electoral fraud in Mexico. But if the government persisted in its traditional tactics, it would face serious obstacles in the U.S. press, academic circles, nongovernmental organizations, and Congress. The United States would not save Mexico from fraud, but it would not be able to spare Carlos Salinas the consequences, either.

Given the Barcelona Agreements, two distinct, hypothetical electoral contests were possible. One favored the opposition: it took hold, especially after the events in Chiapas, until the assassination of Luis Donaldo Colosio in March 1994. It included a campaign criticizing the previous administration, the outgoing president, and the mistakes and violations that had led to disaster: an excessive emphasis on cutting inflation, the lack of growth in the economy and employment, the concentration of wealth, the absence of democratization, corruption, an undue submissiveness vis-à-vis the United States, the government's intellectual arrogance and neglect of social policy, and so on. In that debate and contest, the critics of the regime would undoubtedly win: it is easy to criticize a government that has committed indisputable errors and difficult for the government to defend its record, even if the opposition's alternatives to those errors, in many cases, would have been neither pleasant nor easy. If the election had been clean, if debate had focused on the final balance left by the previous administration and the countless mistakes and violations committed by the Salinas government, the opposition might have won.

For the race to favor the PRI candidate, the second possible contest would have had to be imposed. In this option, the focus would have to be on the future instead of the past—what *would* happen, instead of what had already transpired.

When a contest is centered on the future and not the past, the opposition to a party entrenched in power for a long time—anywhere, and certainly in Mexico in 1994—faces a very real problem: by definition, the opposition lacks the cadres, resources, experience, and information needed to formulate government programs and specific proposals and to present them convincingly. Also by definition, a party that has been in power for over half a century —and that uses and abuses government resources—can generate ideas and strategies with greater ease. As is well known, the best argument in favor of parties perpetually in power is that their adversaries do not know how to govern. How can they, if they've never had the opportunity to learn?

The government had its way: the campaign focused on the future, not the past, but without forcing the official candidate to reveal his intentions at any time. Ernesto Zedillo was able to dodge all questions and challenges without ever explaining how he would solve any of the great dilemmas facing the country: growth or controlling inflation, domestic or foreign savings, trade liberalization or industrial policy, democracy or the continuation of the PRI's power, less inequality or more concentration of wealth, and so on. The PRI's clever departure from what should have been the focus of the campaign succeeded, thanks to one single element: fear. Through a campaign based on fear, the government and the PRI focused the country's attention not on the future under Zedillo nor the past under Salinas, but instead on the future under . . . Cárdenas or Diego Fernández de Cevallos. Fear became the spearhead of the campaign. Voters were induced to ask themselves whether they wanted to live under an opposition government, with the ensuing chaos, violence and decomposition. For its part, the opposition proved incapable of breaking this stranglehold. It was unable to expose the government or to persuade voters that the violence and instability already rampant were the fault of the dominant political system—that they were not in the future and had nothing to do with the opposition's possible victory.

The author of this skillful manipulation of public opinion was obviously the president. At bottom, he continued to hold the balance, deciding whether the campaign would be substantive and programmatic or just revolve around the accomplishments of his own administration. He chose the latter, for one simple reason: without manipulating public opinion, it would have been impossible to avoid a critical evaluation of the Salinas government. And if that evaluation had taken place, his opponents would have used it to their advantage; in consequence, his friends, and especially his virtual successor, would have had to take his defense instead of adopting their own causes. This would have inspired fears in the PRI that Cárdenas or, after the debate in May, Fernández de Cevallos might indeed win in August.

Under the Barcelona reforms, the race might have been substantive, clean, and fairly contested. This did not happen. Other conditions would have to have been met: a united opposition, a revitalized opposition, or a split within the PRI. None of these materialized, either, and one of the reasons for the anticlimax of the election was precisely that none of these things happened. After the debate among the three principal candidates (Zedillo, Cárdenas, and Fernández) on May 12, 1994, the idea of a united opposition reappeared—but came to nothing. One of the last hopes emerged in March 1994, when it seemed possible for a few days that Manuel Camacho would run for president. His decision not to set the limits of the election and the campaign.

THE POSTMAN DID NOT RING TWICE, IN THE CASE OF CAMACHO, but four times. Once, in November, when Colosio was unveiled as the PRI candidate; again, in January, with the Chiapas uprising; in March, when rumors spread that Camacho would replace a lackluster Colosio; and finally, in June, before the Chiapas negotiations ended amid widespread political uneasiness. Why didn't Camacho run? Speculation about the reasons for his indecision and reluctance soon replaced any discussion of his real chances and the conditions for success. So far, he himself has offered only hints and insinuations. But what he has said, and what has become known, allows us to formulate a coherent explanation, though not necessarily a true one.

Camacho wanted to be president. He said so in public and in private. Indeed, if he contributed anything new to Mexico's traditional unveiling, it was the open expression of his ambitions. He believed until the very last day that he would be unveiled as the PRI candidate, and he was convinced of it for one single reason: he was certain that Carlos Salinas, the friend of his youth, would not have allowed him to accumulate so many handicaps had Salinas not decided to name him as his successor no matter what. Each contact Camacho had with the opposition, each supposed act of populism, each open-minded gesture, cost him points with the system, the business sector, or the Right. At the same time, he discussed each contact at the presidential residence, Los Pinos, and was generally authorized to proceed. For example, on October 19, 1993, Manuel Camacho accepted an invitation I extended him— and many other friends—to celebrate at home the publication of my latest book. Cuauhtémoc Cárdenas also came, and the meeting between them aroused the curiosity of my guests, as well as of other people who later heard about it. I assumed that Camacho had come because he trusted that doing so would not harm him politically, and that he had reasons to think so. But he might have taken tolerance for approval: I am not certain that his attendance was well viewed by those who would soon make a decision about him, which he was anxiously awaiting in those very days. Camacho would doubtless have found it inconceivable that the president would encourage him in his "extracurricular" political activities while he was still mayor of Mexico City only to deny him the candidacy afterward, due to other people's criticism of those very activities.

Thus Camacho's consternation when Luis Donaldo Colosio was named candidate. He had lost, and his defeat was largely due to factors generated by the president himself. But Camacho's trust in Salinas, which led Camacho to believe until the very last day that he would be chosen, paralyzed him in the succeeding months. Each time opportunity knocked, week after week, Camacho found himself in an impossible situation: he was unwilling to take any action against Salinas or without his approval, but he never knew for sure what game the president was playing. In those days of February and March, I was convinced that Camacho would not run as an independent candidate because he would never do so against Salinas's will—and it would be illogical for the president to encourage him to do so. Camacho was never able to ascertain exactly whether Salinas was leading him on (in January, February and early March), as Colosio's followers believed; whether the president was using him to put pressure on Colosio, who was beginning to show too much independence; or whether Salinas, overwhelmed by Chiapas and other factors, simply did not have the energy and concentration to rein Camacho in.

When Camacho finally withdrew from the political arena on March 22 and put an end (temporarily) to all the rumors and speculation, he did so—in his own words, expressed weeks later at a private luncheon—because he had no choice. Without ever recognizing that he had contemplated an independent run, the peace commissioner voiced the following analysis: A run on the peso had begun in early March, fed largely by all the rumors concerning Camacho himself. This uncertainty placed his own future political career in jeopardy. If there were a devaluation, many, especially Colosio's followers, would blame him for it, making him responsible for the fall both of the peso and of the First World illusions of the Salinista middle class. In view of this, Camacho attempted to stop the speculation, first by means of a peculiar self-sponsored interview with David Asman of the *Wall Street Journal.* When this proved insufficient, he decided to withdraw from the game altogether, in order to protect his political future.

The final destiny of Manuel Camacho remains unclear. If his indecision was a character trait, it will be hard to overcome. His personality, the steps along his political itinerary, and his long and eventful passage through the glories and failings of Mexico's political labyrinth, opened a brilliant career for him within the system, but also made it impossible for him to pursue any path outside that system. He will remain a friend for many and an unfulfilled promise for all.

However, if his indecision derived from loyalty to Salinas, that speaks well of him as a friend, but badly of him as a politician seeking change. In any case, that is all in the past; his loyalty to his master ended on December 1, 1994. Camacho might now devote himself to building (with others, and without the stellar role he might have consolidated during the year of surprises) the great movement for democracy that he contemplated with many of his friends and potential allies. Having paid his debt to Salinas, he enters the Zedillo period free of any guilt, burden, or skeletons in the closet. The road for him is open, wherever it may lead.

CHAPTER 6

Colosio, Cárdenas, and the Not-So-Great-Debate

THE ASSASSINATION OF LUIS DONALDO COLOSIO COULD HAVE occurred any time, any place: there is no country or historical period immune to this sort of tragedy. But it happened in Mexico, on March 23, inaugurating the country's worst political crisis since the twenties. The state of the nation in which all this took place was not unrelated to the causes and consequences of that death, so deplorable in a young and decent man.

Political violence—or ordinary violence with political consequences—had been on the rise in Mexico even before Colosio's assassination. Over a hundred political activists from the opposition lost their lives during the government of Carlos Salinas. Cardinal Posadas of Guadalajara was murdered in May 1993, and his killers are still at large. The armed uprising in Chiapas, which began on January 1, 1994, shattered the country's confidence and expectations, as did the series of explosions and bomb threats in the days that followed. The kidnapping of one of the owners of Mexico's largest bank also revealed to what extent order and stability—which had made Mexico unique, for better or for worse, in Latin America for over half a century—were now threatened.

The security apparatus, the succession mechanism, and the loyalties and institutions that had braced Mexican stability for such a long time became obsolete. In this sense, Salinas was right in seeking to fix it. But the machine needed more than a few minor repairs: it needed a brand-new chassis, suspension, tires, and motor. A complete overhaul was necessary—one that would create new mechanisms to rule a nation that had always been hard to govern.

THE AMBITIOUS YOUNG MEN WITH MODERNIZING IDEAS WHO took charge of the country in the mid-eighties were afraid of going too far. They refused to replace the old procedures with

new, democratic ones—and suddenly found themselves in the worst
of all possible worlds. The old system was still in place, but obsolete; and there was no new system to keep things going. Guerrilla
warfare, the kidnapping of two of the country's richest men, and
the assassination of one of its most important political figures—
all within a three-month period—was not what one would have
expected from the renowned stability of Mexican institutions.
Mexico continued to be unique in Latin America; but now the difference lay in its lack of democratic institutions to replace traditional forms of stability.

There are only four things certain about Colosio's death. In themselves, they do not indicate who murdered him; nor do they create
a context allowing us to deduce the reasons for the crime. We may
never know for sure exactly what happened that stifling afternoon
in Lomas Taurinas. The successive governments dealing with the case
may well be caught in a trap, set by the political system that gave
them their power in the first place. For the system, only a "single
gunman" theory is acceptable; but public opinion will believe only
in a conspiracy—with a plausible motivation—and in a master plan
behind the assassination. There is no way out of this dilemma: it
will never be possible to construct a hypothesis satisfying both
requirements. Rather than speculate on the many versions making
the rounds, it is best that we limit ourselves to that which is feasible, even if we are not certain of it. Four events or considerations
come to mind.

First of all, in Porfirio Muñoz Ledo's apt formulation, Colosio
jumped the gun. He hurried the pace of the succession process,
picking fights, and advancing pawns and ideas before he had conquered—much less consolidated—the power to do so. This doubtless had to do with his character—he was somewhat brash and
hotheaded—but also with the necessities of the campaign. For the
first time in ages, or ever for that matter, the presidential succession in Mexico was going to be played out in an election that would
be more or less disputed and that was seen as such by all contenders.

Colosio began to mark his distance from his mentor and friend Carlos Salinas, without yet having the means and resources needed for the weaning, the almost oedipal separation, implied by a traditional succession in Mexico. There was nothing drastic about it: neither his speech at the sixty-fifth anniversary of the PRI on March 6, 1994, two weeks before his death, nor his private conversations or insinuated promises were enough to create the impression of a break. But something was clearly afoot.

I recall my last conversation with Colosio on March 10 (less than two weeks before his death), during a long luncheon that was not the first, and should not have been the last, at the home of a common friend, Margarita González Gamio. After discussing many topics over the hours, we eventually got down to the central issue —the election. The PRI candidate asked me, point blank, for whom I was going to vote. Somewhat taken aback, I answered that, given the circumstances in Mexico, I felt obliged to vote for an opposition candidate—that I could not choose any candidate based on his personal virtues or defects, on any affinity or friendship, but rather on the implications that his victory would have for democracy in the country. I ended by saying that under different conditions I might think differently. Colosio's response was swift and disconcerting: "And what if the three of us (Colosio, Cárdenas, and Fernandez de Cevallos) were opposition candidates?" Our discussion came to an end at that point; we agreed to meet again, alone or with our families, every two weeks or as often as his schedule permitted.

I would not dwell on this anecdote if Colosio had not expressed himself thus to many people in those days. At another luncheon, on February 14, he said something similar, revealing his growing awareness that he did not want to—and would not be able to— govern with the same group of people.

It has been said that, a few days before his death, Colosio had dinner with a group of businessmen in Las Lomas, a fashionable part of Mexico City. According to this rumor, he left the table in a fury after having declared that things could no longer go on as they had been. His mood, a mixture of anxiety, melancholy, and indignation—due to what he was learning about the country—became a political event. The resentment of many Colosio supporters against President Salinas, following the latter's hesitation and flirtatiousness with Manuel Camacho, also played a part. In political opinion, as distinct from public opinion, these facts would provide a first explanation for the second element that stands out.

The second event worth recalling was witnessed by millions of television viewers throughout Mexico. At Lomas Taurinas, as in all his public appearances, Colosio virtually threw himself into the arms of the people, allowing himself to be surrounded and separated from his security detail. This reckless behavior had an undeniable logic to it: in a country in which the public's mistrust and alienation from government reigns supreme, physical contact was the only effective and immediate remedy. It can also be fatal. The risks taken by Colosio derived directly from the political dynamic that carried him and from the astonishing awareness he came to have of his own predicament.

Thirdly, very few people in Mexico believed or believe that Mario Aburto acted alone when he assassinated Colosio. The widespread doubt felt by Mexicans rests upon many pillars, ranging from the age-old skepticism that characterizes this country's inhabitants to the meager likelihood of the explanations thus far uncovered by successive investigations. But one element that doubtless made it harder to sell the idea of a lone assassin was the belief, which spread rapidly among broad sectors of the population, that Colosio had already come into conflict with the country's economic or political powers-that-be and that they were responsible for his death. This conviction was partly due to a self-inflicted blow by the government: it insisted repeatedly on the fiction that the most retrograde sectors of the PRI itself, the dinosaurs (so called for their resistance to change), were somehow responsible—and many people came to believe it. The syllogism was quite simple: if Colosio had already quarreled with some of them, if the "bad guys" were within the system itself, and Aburto could not believably have done it alone, then it was the system that killed Colosio. Thus, the regime was able to sidestep the initial, apparently unsolvable electoral obstacle that this impression should have represented; however, its sequels continue to bear poisoned fruit.

The fourth political consideration arises directly from the first three. Clearly, the idea that Colosio's murder was ordered by the president's office seemed farfetched: no political problem could have grown so critical as to require a solution with such grave repercussions. But there was an abundance of political, economic, and other forces with rational motives to get rid of Colosio. That which is obvious in absolving Carlos Salinas and his top adviser, José Córdoba, is not so obvious in the case of others. The trick was to deflect possible guilt away from other political forces by assimilating them with the presidency or the PRI, or even so-called dinosaurs such as Fernando Gutiérrez Barrios, in order later to dismiss it as unthinkable. Serious arguments focusing on particular individuals or cases were shifted onto others, losing credibility in the process. Colosio's differences with the system did not merit his assassination by the party leadership; but they were enough for other sectors (which for years and decades have reaped the system's benefits) to take radical steps. Drug traffickers, narco-politicians, business sectors linked to drugs and corruption, regional *nouveaux riche* involved in drug trafficking, the privatizations that facilitated luxury money-laundering, sectors in the official party linked to narco-business and narco-politicians, all had more than enough reasons to assassinate Colosio as an act of revenge, a preventive step, a life insurance policy.

Soon after Colosio's death, we all discovered just how well-lubricated the system's succession mechanisms still were: the president's magic finger (*dedazo*) designating the official successor, the stampede (*cargada*) of new converts following that designation. The first worked without a hitch: all the bewilderment and discontent within the PRI after the assassination were not enough to keep the faithful from bowing before the only possible candidate. I recall my answer to a question posed on March 27 by U.S. Ambassador James Jones at a breakfast with several Mexican intellectuals: "Salinas has three options: Zedillo, Zedillo, and Zedillo." Or, as was allegedly acknowledged by Salinas, "It was Zedillo because there was nobody else."

Fernando Ortiz Arana, then president of the PRI, was not sellable in domestic and foreign markets; Camacho was no longer viable as a candidate; others, outside the cabinet and intimate circle, were not trustworthy; and those still in the cabinet were barred by law from making a bid for the presidency so late in the game. Salinas made one change to the tacit ironclad law of the Mexican succession process: the chosen one now had to be acceptable abroad, much more fully and precisely than before when only a brief nod from the U.S. Embassy was required. This time, it was essential that the PRI candidate have not just the neutrality of the United States and foreign market, but their enthusiastic support and wholehearted blessings. Nervous and skeptical foreign investors had to be sold on the idea that Zedillo was a new Salinas (from Yale instead of Harvard) who would provide the same guarantees as his predecessor. The other possible candidates simply did not fulfill this requirement. They were not vetoed by Washington; simply, Los Pinos perceived accurately what the markets would stomach and what they wouldn't.

Following the ad hoc method launched so successfully by José Córdoba years before, Salinas opted for the only possible way to eat an elephant: bite by bite. He solved the problem of who the candidate would be by choosing Zedillo. He would deal later with making sure the inexperienced campaigner won the August 21 election. Only afterward, months later, would he work on the nature of his relationship with Zedillo, after handing him the reins of power on December 1. In the meantime, unity had to be maintained within the system at all cost, taking special care to head off any break toward the opposition. No effort was to be spared; and if it became necessary to use outdated methods or allies, so be it. In crisis situations, everything goes and everything works. It worked.

Since 1988, the greatest weakness of the opposition—especially in the Cardenista camp—was the lack of new, important converts from the PRI government. With skill and cynicism, the regime gave to all those who might have broken away whatever they needed to stay. With little practice and infinite amateurishness, the opposition made it even more difficult to attract members of the system. In the situation created by Colosio's death, both trends could conceivably have been reversed. Due to the decomposition underway and the decisive steps taken by dissidents like former Mexico City PRI congressman Demetrio Sodi, there began to be an outflow, or at least a trickle, toward something resembling a halfway house. There was no guarantee that Sodi's effort to build such a halfway house would succeed, or that other PRIistas disgusted by events would seriously envisage running for political office on the PRD ticket. However, there began to be a drift in this direction. An unfortunate full-page advertisement supporting Ernesto Zedillo, which appeared in all major Mexican newspapers on April 12, was above all an effort to staunch the blood flow toward the opposition. It was, to some extent, successful: those who had signed it could hardly break away, and those who had not would think twice about embarking on any adventures.

After Ernesto Zedillo's designation as PRI candidate, the next big event was Mexico's first and only televised presidential debate. It generated countless analyses and played a crucial role in the election results, though nobody knows exactly what role it played. It also gave rise to various interpretations and questions that deserve to be remembered. To begin with, there is still some doubt regarding its impact. All the surveys done immediately after the debate and on election day, as well as the election results themselves, suggest that it effected only a very small change in voters' intentions. Cárdenas and Zedillo, whose performances were beneath their abilities and their expectations, lost only three and eight points, respectively, in the focus group sponsored by the daily newspaper *Reforma*. The PAN candidate, Diego Fernández de Cevallos, did much better and was the great winner in terms of voters' intentions, though his gain was much less when compared with viewer expectations (that is, the difference between those who thought Diego would win the debate and those who concluded that he had indeed won it.) In the long run, however, if we adhere—cautiously—to the official election returns, he gained about seven or eight points.

Beyond its impact, the debate generated a number of interpretations, none of which garnered a consensus. First reactions to the debate soon identified the true winner: none of the above. I believe that if it had been possible, in the surveys and discussions following the debate, to express dissatisfaction or discontent, that option would have received a large measure of sympathy. Unfortunately, Carlos Fuentes was right in this as in so many things: the three contenders were not those most popular with the electorate. Several noncandidates who watched the debate in May must have asked themselves the sixty-four-thousand-vote question: "What if I had thrown my hat into the ring?"

A second observation arising from the televised encounter was that the two candidates who did poorly were both badly prepared (one was overprepared, while the other was underprepared). In Zedillo's case, the all-out effort to sell him and create an image cost him spontaneity, authenticity, and a certain freedom of action. This reflected the PRI strategy, which was to maximize the debate's formal rigidity so as to minimize the opposition candidates' room for maneuvering. Zedillo was so highly trained that he appeared neither sensitive nor sympathetic; however, he did not even do well in terms of agility or mastering the issues, in which he might have stood out. Clearly, the enormous effort, money, and time invested in preparing the PRI candidate were of little use.

The case of Cárdenas was almost at the other extreme. At the end of the day, the PRD candidate had devoted little time both to formal preparation (cameras, lighting, rehearsals, image, smiles, and so on) and to content (feeling comfortable with proposals, rebuttals, and attack strategies against his two rivals, which he did prepare). Possibly the best example is that Cárdenas mentioned only once the three planks in his platform: economic growth, democracy, and social justice. The three points should have been repeated and developed ad nauseam. However, there was not enough time—or awareness that improvisation in this area can be costly indeed.

Finally, the debate provided a glimpse into an underlying problem, beyond those already mentioned. There were two candidates with a consistent platform, identified with a more or less well identified social base: Zedillo and Cárdenas. The former offered a Salinista program and a hope: everything that had been promised would eventually come to pass, with a little more time. Many people had their doubts, but it was a consistent and logical thesis, shared by many Mexicans belonging to the country's most informed and prosperous sectors. Zedillo was fully and sincerely identified with that program, and he defended it articulately and intelligently throughout his campaign. One could agree with it or not, or believe that it simply wasn't viable in a country like Mexico, but there was no denying its existence.

Cárdenas also had a platform, which was not the one attributed to him by deceitfulness and bad faith—with the help, sometimes, of himself and his followers. It did not call for a return to the past, but for a social and democratic revision of the Salinista program. That revision was necessarily placed within the parameters of a market economy, NAFTA, a downsized public sector, but it still represented a significant departure from the status quo. It implied democratizing the country, redistributing wealth and income, reactivating the economy through government investment, and redistributing the burden of a national effort to go from adjustment policies to growth in an orderly fashion. As with Zedillo, one could agree with the platform or not, see it as viable or not, but its relevance was undeniable both in Mexico and other parts of the world. Cárdenas was not able to articulate this proposal effectively; in general, he projected a feeling and an attitude more than a formal, technically polished design. Nonetheless, many Mexicans identified with the man and what he symbolized.

The country's great dilemma revolved around an absence: neither Cárdenas nor Zedillo seemed able to attract votes by themselves, or to build the electoral coalition required by their respective projects. They are both politicians who perform poorly in the setting of a modern election campaign: television, debates, the mixing of the personal and private spheres. Despite the enduring authoritarianism and antidemocratic political culture of Mexico, these are perhaps already the main criteria for success or failure in a Mexican campaign.

Cárdenas was the great leader of a political movement opposing a near dictatorship. He did not become a winning candidate according to the election criteria of a country where over 90 percent of all homes have a television and where the only sources of information for most people are radio and television. In what turned out to be a typical election campaign leading up to an atypical election, it was difficult for Cárdenas to build the electoral base that his project required and deserved.

Ironically, Zedillo found himself in the same situation. He is doubtless a competent administrator and a serious economist. If he weren't, it would be hard to explain how a young man of modest origins could have obtained the education and positions that he did, in what is not exactly a land of opportunity. But it is another story to win votes without the official state apparatus, without the Solidarity program, without the Confederation of Mexican Workers, without the Presidential Guard—that is, to win only by virtue of his own qualities, talents, proposals, and charisma. Like Cárdenas, Zedillo was a candidate with a project and without the necessary means to attract voters cleanly and freely—without the government machinery that distorts the electoral process from the outset—so as to make his project into a program of government.

Diego Fernández did have the means at his disposal. He was a modern, telegenic candidate, with all the required resources, talents, and cunning. He was also devoid of any sense of fair play or the knowledge needed by any presidential candidate, anywhere. He had everything except the project. The salient feature of Fernández's victory in the debate was that he achieved it without a single substantive argument. If neither Cárdenas nor Zedillo presented credible, specific proposals, Fernández did so even less. If economists did not like Cárdenas's economic ideas (with good reason), what might they think of "a humanistic economy"? Amid all the verbal fencing and acrobatics of the PAN candidate, there was not even the glimmer of a solid thesis, a vision of the future, or a minimally coherent solution to a specific problem. Fernández, I insist, had everything but the project: his deficiency was no smaller than that of the other candidates. Perhaps that is why it was relatively easy for him to withdraw from the race for nearly a month and finally to renounce any chance of winning. If his project was nonexistent, or was so similar to Zedillo's that a PRI victory would essentially fulfill it, there was no good reason to fight to the death for a prize that was not that important. That was the situation Mexico awoke to on the day after May 12: it found itself forced to choose between the two candidates who had a program but who lacked the means to win freely and the candidate who could secure the votes but did not know what to do with them.

CHAPTER 7

An Expected and Frustrated Transition

THE SEQUENCE OF EVENTS FOLLOWING ZEDILLO'S NOMINATION as the PRI candidate and leading up to the dejection that swept through Cardenista circles after the debate of May 12, 1994, gave rise to various ideas within a small sector of the Mexican intelligentsia. The way the PRI candidate was selected, the disappointing performance of Cárdenas in the debate, the alarm generated by several runs on the peso, kidnappings and violence throughout the republic, brought together a group of writers and academic figures, together with various politicians from within the system and social activists more or less distanced from government, to promote a transition in Mexico. The amount of ink spilled over the San Angel Group, as it was immediately baptized, accurately reflected not its real importance or its imaginary pull, but rather the political and intellectual void into which the country had sunk, and which any novel, conspicuous initiative could have filled.

One of the ideas supported by several of the group's members was the need for a negotiated transition—to be accepted by the three presidential candidates and the outgoing government—to launch a process of democratization, which the elections alone, for a series of reasons, would not initiate.

The basic goal was a set of agreements on the program of the next government, its composition, and a calendar for the transition—all before the elections. The reason for attempting this before August 21 was obvious: uncertainty would induce the candidates to satisfy certain demands before crossing the Rubicon of the ballot, since by definition two of the three candidates would lose, but each had a chance to win.

In my own view, the obstacles in the electoral process generated both dangers and opportunities. These included the decreasing chances for a Cárdenas victory; the incomprehensible attitude of

Diego Fernández de Cevallos after the debate; and the difficulty Zedillo would have in winning over the opposition's candidates and voters if he won, given his campaign's links with the PRI's most recalcitrant hardliners.

There was indeed the danger of "two locomotives colliding," but also people's awareness of the need to avoid it. The winner might obtain less than required for a mandate, giving rise to a problem of governability under current conditions; but this could also pave the road to a new way of governing, a democratic way. It is perhaps worth emphasizing the congruence between the San Angel Group's ideas and actions, no matter one's own affinity with those ideas or the usefulness of what was actually accomplished. There was an agreement of ideas and actions, and it is worth examining both in succession.

THE STUDY OF DEMOCRATIC TRANSITIONS IN LATIN AMERICA reveals a relative similarity among recent experiences and others not so recent. There are several paths from authoritarian regimes to representative democracies, but two of them stand out for their frequency and simplicity. The first—the least common of the two—occurs when a society that is profoundly divided in social, ideological, and political terms, but whose fractures have been concealed for years by a regime lacking the democratic channels to resolve them, is suddenly forced to settle those differences through elections. Due to circumstances that are usually gratuitous—the death of a dictator, the military defeat of an outgoing regime, the end of a dynasty—that society's different political, social, ideological, and institutional forces agree to hold elections to decide who will govern, and how.

There is no agreement on how the country in question should be governed, or by whom. But everyone agrees that the issue must be solved through the ballot, and on how that should be done (majority or proportional representation, electoral authorities, voters' list, and so on). Examples of countries that have recently taken this path include Spain (1975-77), Argentina (1983), Chile to a certain extent (1988-89), and El Salvador (1992-94). None of these experiences involved governments of national unity, common fronts, or a governing consensus. But agreements were reached on the meaning of the break with the past.

The two paths are doubtless impure. Under the first scenario, though the issue of power is left to the ballot, contending forces readily agree on various aspects of the future: there will be no "Night of the Long Knives" (Spain, Chile, El Salvador) and no radical challenge to the economic course followed in previous years (Chile), though there may be deep disagreements about the future or even severe punishment for previous behavior (Argentina). But the logic of the transition is elsewhere: the consensus concerns not the future course of events, but rather the way in which society is going to choose between the different options available to it.

The second path is different: despite their differences, all political forces join in government for a while, on the basis of a provisional consensus, until the rules for competing for power are established. Perhaps its first modern-day expressions were the pacts that emerged in France and Italy at the end of the World War II, an example of which was the Liberation period in France between 1944 and 1947, thanks to the program of the National Council of the Resistance or the so-called triparty system—consisting of the Communist and Socialist Parties, and the Christian-democratic Popular Republican Movement, and Charles de Gaulle's leadership. For three years, the forces that had led the resistance governed together, with a common program and a coalition government. Despite the country's wish to extend national unity under de Gaulle, the outbreak of the Cold War made this impossible. By then, however, an agreement had been reached about the means of separation and the future rules of the game.

In Mexico since 1988, both the opposition and government have emphasized the first path in the transition toward democracy. The essential point was to have clear rules, accepted by all, regarding the settlement of disputes. Thus, throughout the entire term of Carlos Salinas and especially during the campaign, the main issue was how to hold elections (electoral authorities, voters' list, financing, media, the link between the PRI and the state) and not what each party would do if it won. This emphasis was due in part to the government's attitude and its certainty that the PRI would win clean elections: there was no reason to discuss the future with an opposition headed toward defeat. For its part, the Cardenista opposition believed the PRI would lose in clean elections, beyond a shadow of a doubt; so it had no reason to negotiate future plans with an obsolete, authoritarian government on its way out.

There was also a certain innocence on the part of Mexico's political players. They behaved as if they really believed that winning clean, or at least credible, elections was enough to implement any agenda—as if the mere fact of winning at the polls would make any major concessions to their opponents unnecessary, the latter having been soundly and definitively defeated. Strangely enough, in a country where power had never been transmitted through elections, people seemed to think that victory in a clean election would obviate those concessions that neither the government nor the opposition wished to make. In hindsight, it was naive and unrealistic to believe that divisions as deep and severe as those afflicting Mexican society would simply disappear overnight thanks to elections, in a country so lacking in electoral traditions. The fact that various members of Ernesto Zedillo's cabinet persist today in these celebratory delusions did not make them any more real or believable than they had been before August 21. In hindsight, it is now obvious that the August elections could not be the arrival point of Mexico's transition.

During the administration of Carlos Salinas, it was impossible for all the nation's political, social, and ideological forces to agree on the rules for holding elections. Nor were they able to reach accords reliable enough to withstand any possible outcome, as opposed merely to making a particular result more feasible or credible. Either because there was not enough time, or because the country's social and political forces could not resign themselves to betting solely on election returns, or because the government never really accepted the possibility of alternation in power, the elections of August 1994 did not play the key role in Mexico's hypothetical transition as prescribed by the first path.

This gave rise to two possibilities. Either the transition would have to wait for another election, and one could only hope that the conflicts arising from this one would not shatter what little stability was still left in Mexico. Or else the August polls could serve as a stepping-stone toward democracy along the second possible path — that is, through broad national agreements based on a consensus previously built and simply ratified by the election.

But this was not the view espoused by most of the country's social, political, and ideological forces. Instead, all the conceptual weight of the transition fell on the mechanics of the elections and who would win them — not on what the winners would do to heal the wounds afflicting the country. Choosing the other route would have meant recognizing that the August elections could not heal those wounds. The vote would serve to define who would be president, but not to determine his program or governing team or the steps needed to build a democracy that would eventually render such pacts unnecessary.

If Mexico had chosen the second path, three important, linked accords would have been necessary: a common program of government, a broad coalition government to implement it, and a calendar to move gradually away from the exceptional situation inherent in this type of transition. The three accords are as relevant now as ever, perhaps even more so than before. Arguably, without them Mexico will not emerge from its current travails.

It would not have been hard to define the main features of a common program to be executed by a transition government. By definition, they would have included economic, social, political, and international components. Any common agreements concerning the economic, social, and international aspects would have involved a judicious combination of existing factors and significant changes, but within the current framework. In the political sphere, in contrast, any agreement would have required the transformation of the existing framework, even while guaranteeing fully that certain changes would not be retroactive.

In the economic sphere, a national agreement would have rested on two basic premises: First of all, the stability of certain parameters for the duration of the agreement. These would be, on the one hand, the structural characteristics of the Mexican economy today: trade liberalization; downsizing of the public sector; recourse to external savings, especially foreign investment to finance development; autonomy of the Central Bank, and the curtailment of generalized subsidies. On the other hand, the agreement would have to maintain the equilibrium already attained, especially in terms of price and exchange rate stability. No agreement is possible if the country's social and political forces do not adhere to these basic premises.

Within these limits, however, a number of changes would be needed to attain the two major goals still pending: economic growth and the beginnings of redistribution, in order to start reducing the country's abysmal inequalities. Growth and the movement toward social equality would take place within the current framework, but would derive from a deliberate policy instead of being mere by-products of already existing policies. The main defect in the economic program outlined by Ernesto Zedillo during his campaign was precisely this omission. He assumed that more of the same, aside from some additional support for small businesses, would automatically solve the huge problems facing the national economy. If Zedillo's economic strategy was, inevitably, the main dish in his campaign; if he was an expert in the field; if he had unlimited human, technical, and material resources to design his program, then the huge gaps in his economic platform were presumably of a political nature. And they derived from the difficulty of choosing between several solutions, all unpleasant, to problems which could no longer be postponed.

Zedillo did not say where he would get the funds to raise government investment in a healthy and lasting way, so as to reactivate the economy. Nor did he mention the dilemma of the external accounts: How could there be growth without immediately incurring a much higher foreign deficit or devaluation? According to Rudiger Dornbusch and Alejandro Werner's essay *Mexico: Stabilization, Reform and No Growth*, published in September 1994 (three months before the devaluation), this was not possible.[14] However, it would have been difficult for the government to adjust the exchange rate significantly without an agreement like the one described above, so that the adjustment would indeed be an instrument for reactivation and not just the symbol of a failed economic policy.

The first goal—to resume economic growth—requires several conditions to be achievable in the short term. To begin with, it calls for a healthily financed increase in government investment in public works, housing, and education, creating jobs and laying the bases for future growth and competitiveness. Secondly, there must be a sustainable reduction in domestic interest rates in order to stimulate demand and allow small and medium-sized companies (which do not have access to dollars) to invest and grow. Thirdly and finally, the government must take precise but forceful measures regarding the country's foreign accounts, to ensure that economic reactivation does not worsen the trade imbalance and to finance the remaining gap appropriately.

But, as many people have noted—among them Sebastian Edwards, the World Bank's chief economist for Latin America— the consolidation of economic reforms in the hemisphere, and obviously in Mexico, requires three great transformations. First of all, there must be high and lasting growth. In order to check the spread of poverty in Latin America, the region's economies must grow 3.4 percent a year. After the complete stagnation registered in Mexico during de la Madrid's term (1982-88), the economy grew an average of about 2.5 percent a year under Carlos Salinas. According to the World Bank, such low rates of growth indicate that poverty increased during that time. In the second place, reforms cannot be consolidated without a significant increase in Latin America's savings rates, which remain 30 to 50 percent lower than in southeast Asia. This applies both to private and government savings. In other words, governments' tax revenues must increase substantially in the short term, allowing them to spend more without incurring deficits. Depending on the country, this can be done by improving tax collection (though there is now little room for further improvement), increasing tax rates (which implies problems in terms of international competitiveness), or taxing new forms of wealth and income (the World Bank's preferred solution). Finally, Latin America must undertake a process of "export substitution": it will not be able to finance its innumerable purchases abroad just by selling raw materials, fruit, and oil. It must incorporate higher levels of value added into its exports, and implement industrial and industrialization policies. In sum, a national pact in Mexico would have to reconcile these goals with economic reactivation in the short term, while preserving macroeconomic balances. If this were easy, it would not be necessary to have everybody involved in the effort.

In social terms, any transition pact would obviously have to target poverty and inequality, and prepare for the future. This chapter of the agreement would include a fiscal reform making taxes more progressive and raising tax revenues in relation to GDP, while decentralizing collection and spending to finance a vigorous program for employment, housing, and infrastructure in the short term, as well as education, with a view toward the future. It would also imply a minimal social safety net: housing, health, secondary education at least, a tolerable environment, protection against unemployment, and the attainment of higher salaries. Without a free, combative, and renewed labor movement and unions, such a social policy is impossible. Honest, combative, democratic unions are the first condition for flexibility in the labor market without greater inequality.

Also on the social front, there must be imaginative ways to combine scholarships, training and learning to face problems in employment, education, and the reconversion of part of the country's labor force. The decentralization of responsibilities, through the decentralization of tax collection and spending, must also play a key role in the consensus required by the new social policy.

In the international sphere, a national transition agreement would first of all have to respect existing commitments. In order to maintain flows of foreign capital and the country's credibility, the government would have to send signals of continuity and seriousness. This obviously refers to the country's financial obligations and the North America Free Trade Agreement with the United States and Canada, but also the more or less tacit agreements it has with the United States regarding drug trafficking and the regulation of migratory flows, at least from third countries. It is not acceptable that all commitments made by an authoritarian regime during previous administrations should be permanent and unchangeable; but the transition period should not be overburdened with too many tasks or pressures. A transition regime in Mexico would have to make certain adjustments to existing policy, whether regarding NAFTA or the foreign debt. The transition government would also have to take a firmer stance with the United States regarding migration: this is indeed the great negotiation Mexico has pending with its northern neighbor. Likewise, as a counterweight—albeit minimal —to the asymmetry between the two countries, Mexico should push for the democratization of supranational institutions as they appear and for a Central American and Caribbean common market based on the complementarity between our economy and those of Central America and the Antilles.

In contrast with the three transformations already mentioned, there must be a profound transformation of basic parameters in the political sphere. A transition agreement should focus on two major changes: the state must be democratized and civil society must be strengthened. This must be done while providing guarantees for those adversely affected by change, so that they will not pose insurmountable obstacles. The democratization of the state must begin with the electoral reform still pending in Mexico. Some progress was made before August 21, but the election returns show that the contest was neither moral nor fair, though it may have been cleaner than on other occasions. Such a reform would have to reexamine matters already discussed and go more deeply into those areas left outside the scope of previous negotiations: voters' lists, election authorities at all levels, regulation of party and campaign funding, and the generalized wish to end the symbiosis between the PRI and the state.

But the country's political mutation cannot be limited to the electoral sphere. Fair and effective law enforcement and the establishment of an honest and independent judiciary with sufficient resources are the indispensable conditions for combatting corruption and founding something that has always been lacking in Mexico: the accountability of those who govern. It is also a condition —necessary though not sufficient—for building an honest and competent security and law-enforcement apparatus to protect citizens instead of constantly entrapping and endangering them. Accountability would, most importantly, be a first step toward the clear separation of state and government—a distinction that has never existed in Mexico.

However, the democratization of Mexico should not be limited to the state. No democracy can survive in a country with little democratic experience, if it is limited to the sphere of the state. And there is no democracy in existence that can accomplish the redistribution of wealth which our country requires if the reach of reform does not extend beyond the state and into civil society. That is why a national transition agreement would have to include a series of changes and innovations over and beyond the pale of the state, to direct and encourage the revitalization of civil society. This implies an in-depth reform of the regulations, legal framework, and performance of the media, labor unions, political parties, and regional and citizens' groups in general. The state should not attempt to change behaviors, but instead build a context in which all expressions of civil society can flourish and multiply. The television monopoly must be eliminated; citizens' groups must have access to local or sectoral media; there must be an end to the practices and legal dispositions that have stifled labor union activity in Mexico since the forties. These are all urgent steps to ensure the flowering of civil society. Organizations of students, women, indigenous people, neighbors, and farmers must receive state support; administrative and bureaucratic red tape, and its abuse, must be eliminated. The end of Mexican corporativism, and its replacement not by a new state paternalism (for example, the Solidarity program) but by a true explosion of autonomous groupings and organizations, reflecting this society's great diversity, is the central challenge for the building of democracy in Mexico.

This program would be a first step, but it is not enough. The prevailing mistrust, political polarization, and grievances real and imagined would force Mexico, like many other countries, to complement the transition program with a government to execute it. The possibility of "letting the ball through but not the player" is a very real risk for all the social groups, the eternal losers, traditionally excluded by this type of agreement. Broad sectors of Mexican society have no reason to trust the traditional powers-that-be to do things differently, or to accept automatically the word of a new government that it will implement the program as agreed. There can be no transition accord without a commitment to share power among the representatives of the various political, ideological, and social forces that have joined in adopting the program.

The election returns, and the opinions expressed by Ernesto Zedillo even before the vote, effectively canceled this option. The administration that was inaugurated on December 1, 1994, was not a transition government. But this should not prevent us from wondering what might have happened if the ballot and the national mood had so dictated, and what might still occur given all the surprises the country has experienced since then.

However, the pressing need for a transition in Mexico does not stem solely from the elections and the country's exceptional situation, nor does it derive only from August 21 and its sequel. This narrow view subjects the democratic transition of Mexico to the election, seeing it both as a starting point and a goal—as fulfilling the transition in its entirety. In reality, the achievement of a structured transition with an idea, a program, a government, and calendar is not a function of clean elections. The election itself is but an isolated moment in the transition. Clearly, Mexico's transition will consist in going from an authoritarian regime to a democratic one, and clean presidential elections will be an essential part—but not by any means the entirety—of that transition.

The key is in the transition itself, not in any particular election outcome; the aspiration for a transition government is not born of violence, fraud, or a close election, but from the need to join political, social, and cultural forces during an exceptional period leading into a real alternation of power.

But if the causes and origins of the idea of a coalition government were distorted, so were its nature and composition. The real problem was never one of quotas, names, or a plurality generously accepted by an enlightened president. It is a matter of consensus and actions reflecting the awareness that commitments cannot be fulfilled without the participation of all. Many sectors long excluded from power would not enter into a consensus without some significant—as opposed to symbolic—participation in the exercise of power. Thus, a transition or coalition government would not consist in a distribution of posts among parties or groups linked to the candidates; rather, its purpose would be to implement a program previously agreed upon by a majority of the country's political, social, and economic forces.

The coalition could—and should—include the private sector in promoting exports, making long-awaited microeconomic adjustments, and ensuring the autonomous management of those state-owned companies that outlived the privatizing frenzy of the previous administration. Thus, competent and successful business leaders could hold cabinet-level positions in Trade and Industrial Development, Pemex, the Federal Electricity Commission, and the External Trade Bank—not to dismantle the state, but to save it from the neoliberal clutches of government technocrats. Similarly, representatives of prominent nongovernmental organizations would be invited to take part in the social and political reform, and cultural figures and groups to participate in education, culture, and the arts, so that they stay in the hands of creators, not bureaucrats.

But a true coalition government would also have had the support of all the opposition. Taking into account the vocation, talent, and experience of the two relevant opposition parties, the PAN could have been entrusted with delicate posts such as those of attorneys-general of the republic (already the case) and Mexico City, the federal comptroller, the independent tax agency proposed by Zedillo, the Federal Commission for Competitiveness, and the National Security Coordinating Office, if it were unfortunately to survive. The PRD, or in any case the Cardenista movement in its broader definition, could have been in charge of social spending, the unions, and reforms of the labor sector and the Human Rights Commission, for instance. A coalition government would have had to include local interest groups in areas with clearly regional tasks: indigenous communities and the northern border are cases in point.

Just as the entire state should not overlap with government, the agreement on a national coalition government should also encompass autonomous posts and responsibilities, such as the Bank of Mexico, the Comptroller's Office (if it becomes autonomous), regulatory agencies, the judiciary, Congress, and other state agencies headed by presidential appointees.

A frequent objection centers on the difficulty for a government to function effectively without previous experience and affinity among its parts. There is no doubt that maintaining cohesiveness and competence in government is a prerequisite for financial stability and public security. Fulfilling that requirement would be a major challenge for the transition government, whatever its duration. Clearly, the members of this hypothetical government would need to possess a minimal level of expertise. The latter can doubtless be found among the opposition and civil society, though perhaps not in great abundance.

The transition calendar is extremely important. To set a precise calendar with steps, changes, and deadlines is a fundamental part of the process. There must be deadlines to fulfill certain tasks and goals, so that citizens know what to expect and how to evaluate the progress of reform. A common program, and the coalition government based on it, constitutes an exceptional situation or solution. It is not, and should not become, a permanent fixture. The Colombian precedent of the National Front is a good example of what to avoid. When a temporary arrangement becomes permanent, there is eventually a high price to pay. In order to put an end to the military regime of Rojas Pinilla and the so-called violence, the National Front (an agreement between the liberal and conservative parties) was formed in Colombia, which contemplated the joint exercise of power within a future constitutional government. The front allowed the two parties to alternate in the presidency every four years, until 1978. But because the liberal-conservative pact was practically devoid of any social or economic components, it eventually became a closed hunting preserve for the Colombian oligarchy. It actually excluded a majority of the population from democracy and precluded much-needed reforms for many years.

In Mexico, an agenda for transition must be explicitly temporary. A coalition government should last only as long as necessary to carry out the tasks on that agenda—not one day more or one day less. The term of the transition government should be set in accordance with the tasks ahead. If less than six years are sufficient to lay the bases whereby the social and political pluralism of Mexico might be reflected at the polls, all the better. If not, the joint effort will have to continue beyond one six-year term.

This is not the only criterion for setting the calendar. Another is the necessarily gradual nature of any transition, so as to avoid one inherent, mortal danger: an excess of demands, concentrated in too brief an interval between authoritarianism and democracy. Especially in a country like Mexico, lacking a tradition of clean and meaningful elections, there must be a chance for society, political players, and government to learn. There must be enough rehearsal time for opening night to be a success, when the new play of democracy comes to town.

It is best to advance step by step. Risks that should not at first be taken nationally or at the executive level might be feasible in the medium term. Thus, direct elections (like those still pending for the office of Mexico City mayor) might be held, thanks to a legislative consensus, ahead of schedule. The indispensable step of having simultaneous elections for governor in at least half the states, through revision of their respective constitutions, could be scheduled for the second year of the current administration. Finally, the election of a Chamber of Deputies that would actually have a constitution-drafting status in 1997, would be a third intermediate step toward the full "electoralization" of Mexican society. As the mechanisms and legislation for these elections are perfected, we would gradually advance toward the mother of all elections, the presidential one.

CHAPTER 8

Anticlimax: The Election of August 21, 1994

IN ORDER TO FORM AN OPINION OF THE AUGUST 21, 1994,
election outcome, we must distinguish between different levels of
explanation. The fine detail of the results will be known only in time,
if ever. We may take as an illustration of this the disclosure by Jorge
Alcocer, who was in 1988 the Mexican Socialist Party's representative before the Federal Election Commission and became a principal adviser to Interior Minister Jorge Carpizo in January 1994. In
an article published on July 10, 1994, in the Sunday supplement to
the Mexico City daily *Reforma*, Alcocer revealed that he and the
political scientist Leonardo Valdés had gone over all the 1988 pres-
idential-election data precinct by precinct and had concluded that
"the results favoring the PRI had been distorted upward between
six and eight percentage points" but that there was no evidence of
a Cárdenas victory. This is worth noting because, as far as I know,
nobody else was able to examine the documents in their entirety
(fifty-five thousand precincts) and, regardless of whether Cárdenas
won or not, an alteration of six to eight percentage points would profoundly distort the result of any election.

For the moment, it is impossible to know whether there was any
significant distortion of the voters' will in the election of 1994 and
if so, to what degree. Although we did have two fairly reliable exit
polls, they both pose several problems. That of Mexico's Chamber
of the Radio and Television Industry, was allegedly misused by the
chamber itself when it announced the results of a supposed quick
count at ten o'clock on the night of the election, when there were still
too few results available. Additionally, the formulation of the questions asked was itself problematical. The exit poll conducted on
behalf of the U.S. network Telemundo and the Los Angeles daily
La Opinión, raises other questions. This survey gave Cuauhtémoc
Cárdenas 24.5 percent of the vote in Mexico City; official results gave

him only 20.5 percent. However, in the cases of the PRI and the PAN, the poll was remarkably accurate. Only Cárdenas's share of the vote turned out different, and that difference came to more than twice the margin of error. Either the poll was wrong or else the final result was manipulated.

In sum, any analysis or conclusion drawn from the questionable official results must be taken with all due caution. We are to some extent working in the dark, without any lighting worthy of the name. With all these doubts, one should distinguish between two types of explanations of the election results: those related to the electoral process itself and those referring to the candidates and their campaigns. In another time, in another language, the diagnosis might have been divided into objective or structural causes and subjective or contingent causes.

Perhaps the best way to elucidate what happened on Sunday, August 21, is to compare it with another Sunday, that which six years ago brightened the eyes and the hopes of millions of Mexicans: election day, July 6, 1988. According to official figures, the results of both elections were almost identical: approximately 50 percent for the PRI; the largest opposition party received about 30 percent, the second largest, 16 to 17 percent. The great difference between the 1994 election and the previous one resided in the magnitude and impact of the electoral fraud, to call a spade a spade in this country of euphemisms.

In 1988, the manipulation of the vote not only affected the result of the election, it probably reversed it. There is still, in the minds of millions of Mexicans, the suspicion or certainty that Carlos Salinas de Gortari lost the election and Cuauhtémoc Cárdenas won it. In contrast, in 1994 the undeniable irregularities that took place on election day and the scandalous unfairness which permeated the electoral process as a whole do not seem to have altered the final outcome of the presidential election: Ernesto Zedillo did indeed win at the polls. Neither Diego Fernández de Cevallos nor Cuauhtémoc Cárdenas claim they were stripped of a victory that was morally or legally theirs. Another story entirely is how the votes giving Zedillo his victory came to be. Understanding this is a first condition for explaining what happened.

A second recognition concerns the link between the election process and the election proper. It is neither honest nor possible to evaluate only what happened on August 21, without placing it in the context of the election campaign beginning in October 1993. To examine only the day of the election is to see only part of the problem, a small token of the persistent authoritarianism in Mexico. If one looks at the process as a whole, a long series of tricks and inequities comes to light, and those "irregularities" inevitably altered the events of the day itself. Perhaps the opposition should have measured more lucidly the consequences of playing in a soccer match where the goalposts were of different heights and breadths and where one team included eleven players plus the umpire and the other a mere six or seven players. But that is a completely different matter.

Three flaws in particular vitiated the origin and content of the electoral process from the outset, placing on it an irrevocable stamp of injustice and distortion of the people's will. The first, due to its importance and longevity, is the link between party and state in Mexico. Some limits were set, a few boundaries achieved, but the 1994 electoral battle in Mexico did not take place between several parties or candidates, but instead between the state and its party on the one hand, and the (divided) opposition on the other. Material and human resources, national information and international relations, logos and colors (the PRI symbol bears the same colors as the Mexican flag), complicities and collusion, government officials and supporters: the umbilical cord between the PRI and the government has never been cut, and no electoral contest in Mexico will be truly fair until it is. That this symbiosis should give rise to a vicious cycle only highlights its importance: there is no way to separate the PRI from the state until the PRI loses, and it seems the PRI cannot lose until it is separated from the state. No wonder it's so difficult to put an end to this system.

Those who argued sarcastically that the PRI would have won with any candidate were right: the real contender was the system and the government. Nor was Angel Gurría, currently Mexico's foreign minister, wrong when he boasted to a U.S. journalist that the PRI is like a Transformer toy because it makes anybody into a winning candidate. The only argument against this thesis—that the opposition almost won in 1988, although the system was the same—has its grain of truth but suffers from a serious defect: it is abstract, that is, partial and deformed.

There are many intelligent explanations regarding the surprise of 1988. Almost all of them are partly right, but also incomplete. The thesis of the unexpected blow to the system is valid but insufficient: How could Cárdenas possibly accumulate the strength needed to strike such a great blow to the system, without the latter knowing about it beforehand? The notion of a miscalculation—whereby the government allowed Cárdenas to grow and thrive because it was more afraid of the PAN candidate Manuel Clouthier—explains Cárdenas's growth, but not the amazement and paralysis of the system when the initial returns came in on July 6. In my view, the most accurate interpretation is to be found in a comment made by Carlos Salinas in December 1993, when Carlos Fuentes insisted that the PRI should hold primaries or some sort of open competition for the presidency. In so many words, President Salinas answered that if there had been an open struggle during the succession process in 1993, it would have caused insurmountable divisions. Even the sedate, harmless contest opened in 1987 among precandidates for the PRI nomination (with carefully orchestrated television appearances by the six contenders, all government officials) generated huge problems and had lasting effects.

In 1988, the Cardenista movement was almost able to defeat the PRI in a first vote count, despite the enormous power of the apparatus, the state party, and Televisa, the privately held but pro-PRI broadcast network. This was due in part to the government's lack of preparedness, but also to divisions within the system. The Interior

Ministry's passive or even helpful attitude toward the make-believe parties when they ran out of control, toward oil workers' union leader La Quina, and toward local PRI leaders (at least in Michoacán, the state of Mexico, and Mexico City) and the government's neglect of the foreign press, all point to an internal conflict, which led to the famous collapse of the computer system. Salinas was determined not to let it happen again unless he did it himself, as part of his own strategy. He did not tolerate any dissension before Colosio's designation, or before or after Zedillo's, because he knew it would unleash the winds of his misfortune. One rarely makes the same mistake twice.

A second serious and lasting flaw in the electoral process: the problem of the mass media. Again, it would be absurd to deny the progress that has been made. At the end of the 1994 campaign, in particular, there was some openness on television, and the radio, too, allowed some small degree of equity. But these improvements pale before the dimensions of Televisa's pro-government slant and the power of that corporation's near-monopoly in a country that has no tradition of newspaper reading and where over 90 percent of all homes now possess a television. Televisa thus had one candidate, Ernesto Zedillo; one enemy, Cuauhtémoc Cárdenas (and, for a few days in May, Diego Fernández) and one strategy: to identify the PRI with peace and stability, and the opposition with violence and chaos. Fear might spread like wildfire, but it certainly doesn't arise from spontaneous combustion. People were terrified of change and of Cárdenas because they were persuaded by the media, which never allowed any opposing or even different points of view to challenge their slanderous approach. That a party should set out to build such a set of equivalences is more than legitimate. That a government in office should do so on behalf of its supporters is less so. That a franchised private company should attempt to do so, and succeed, is such a distortion of electoral fair play that there cannot possibly be a fair contest while such practices persist.

The third flaw concerns the six make-believe parties and their candidates. As was to be expected, they did not take many votes away from the other parties; however, they did take away from their time and resources. Among the pygmies (as they were called), the five smallest garnered only 3.2 percent of the vote. Cecilia Soto of the Workers' Party got 2.8 percent, but they probably turned out to be the world's most expensive votes in relation to the resources at her disposal. None of the minor candidates represented an independent or respectable political option or even a significant portion of the electorate. To say that they received a fitting punishment at the polls ignores the equal time they were given in the news, in the government's machinations (such as the Pact of Civility sponsored by Interior Minister Jorge Carpizo and subscribed to by "eight of nine candidates"), and at the polls. Their presence in the race was obviously meant to distract voters' attention, to split the opposition vote to some degree, and, above all, to divide among many the resources and time allotted the opposition, thus ensuring a (superficial) legitimacy and an overwhelming majority in the Electoral Council on election day.

It is in this context, permeated with inequity and distortions, that one must understand the election itself. The irregularities and anomalies registered on election day were substantive, numerous, and sufficient to change the balance of power among the candidates, though not the final outcome. And as Alianza Cívica, the citizens' watchdog organization, noted in its final report, the irregularities also altered the political climate. The sheer magnitude of the opposition's defeat discouraged it profoundly and promoted the idea that people had voted for continuity and thrown their support behind the system—which a smaller defeat would not have prompted. The tricks, machinations, and shortcomings appeared, as always, little by little. People "shaven off" the voters' list, double or triple voting, sums that didn't add up, pressures on voters, the countless small and not-so-small distortions of the vote which can, as a whole, make a difference, were documented only gradually.

There were many more of them than appeared in the first few hours, when some observers hastened to qualify as "crystal clear" an election that clearly wasn't crystalline. And the quantity of abuses ended up being less than those denounced by the PRD, which insisted on blaming its defeat solely on a fraud, which, though undeniable, was not the only reason for Cárdenas's loss.

Every passing day brought forth new instances of electoral fraud. August 21 was not, as Cárdenas proclaimed, one gigantic fraud; rather, it was—due to its scope and variety—a truly impressive multiplicity of small frauds that, taken together, did indeed affect the correlation of forces. The investigation conducted by the local PRD candidate Carlos Imaz and his friends in voting booth 719 in Coyoacán (District 39 of Mexico City) is revealing. Their interview of 433 out of 440 voters showed that one deceased and two absent persons voted on that Sunday, as well as twenty people who did not inhabit and were not even known at the addresses registered on the voters' list and two persons whose addresses simply did not exist. Altogether, these anomalies represented 6 percent of the vote. The PRI defeated the PAN by seventy-two votes; even if all the anomalies had taken votes away from the PAN, it would have lost at that voting booth. But if this happened in one of the most highly monitored districts of Mexico City and things like this took place throughout the country, we may conclude that transparency was one of the lesser attributes of this election, especially in rural areas with strong Cardenista leanings. As Jaime Avilés noted in an extraordinary article, published in the Mexico City daily *El Financiero* on October 4, 1994:

> Oaxaca public opinion, in its most discreet manner—that is, in mere whispers—knows and says that on August 21 there was enormous fraud among the indigenous communities and cites the testimony of foreign observers who witnessed abhorrent situations: PRI organizers who set up shop alongside the ballot boxes and demanded that voters show them their ballots

before depositing them; voting-booth presidents who despite the random drawings were always PRIistas; supervisors who stood beside the curtains serving as screens, showing voters the symbol they should mark on the ballot. But, as in the entire country, ignorance, poverty, threats, and bribery made the fraud possible and invisible at the same time.[15]

THAT IS WHY THE HISTORIAN LORENZO MEYER WAS RIGHT when he claimed that: the election of August 21 was perhaps the cleanest in Mexican history (which doesn't say much), but it hardly bears any comparison with elections in the rest of Latin America, much less Europe. Documented election day irregularities could not, in principle, have altered the final outcome. They could, however, modify the electoral balance of power. If they altered it significantly, then the hypothetical question becomes: If the process had been fair, would the PRI have won?

Among those aspects pertaining to the process and those concerning the candidates is the "Diego effect" and the problem posed by a race in which not everybody shares the same goal. From the night of the debate—except when he was overtaken by his tantrums and rages—Diego Fernández de Cevallos toned down his campaign, in every the sense of the word. At the end, certainly, he quickened his pace: he made several public appearances a day and the intensity of his effort was doubtless impressive. But Diego's discourse—whether implicit or explicit—became far more moderate after the debate. In the final analysis, his central message was that it didn't matter if the PAN didn't win, so long as the election was clean.

But this caution and moderation did not reflect the feelings or demands of the PAN electorate. The PAN faithful I saw in Culiacán in a torrential rainstorm and in Mazatlán under a blazing sun had little to distinguish them from the impassioned Cardenista masses of Michoacán, Veracruz, or Tabasco. And the connection between Diego and his followers was no less emotional than that between Cárdenas and his. For National Action voters, the issue was not whether Zedillo won cleanly or not; the point of the election was to defeat the PRI, no matter what it took. Diego's divergence from his electorate was reflected in the gaps between his public discourse in the streets and his discourse to the press or in private. Before the cheering throngs of his supporters, Fernández de Cevallos railed against the PRI, the system, and Zedillo, "the straight-A youngster"; but in more private settings, he was the epitome of moderation. With reason: his electorate and audience wanted to hear calls to arms and battle cries; but in his own heart and ideology, Diego seemed to think that there was no alternative but to accept, and support, Ernesto Zedillo.

The problem is that a democratic race requires, among many other things, the contenders' complete dedication and determination to win. If the polls were partly accurate in August, there is no reason to doubt their accuracy in May or June. We learned afterward that they were right: after the May 12 debate, Diego Fernández surpassed Cárdenas and even Zedillo, according to several polls. We also discovered later that between that time, when he peaked, and the August election, the PAN candidate lost about ten percentage points. And we realized that Diego's fall was different from that of, say, Ross Perot in the United States between May of 1992 and the November election. The Texan's fall was due to his glaring blunders, the meticulous and malicious scrutiny of the press, and a U.S. electorate weary of twelve years of Republican conservatism. None of these factors seems relevant in Diego's case. He did not say or do anything more outrageous than before; he was not examined by the press or his enemies with any particular severity; and his supporters did not choose to vote more usefully by favoring another candidate.

What Fernández de Cevallos did was to withdraw from the race for almost a month. The difference of slightly more than twenty points between him and Zedillo corresponds almost exactly to the ten points Diego lost, and the ten points Zedillo won, as a result of Fernández de Cevallos's campaign moratorium from May 15 to early August. A chart published on August 5 by *Reforma*—whose unabashed sympathy for Diego's candidacy places it above all suspicion—depicts the magnitude of his campaign's free-fall. According to *Reforma*, between January 8 and May 12 (the day of the debate), Fernández de Cevallos held 48 rallies in 45 cities, gave 45 interviews on the radio and 31 on television, and had only 16 days without any public activity. However, during the 82 days between May 13 and August 13—that is, in the final stretch of the campaign—he held 39 rallies in 29 cities, did only 20 interviews on the radio and 12 on television, and had 34 days without any official activity.

No wonder *The New York Times*, in a long report on Fernández de Cevallos published on July 27, noted with some perplexity: "Barely two months after he came out of nowhere to mount what many Mexicans considered the most serious challenge to the governing party in 65 years, Diego Fernández de Cevallos has done something nearly as astonishing. He has almost disappeared." There cannot be a fair race when one of the candidates, especially the frontrunner, has a hidden agenda or some ulterior motive. If Fernández de Cevallos was ill, he should have said so; if he was threatened, he should have withdrawn and been replaced by another member of his party or else thrown his support behind one of the remaining contenders. And if he did strike some secret deal, then he brought into the race the greatest and worst possible distortion of the people's will in the entire electoral process. For a race to be fair, all the viable contenders must seek to win, and they must devote themselves fully to that purpose.

A second characteristic of the opposition candidates was the divisiveness among them, a responsibility borne equally by Fernández de Cevallos and Cárdenas. Octavio Paz said it before and after the elections, as did many others: with a divided opposition, it was virtually impossible for the PRI to be defeated. Of course, the problem was exceedingly complex. The highly charged question of who might be the possible candidate of a united opposition was inseparable from the more or less pious wish of seeing the PRI's opponents join together. One obstacle was clear from the very beginning: Cárdenas could never be the PAN's candidate, nor would he ever renounce his own candidacy on behalf of a PANista.

The PRD candidate refused to cede his place to a PANista for many reasons, but especially one that we have already mentioned on several occasions: he was convinced that he, and he alone, could defeat the PRI candidate. He was wrong, but that was his belief. The PAN, for its part, would have stepped down in favor of Cárdenas if its central goal had been to defeat the PRI—but that was not the case. So the only chance of a unified opposition lay in the emergence, or the deliberate manufacture, of a third candidacy: somebody who was neither Cárdenas nor an institutional PANista.

The logic behind several attempts to launch "another" candidate —the most talked about were Jesús Silva Herzog in 1993 and Manuel Camacho in 1994—was precisely that. The point was to "invent" a candidacy acceptable both to the leadership and the electorate of the PAN and the PRD. The trick was to avoid the double jeopardy inherent in this sort of situation: a divided opposition tends to lose, and the only candidate with any chance of winning tends to be the one closest to the center of the political spectrum. But the closer the candidate is to the center, the greater the resistance within the parties involved. That third candidacy never left the ground, for many reasons, once again, but mainly one. In the best of cases, none of the possible candidates would have ventured to throw his hat into the ring without being certain of the support of both parties; and neither the PAN nor the PRD would have offered their respective tickets to anybody without being certain, beforehand, that he would be accepted. How could all these circles be squared? Only with an ideal candidate, proposed by ideal parties—perfect elements that, in Mexico in 1994, were simply not to be found.

WHAT SHARE OF THE CARDENISTA MOVEMENT'S DEFEAT WAS due to the government's machinations and the unfairness of the process, and what part to its own mistakes? The responsibility for the crushing defeat of Cuauhtémoc Cárdenas rests, at least in part, with the main players in his candidacy and the forces supporting them.

Like the vast majority of Mexicans voting on August 21, 1994, I voted for one of the real candidates on the ballot—not for any of the six pygmies or any imaginary and nonexistent candidate whose absence I might have lamented at some other moment (Comacho, Silva Herzog, etc.). Obviously, one's choice could be based on the candidates' virtues or defects or on the political effects of each one's victory. If the voter believed, as I did, that the point was to change the political system, then that had to be the major criterion and one had to vote for an opposition candidate. It was not a matter of persons, but of historical direction. In other countries, under other circumstances, one's vote may solely be a function of candidates or parties; the impact is less important than the choice. But in special circumstances this is not the case. South Africa is a case in point: for somebody wishing to end racism and apartheid, it would have been absurd to vote for de Klerk or Buthelezi instead of Nelson Mandela, just because one seemed the better candidate or the other had a more consistent program. In Mexico, it never occurred to me to vote for a candidate rather than a cause. I knew, and came to regard, Luis Donaldo Colosio; but I would not have voted for him, precisely for those reasons. I had but a passing acquaintance with Ernesto Zedillo; but over and beyond his personal merit or talent, I never contemplated voting for a candidate of the system rather than for a cause.

From the perspective of those in power in Mexico, there were two opposition candidates on the ballot. The victory of either one would have meant the end of the PRI and of Mexican politics as we know it. I gave my vote to Cárdenas because of his tireless and determined struggle for democracy in this country, his emphasis on social justice, and finally my conviction (born of the friendship with which he has honored me for several years) that Cárdenas is a completely honest man. Diego Fernández de Cevallos was, in my opinion, a serious candidate with an undeniable vocation for democracy. But I disagreed so strongly with his apparent cultural beliefs (on education, women, religion, tolerance, and so on) that, despite my convergence with his party in other areas, I could not possibly vote for him.

There is no question about the enormous contribution of Cárdenas to the slow and difficult process of democratization in Mexico these last few years. It would also be absurd to doubt the tenacity and integrity of a man who has for seven years devoted himself heart and soul, like none other, to transforming this country's political structure. The daring and bravery of his radical break with the system should not be underestimated in a country where nobody breaks away and where so many who might have did not have the courage to do so. The enormous merit of Cárdenas is undeniable, as is his responsibility for the final outcome of his crusade. Cárdenas made four basic errors in strategy and several secondary tactical mistakes, which partly explain the results of the election.

The first strategic error was one that Cárdenas himself recognized in his speech at the Zócalo, the main square of Mexico City, on the Saturday following the election, and it consisted in having entered a tainted electoral process. Ever since the local congressional elections in Michoacán in July 1989, Cárdenas underestimated the regime's willingness and capacity to go to any length to prevent him or his party from holding any elected office, whether a seat in state congress, an important municipal presidency, a governorship, or a Senate seat. The same drama repeated itself at each and every election: Cárdenas and the PRD denounced the process beforehand, with good reason, and then proceeded to participate in it. For its part, the government acted exactly as expected. The PRD then lost and protested all over again. The same thing happened time and again. Aside from projecting an image of unceasing negativism and impotence, this pattern gave rise to an undeniable exhaustion. Even worse, it did not derive from any conscious decision, but from the difficulty Cárdenas and the PRD experienced in choosing between their two sole viable options. Either they stopped participating in elections until the link between the PRI and the government was broken and the state-party structure was dismantled, or else they negotiated with the government specific conditions for participating in each election, as the PAN was doing, but from a stronger position now that two parties would be exerting pressure.

As Cárdenas and the PRD did not want to choose between these two admittedly unpleasant paths, they inclined toward (but never clearly decided on) a third path, even less auspicious: to participate in the process while simultaneously denouncing it, thus falling into a hopeless contradiction. There were many opportunities for them either to negotiate in depth and renounce their accusations or else simply to withdraw from the process. Many suggested other alternatives to the PRD candidate, including withdrawal from the race after a massive rally on March 18 (the anniversary of the nationalization of the oil industry carried out by Lázaro Cárdenas, the PRD candidate's father) and the thwarted meetings with Luis Donaldo Colosio in January, as already related. The last attempt took place in the days before and after the meetings held by the San Angel Group both with Cárdenas and Salinas. Prior to the first meeting, several of Cárdenas's advisers suggested that, during his luncheon with the group, he set forth a series of specific demands for the election. If the San Angel Group was able to convince the government of them, then Cárdenas would meet with Salinas in the presence of the group in order to ratify an agreement. Cárdenas rejected this idea a couple of days before his lunch with the Group; his reasons were never clear. At the luncheon with Salinas, Amalia García, a PRD member, asked the president whether he would be willing to meet with Cárdenas; Salinas answered that he would. Messages and couriers went back and forth for several days, but again in vain. There was probably less doubt and hesitation concerning the second option, withdrawing from the elections. But it became known that the idea was discussed repeatedly within the Cardenista inner circle. Of the three potential routes, Cárdenas chose the path of least resistance, the worst possible choice.

He should have withdrawn from the race after Colosio's death, or, after the Chiapas uprising, he should have negotiated an electoral reform down to its last consequences. Though not ideal, either of these courses would have been preferable to the one he chose. And this is not a matter of hindsight: many people advised Cárdenas to follow a different path before August 21.

The second strategic error was to leave undefined the race's ultimate target. In modern election campaigns, in countries where several candidates compete for each of a variety of elected positions, nobody can hope to win all of the votes. Campaigns take place within a framework of limited time, resources, and voter availability. Certain sectors of the electorate are out of bounds to certain candidates, no matter what they do. For instance, Republicans in the United States cannot win much of the black vote; over 90 percent of all African-Americans have voted for the Democratic Party since the thirties and will continue to do so for years to come. That is why one must choose targets—which is precisely what Cárdenas's campaign was never willing to do. In its major speeches, in the allotment of its time, in its statements on various issues, the Cardenista campaign never ventured to define its priorities clearly. The candidate never chose among several electorates (for example, the dispossessed versus the middle classes, the city versus the countryside), or among possible discourses (radical left versus moderate center). The choice between electorates and discourses did not coincide exactly, but it overlapped in part. To define one would eventually imply defining the other, as well.

In particular, Cárdenas was never able, or willing, to resolve the central impasse in which he found himself concerning his electorate. He could focus on the diehard PRD supporters—basically low-income, or else concentrated in Cardenista strongholds like the states of Michoacán, Guerrero, Tabasco, Oaxaca, Chiapas (surprisingly) and Veracruz (less so)—and concentrate on the vote in the countryside, small cities, and large towns. Or he could direct his efforts toward the middle classes, which in 1988 had given him almost half their votes in Mexico City and the state of Mexico and 25 percent in Guadalajara. Obviously, it is not enough just to want the votes, but it is impossible to get them without seeking them. The discourse, methods, positions, and image required to secure the vote of the middle sectors in large cities were not compatible with those aimed at a rural, poor, and irate population, regardless of the sympathy one might have for that anger.

The fact of the matter was that Cárdenas saw his options increasingly limited to the so-called peasant strategy in the final months of his campaign, not necessarily due to any conscious, deliberate choice. That strategy consisted in seeking massive rural or *campesino* support. The voters' list included about fifteen million rural dwellers —that is, people living in rural election precincts. Even at the enormous urban rallies Cárdenas held in numerous cities (Córdoba, Xalapa, Orizaba, Tapachula, Morelia, Salamanca), many of the participants came from nearby rural areas with paved roads. They had traditionally voted for the PRI—or rather, the PRI had voted for them. Cárdenas banked heavily on their support. His positions on agrarian policy, as well as the amount of time he spent campaigning in villages and *ejidos*, make sense only within this framework. I personally doubted the strategy's soundness, but one must acknowledge that it was both astute and plausible.

The countryside was the part of Mexico most devastated by Salinista policy. Millions of *campesinos* were impoverished, humiliated, and ruined by the implementation of Finance Minister Pedro Aspe's "brilliant myths." The low prices of many products, competition from abroad, the high cost of credit, and the termination of subsidies and the whole panoply of state support all led to a genuine devastation of the Mexican countryside such as had not been seen within memory. The breeding ground for anger and mobilization was more fertile than ever. The destruction of traditional mechanisms also meant the disappearance of many instruments of control. The virtual elimination of farm-support institutions like Banrural, Pronase, Anagsa, most of Conasupo, and the whole system for the corporatist manipulation of the countryside implied the loss of means to pressure voters, despite the last-minute Procampo producer-subsidy checks. It would no longer be as easy to stuff ballot boxes, truck *campesinos* to the voting booths, and force Mexicans throughout the countryside to perpetuate the power of the state party. It was still possible; as Procampo proved, one lark does not democracy make. But the PRI's peasant vote was becoming a thing of the past.

Besides, it is in the countryside that the memory of the original Cardenista movement still endures: the memories of land being distributed in La Laguna, Michoacán, and the entire Mexican countryside have proven longlasting. Nobody had ever given much to the *campesinos*; their destiny has been tragic since time immemorial. Their only brief moment of dignity and pride, with some small fulfillment of their demands, was when they were given land and treated as human beings. Their lot might not have improved, from a strictly economic point of view; but as Mexicans, they lived an hour of glory that they obviously have not forgotten. Cuauhtémoc Cárdenas is the present embodiment of that memory; it was to be expected that their affection and nostalgia would be reflected at the polls. Finally, the campaign's shift toward the countryside introduced a new tactical element into the so-called run-off in the streets: in rural areas, Cárdenas's followers were more combative; they had proved more willing to block highways, take municipal offices, and mobilize after elections.

For the thesis to prove correct, however, various conditions had to met, and they were not at all assured. First of all, the Cardenista *campesinos* had to be registered to vote. The regime's arguments regarding the voters' list left many people skeptical; but so did the opposition's. However, if the list was as tainted as Cárdenas and the PRD said it was, then the peasant strategy was not realistic.

A second problem was to ensure that those *campesinos* who were registered actually voted. Neither surveys nor precedent would be very helpful in this regard. The electoral history of the Mexican countryside has been a history of fraud. So no one knew whether Mexicans in rural areas would actually vote if it were, for once, left in their hands. They might decide it was too risky in a country where nothing has ever been solved through the ballot, that it was not worth facing the dangers involved, just to fulfill an act of civic duty devoid of any real significance. Or they might judge, as many did, that, under conditions of coercion, with no guarantee that their vote would be private, it was best to vote for the PRI, "since it always wins anyway." It is now clear that Cárdenas underestimated the weight of Procampo: the massive delivery of direct subsidy checks in the weeks preceding the elections must have been one of the most important illegitimate factors brought to bear on the vote.

The third and final issue: Even if the *campesinos* voted, who would protect their vote? The political parties were barely able to monitor a majority of urban voting booths (probably not even all of them). A high proportion of the rural sectors was not covered. Despite their good intentions, Mexican observers from organizations such as Alianza Cívica would not be able to make up for their shortcomings, divisions, and lack of consistency with foreign money and public relations. And foreign visitors would not be present, either, thanks to the hesitation and inconsistency of the Mexican watchdog groups. Furthermore, the United Nations would argue that monitoring the Mexican election was not within its mandate.

Many of the urban middle-class voters supporting Cárdenas in 1988 had already gone over to Fernández de Cevallos or the PRI due to the regime's fear tactics. Those voters were to be replaced by the rural peasantry: among these voters Cárdenas saw the margin of victory and the capacity for mobilization. And, indeed, the PRD did much better in the countryside this time than in 1988; the PRI got far fewer votes. Of course, one can compare official results only with great caution, as the manipulation of the vote was scandalous in the countryside, especially in 1988 and particularly in states such as Chiapas, where Cárdenas's vote increased by 724 percent from one election to the other. Despite electoral fraud, the PRD did become a major force in typically rural states like Oaxaca, where its support rose by 46 percent; Guerrero, where it was already strong but still got 48 percent more votes than in 1988; and Tabasco, where, despite its previous strength, the PRD got 284 percent more votes. If we suppose (without, however, accepting) that Cárdenas got essentially the same number of votes as in 1988, but that he lost votes in the big cities (as the numbers indeed confirm), then his new supporters must have been from rural areas. So the peasant strategy worked. What is less clear is whether it was a deliberate, winning strategy or merely a consequence of inertia and the difficulty of doing anything else.

It was, in any case, a contradictory strategy. Two observations illustrate this fully. In the first place, the protest marches, rallies, and radical agrarian stances did indeed attract the aggrieved Cardenistas of Michoacán, Guerrero, and other areas. But those same elements alienated the less aggrieved voters of the middle class, more subject to the influence of Televisa and the government. They did have something to lose, even if it was only the time they wasted in traffic jams caused by protest marches. A second observation: constant criticism of a government that did enormous damage to the poor sectors of the population might be an excellent tactic to gain those voters' support, but antigovernment rhetoric's inherent negativism can be distasteful, even irritating, to the Mexican middle classes who enjoy lower inflation and a stable exchange rate and who are conditioned by unceasing propaganda. With these voters, a more positive, solution-oriented, and realistic discourse would perhaps have been more effective. Both paths were logical and dignified, but Cárdenas had to choose. He never did. One day he would present a moderate, centrist economic program; the next he would promise to reverse the agrarian counterreform, and on the third day denounce the "gigantic fraud" being prepared.

The dilemma was apparent from the beginning of the campaign, in the text of Cárdenas's speech on October 17, 1993, when he accepted his party's nomination. At his request, a group of friends and supporters (including myself) prepared a complete draft, aimed mainly at the public outside the Palacio de los Deportes: those who were not yet convinced, the middle and neutral sectors. The draft was shown to several persons outside the candidate's inner circle, and later drafts incorporated a large number of suggestions made by them. The working group attempted to make the text sound more modern and personal, while outlining a more moderate and centrist economic and political platform. We also tried to build a structure that would last, a framework that would work throughout the campaign, so as to develop a number of constant themes, with a permanent underpinning for all the different statements the candidate might make. The proposed text was so different from Cárdenas's usual message and approach that an assistant of his who read it commented, "If this is what it's all about, I'd rather vote for the PRI." Leaving exaggeration aside, the intention was indeed to draw Cárdenas nearer the center of the political spectrum, where the votes were.

The candidate used part of this group's draft, but also drew on many other outlines and collections of notes, shaping it all into a structure of his own, as he was fully entitled to. The eclectic result of this exercise was an excellent speech, with entire paragraphs aimed at each group of sympathizers crowded into the Palacio de los Deportes; but the moderation aimed at some contradicted the fervor aimed at others, and all structure disappeared. What remained was a litany of demands and denunciations, well formulated and legitimate, but without priorities. From that moment, any doubts still held by the group were put to rest: Cuauhtémoc Cárdenas would never opt for a campaign platform aimed at the middle sectors of the population. He would oscillate from them to the most dispossessed; from irate PRD militants to the undecided; from the middle classes to the *campesinos*; from workers to the unemployed. But that hesitation was not gratuitous: in fact, it meant opting for the most radical message, simply by virtue of the reality of things.

As Televisa and the government highlighted the incendiary

parts while suppressing the others, and as the candidate's accusations tended to cancel out his proposals, the most radical and incendiary tone prevailed. This was reflected in the official election results: in Mexico City, Cárdenas lost over a third of his support (five hundred thousand votes, or 35 percent); much more than half in Jalisco (in the state capital, Guadalajara, he got 115,000 fewer votes or 41 percent of his result in 1988); and almost a third in the state of Mexico (30 percent less, or 359,000 fewer votes). But, in Michoacán he got 107,000 votes more than in 1988 (although his percentage of the vote also fell there); he also improved considerably in the southern states, as already noted.[16] If Cárdenas's intention was to build and organize the power of the poor, then his strategy was correct. However, if his goal was to win the 1994 election, he should have focused on winning the middle-class, ideologically centrist electorate. Those Mexicans doomed to poverty by the regime and the country's history were not going to vote in large enough numbers for an opposition candidate, bound as they were by the political system; and those Mexicans affronted by and determined to vote against the Salinas government had nowhere else to go. Furthermore, the electoral participation of middle sectors is much greater, even without fraud, than that of the dispossessed.

A third strategic mistake: Cárdenas chose the village square over the mass media. In an ideal world, in a perfect democracy in which all candidates enjoyed equal access to communication with the electorate, perhaps it would not have been necessary for Cárdenas to choose carefully among the different ways of broadcasting his message. But in the Mexico of 1994, it was. Obviously, it was not an easy choice: the mass media were not exactly willing to make room for the opposition; Cárdenas did not feel comfortable on television, though he always did well on the radio; and forsaken towns and villages throughout Mexico beg for attention and deserve to have it.

Despite these disadvantages, Cárdenas made the wrong choice.

He systematically devoted more time and attention to villages than to the mass media. He preferred to visit a semi-deserted village than to prepare, or even accept, an appearance on radio or television. His political instinct and intelligence obliged him to accept many such invitations—but always reluctantly, at the last minute, and often without setting himself clear and specific goals. The proof that it was only a matter of decision and preparation was provided by the candidate himself: his last appearances on the small screen revealed a Cárdenas far more skilled before the cameras than he had been previously. And the proof of a mass-media-oriented strategy's effectiveness was given, in turn, by Diego Fernández de Cevallos: all the exit polls and everyday public feeling indicated that his advantage over Cárdenas stemmed from the televised debate of May 12.

That same debate revealed the inconsistency in the communications strategy of Cárdenas himself, not his team. The problem was never in the format or the supposedly mistaken way in which his communications team advised him. The main reason for Cárdenas's failure in the debate was the little time and meager organization he devoted to its preparation. The record shows just how difficult it was for his communications team to help Cárdenas not only prepare for the debate but build his image throughout the campaign—and this despite their undeniable talent and dedication to the cause.

Perhaps Cárdenas would not have won the election anyway, but his chances were severely damaged by the May 12 televised debate. He revealed himself acutely aware of the debate's crucial character, in his way: he made an enormous effort to arrive at the site of the debate in the best of conditions. To that end, he organized brainstorming sessions: advisers, assistants, friends, and even people unknown to Cárdenas exchanged ideas and suggestions among themselves and with the candidate. The meetings were disorderly and unproductive but absolutely indispensable in the early stages of preparation for the debate. The problem that emerged was the same as always: the real organizer of the whole effort, the only person to see the complete picture, who led the discussion and was also its object, was Cárdenas himself.

As the drafting group drew up the texts or script supposedly based on previous meetings and on the decisions and rulings of Cárdenas himself, the candidate was to rehearse his statements based on those texts—without, however, actually reading them. So far, so good.

Things got complicated when it became apparent that the group of sympathizers involved in this effort had simply set in motion a vicious cycle. The ideas and texts submitted to Cárdenas by the drafting group were not to Cárdenas's liking: he didn't feel comfortable with the material. As a result, rehearsals in the studio went poorly and he became more and more upset. Then he would go to his private quarters and revise the material, punctuation and all, instead of using that time to rehearse before the cameras. And while the candidate's manuscripts clearly reflected his views and state of mind, they also revealed a lack of familiarity with television. So these meetings did not generate the texts to be used by Cárdenas (though he did, as always, use some of the material), nor a strategy, nor effective techniques. The last meeting at the studio began late; the candidate left early and was not able to use the equipment set up for him.

I describe these meetings because those of us who attended them always wondered about the number, composition, and impact of other meetings, more or less similar, which we suspected were also taking place; but we never really knew. However, their existence was the only logical explanation we had for what we saw on television the night of May 12: a few elements proposed by our group, accompanied and obscured by many other themes, and, especially, a completely eclectic structure.

Whatever it's origin, the eclectic structure also explained Cárdenas's collapse in the debate. Lacking a natural talent for the media—which Fernández de Cevallos has and Zedillo does not—Cárdenas had to prepare himself technically and define and convey the core message of his candidacy. If to this we add the necessities of the campaign—which was not entirely suspended—it was obvious that Cárdenas was caught between two lines of fire. He had two basic choices for the debate. He could designate some body to formulate his substantive message after a minimum of discussion and then simply prepare on a formal level without intervening any further in matters of substance, already entrusted to a loyal adviser. Or else he could devote himself to preparing his statements, while inevitably neglecting the form; in this case, the content might also suffer from his haste, nervousness, and discomfort with the medium. This is what actually happened. It was nobody's fault; in fact, it could not have transpired any differently.

In contrast, the PRD candidate never had any qualms about spending endless hours in buses and vans to visit some god-forsaken village and address a few dozen supporters. Their lot was indeed a dreadful one, but this did not make up for the time and effort that went into accompanying them in their misfortune for a few brief moments. For a moral crusade, visiting villages is both dignified and indispensable. For an election campaign in a country of Mexico's size, where television reaches over 90 percent of all homes, it cannot be justified. Cárdenas should have chosen a strategy based on the media, not the village square: he should have done what Fernández de Cevallos said he would do but never did.

A final weakness in the PRD campaign was its lack of coordination. From the middle of 1993, Cárdenas faced the central dilemma of his campaign organization. Either he delegated to a powerful and autonomous group most of the tasks in the race, keeping for himself only major decisions and daily campaign activities, or else he took charge of everything, from scheduling to the stylistic details of his speeches. The first option, the Clinton-style "war room" or the Chilean-style "campaign command" was discarded at a high cost. Instead, Cárdenas selected a low-intensity coordination team, with Cárdenas serving as his own campaign manager, chief adviser, and speechwriter. The first path meant transferring real power to one or several persons; the second implied a dispersal of the candidate's time, energy, and talent. But to name a team with authority and give it the real power it required to carry out its task would have forced Cárdenas to choose among PRD personalities, between the PRD and other groups, and between longstanding and loyal but inexperienced supporters and new companions, who were possibly better suited to the task but of unproven loyalties.

Cárdenas opted for the path implying a concentration of authority, information, and ultimately power in his own hands. In a country of betrayals and reversals, this decision was understandable, but it proved fatal: it is probably impossible to conduct a modern presidential campaign without delegating responsibility. It is extraordinarily difficult for one person to direct and execute such a complex process of organization, confrontation, negotiation, mobilization, and persuasion. From the moment that Cárdenas decided to navigate alone, the course was set for all of his endeavors. He would allow the inertia of 1988 to shape each and every decision that presented itself. It would have been preferable— indeed, indispensable—for the candidate to delegate his authority to a team with a single direction, voice, guiding principle, and command. But Cárdenas rejected that option from the outset.

The campaign's tactical blunders, though not insignificant in themselves, almost all derived from the larger strategy. The last mistake was Cárdenas's refusal to meet with Salinas a scant few weeks before the election, to discuss an agenda previously negotiated. In contrast with previous possible meetings, which would only have benefited Salinas, this one made possible a change in Cárdenas's image. It might have neutralized—at least in part—the notorious fear factor that later proved decisive. Another questionable decision was Cárdenas's trip to Chiapas and his meeting with the Zapatista rebels' leader, Marcos. The meeting was immortalized in a photograph that appeared not only on the front pages of newspapers and on television screens, but also on posters later put up by PRD supporters—even in the middle-class areas of Mexico City.

In an apparent response to an article of mine, *subcomandante* Marcos remarked to *La Jornada* (September 22, 1994) that that photograph was one in which "Salinas, Camacho, and Zedillo would have liked to appear." Doubtless, but Camacho had already had his picture taken with Marcos; indeed, that was part of his job as peace commissioner. And if either Salinas or Zedillo had appeared in a picture with Marcos, it would not have hurt their chances for election: the one, because he was no longer seeking office, and the other, because there was little chance of his being mistaken for a leftist. Not even *The New York Times* would have bought that story.

I agree with Marcos that my doubts about Cárdenas's performance actually boil down to criticizing him for being himself. The problem is that to win votes, aside from any sympathies or front pages, and especially in order to convince those who are *not* convinced—an inescapable task for any candidate—it is not enough to be oneself. One must also, to some extent, be what others want one to be. Many may think that is too high a price to pay, to win an election, and I tend to agree; but in that case they should not run for office. Marcos chose not to; Cárdenas decided to try. Actually, the two paths do intersect at times. The day Marcos appears on *Sixty Minutes* without his mask, he will have to use makeup just as Cárdenas did when he was not traveling to remote villages. The irony is daunting: he who attacked Cárdenas as few ever did, before the election, turns into his indignant supporter afterward, when it no longer matters; and he who supported Cárdenas for six long years is now criticized for . . . criticizing him without reason.

THE ERRORS OF CÁRDENAS AND THE RIDDLE OF FERNÁNDEZ DE Cevallos do not, however, complete our explanations of the election results over and beyond the electoral process as such. Zedillo, the PRI, and the government also did a lot of things right, in contrast with 1988. I return to the prescient answer that Carlos Salinas gave Carlos Fuentes in December of 1993: what most complicated matters in 1988 were the internal divisions within the PRI and the system as a whole. It is a paradoxical response, when one recalls the dance of the seven veils, the insinuations surrounding Manuel Camacho, Colosio, and Salinas until Colosio's assassination. But it is a perspicacious observation if one recalls how Zedillo devoted himself, from the time of his nomination and doubtless with the help of Salinas, to reconciling the various groups within the system so as to avoid at all cost the slightest hint of a justified division. The offensive against Camacho beginning in early June, the reconciliation with the PRI dinosaurs and Carlos Hank González, the orchestration of a completely traditional campaign with bused-in supporters and guests, massive rallies and little direct contact with the population, were undoubtedly the official party's best bet to remain in power no matter what.

Ernesto Zedillo had to learn in four months what his predecessors had a whole year to absorb: how to become a familiar, attractive, and believable candidate. Even worse, he had to accomplish this in the midst of a full-blown economic, political, social, and even psychological crisis, and in the wake of the Chiapas uprising and the assassination of Colosio. The task seemed formidable, if not impossible. The system's inertia, the fear of change, and the incredible inequity of the electoral process led Zedillo to victory; but the cost of that achievement remains to be seen.

The candidate presented several contradictory traits during his campaign. One could see, and one of his most honest advisers confirmed, that he had changed in four months. He became a better speaker and began to change his relationship with the public and to consolidate his understanding of the country's complexity, its contradictions and divisions, and the countless wrongs inflicted on the Mexican people. It would have been odd for a man of Zedillo's education and experience not to undergo the same process of change and assimilation as his predecessors. Everything suggested that this was indeed the case, at least in terms of his social awareness. Over and beyond the campaign oratory, toward the end of the race one could feel in Zedillo a growing perception of Mexico's harrowing inequality.

Yet his speeches showed a disturbing lack of substance, with the (debatable) exception of his major statements on the economy, foreign policy, and democracy. His campaign speeches were mere harangues, completely devoid of content, full of facile and more or less effective rhetorical tricks. His speeches to the PRI masses— mostly bused in, mainly indifferent, though occasionally roused by an unquestionably festive atmosphere, at one rally or another— had little to do with current events or the general situation. Clearly, no candidate in the world can make three or four substantive speeches every day. But the process of the campaign itself, daily national and world events, and the rivalry with other candidates usually enrich to some extent the endless speechifying of a presidential race.

That was not the way Zedillo functioned. Instead of reviewing current events, generating a running commentary in order to earn approval and capture those headlines not for sale, he limited himself to a chorus of facile slogans and phrases. Some were good, some bad; and some worked well, while others left the public indifferent. There were two possible explanations. Either Zedillo was perfectly capable of being more creative, but chose not to take positions on various issues so as to avoid making mistakes or getting into trouble, or else he did not have the political leeway or the self-confidence, to do so. This may eventually become a problem, though. To be president of a country as complex as Mexico implies taking daily positions on countless matters, not all of which pertain to one's field of competence or even the logical scope of the office.

Beyond the lack of substance, another contradiction in the Zedillo campaign was confirmed on the night of the PRI victory on August 21, and succinctly expressed by a standing riddle: Where were the millions of people who had supposedly voted for Mexico's "super party"? Why didn't they take to the streets to celebrate the unexpected landslide of their supposed idol? The converse had already taken place in Guanajuato, San Luis Potosí, Michoacán, and Mérida: when PRI supporters learned that their candidate would not be governor or mayor after all, they resigned themselves to defeat with a conspicuous passivity. The PRI's voters—whether enthusiastic, sympathetic, or simply bused in, for those are the categories—seemed increasingly listless. At the same time, Zedillo's harangues grew more and more strident and hostile toward the opposition. Zedillo wanted to mobilize his party base through a vocal, antiopposition radicalism that was perfectly legitimate. In contrast, although his supporters undoubtedly wanted their candidate and party to win, they were not willing to do very much to make it happen—except vote, often under pressure. If the entire electorate had been in that mood, it would not have mattered. But this was not the case: there was an obvious difference between the PRI voters' meager militancy, combativeness, and dedication and the far more intense involvement of the Cardenista and PANista opposition. This was clear in the four elections settled through backroom negotiations: the PRI's voters did not flinch when their supposedly victorious candidates were thrown out. In contrast, the opposition's voters took town squares and roads and occupied city halls and front pages, in defense of their vote.

As election day approached, people began to feel that clean and transparent elections were no longer the core of the matter. Traveling anywhere in the country, listening to people from different sectors, from the taxi driver to the famous writer or the historian on television, one always came to the same conclusion: there was (and still is) an enormous portion of the population, representing either a small majority or a large minority, that was simply fed up with the PRI and the government. The hundreds of thousands, even millions of people attending the scores of PANista or Cardenista rallies were not only seeking clean elections, a Congress to their liking, and a PRI president who would stop naming his party's candidates, they were anxious to put an end to the PRI and its authoritarianism.

The complete lack of an electoral culture in Mexico, combined with the doubts—most of them legitimate, some invented—surrounding the process and election day, and finally the disgust or even despair of many Mexicans, were all good reasons not to accept Zedillo's victory. For those Mexicans, clean elections were a minor concern: the overriding goal was change. The tragedy for that portion of the population was that the PRI should have stayed in power, despite that great longing for change, due to the system's inertia and the division among the opposition. It will not be easy to allay the terrible blow felt by millions of Mexicans when they learned they would have to continue putting up with more of the same. Opposition voters are neither better nor more valuable than those of the PRI; but they were fired by a conviction, a hunger for change, that the PRI electorate has simply never demonstrated. That is why any reading that sees the two electorates as roughly equal, which bases itself on merely arithmetical calculations, must eventually come face to face with the harsh difference.

The country did not fit into the election. The reasons are many and were noted by various writers, politicians, and pundits. Mexico has no electoral tradition: power has never been transmitted in that manner, though elections have sometimes served to ratify a transfer of power previously settled by other means. The 1994 elections in particular were unfair, rigged, and devoid of the substantive debates that allow societies to feel that their outstanding choices have been examined seriously and responsibly. The candidates were not up to the challenges facing the country, not because of their personalities, but because of the political conditions prevailing in Mexico.

Three examples will suffice to show how the elections of August 21 were too small for Mexico and how the vote was indeed anticlimactic. First of all, where it hurt the most: the situation of the intellectuals. Any analysis of Mexico's autumn of discontent must include its intellectuals. Despite the government's attempt to divide Mexico's intellectual elite through a vicious anti-intellectual campaign led by aggrieved political leaders, paid journalists, and vengeful officials, most of the intelligentsia would have preferred—and hoped for—a different election result. Of course, not all intellectuals belong to this category; several distinguished Mexican writers and painters were pleased with the outcome of the election. But many of the Mexican intellectuals who voted for the PRI candidate did so in the belief that he would win by a narrow margin and that the close results of the race would finally lead into a democratic transition.

A large part—though not all—of the difference between the official result and that imagined by many was due to the fact that voter turnout—especially among the poorest members of society —was unexpectedly large. The gap between them and the intellectuals was clear to see, once again: for the hundredth time in the country's history, but perhaps more starkly than ever before, the wishes and expectations of the academic, literary, artistic, and journalistic elite stood in dramatic contrast with those of "the people." There is nothing new about this: in a country beset by social, ethnic, and regional inequality like few others in the world, it is no surprise that a major gap in living standards, education, and worldview should also translate into electoral behavior. It is important that we know and emphasize this: not only has the supposed modernization of Mexico not narrowed the abyss between elites and masses, it has actually widened it, at least in electoral terms. Mexican intellectuals have never known how to blend in with the rest of the country, though they have drawn from it their inspiration, vitality, and their very breath.

In the second place, the lack of plurality in the election results also shows that the election was too small for the country. Neither the Congress, the government, the governorships, nor the margins for freedom within the media reflect the diversity of the country that went to the polls on August 21. There is no possible doubt that Mexico today is a plural and diversified nation, split into hundreds of currents, regions, sensitivities, opinions, and aspirations. That is its strength and a central reason for the vitality that astounds Mexicans and foreigners alike. But that plurality and wealth of opinions were not reflected in the election results.

Not only did the PRI win the presidential election, it also enjoys a broad majority in the Chamber (three hundred of five hundred seats) and an overwhelming presence in the Senate and the Assembly of Representatives of the Federal District. None of these bodies reflects, even remotely, the diversity that is, quite rightly, a source of pride for the entire country. Since the winner of the presidential election did not feel the slightest need to forge a coalition with the opposition or with other political or ideological sectors of society, Mexico's plurality is not reflected in his cabinet, either. Ernesto Zedillo is right: Why complicate his position by appointing men and women whom he does not know and who did not support him, when he received more than half the vote in an election perceived as clean and transparent by the world community and a good part of Mexican public opinion?

Thirdly and finally, the election did not help create the spaces and channels necessary for popular discontent, and the deep fractures among Mexican elites, to find free and accurate expression. The divisions among the elites (at the origin of countless evils and tragedies in this country) thus continue to manifest themselves in other ways. And the social unrest rampant in the country—among a minority, or those who could not or would not express themselves at the polls—must continue to seek the path of least resistance. Of these two adverse effects of our electoral ills, only the first has become a reality thus far. José Francisco Ruiz Massieu, the secretary general of the PRI who was assassinated in September, 1994, might have died anyway; not even a pristine election can eradicate tensions and violence like Mexico's from one day to the next. But we are only halfway through the film. Still ahead are the repercussions of thirteen years of economic stagnation, a brutal concentration of wealth and income, and the lack of any escape valve for the resentment that must, inevitably, ensue.

Obviously not everybody—and especially not the winners—shares this reading of the situation. On the contrary, many see in the election the ex post facto justification of their hopes and convictions, the final vindication of their support for the efficacy and currency of Mexico's political system. In a country and a year full of surprises, it would be absurd to bet on any one of the possible readings of the August 21 results.

CHAPTER 9

After the Election and Before the Collapse

IT WILL BE A LONG TIME BEFORE MEXICO KNOWS WHO KILLED Jose Francisco Ruiz Massieu. Given the series of explanations and counter·explanations that sprang up around the death of Luis Donaldo Colosio, it was to be expected that many of the assumptions and accusations concerning the second political assassination of 1994 would fade away only to be replaced by others, just as implausible. Nonetheless, it is important not to confuse legal and criminological inquiry with conceptual analysis. To understand what happened in the successive tragedies of Guadalajara airport, Lomas Taurinas, and Lafragua Street (the sites of the murders of Cardinal Posadas, Colosio, and Ruiz Massieu, respectively)—and to prevent such things from happening again—one need not await the public prosecutor's report.

If we reject the thesis of a solitary madman in the Colosio case —a barely credible hypothesis from the outset—and even if the three murders are unrelated and one accepts that they did not derive from an articulated conspiracy, one conclusion is unescapable: the traditional methods for settling disputes and differences among the Mexican elites had fallen into a terminal state of dysfunction. For decades, students of the Mexican political system and its legendary stability formulated two abstract theses to explain the perfect workings of the machine designed in the last years of the revolution and the first years of the post-revolutionary era. One view attributed miraculous virtues to the methods, created since 1929, for settling in a peaceful and orderly way the struggles and quarrels among elites—including the mother of all battles, every six years, to decide who would be the next ruler. The second view followed the first like a shadow: the prevention of violent clashes among those above required the easing of violence and discontent among those below. It required constant, albeit gradual and modest, improvements in the lot of the country's vast impoverished masses. Both conditions were met during the years of the genuine "Mexican miracle," and even throughout its lengthy decline, until the early eighties.

The string of assassinations under Carlos Salinas suggests that the stagnation of Mexican living standards beginning in 1981 (per capita gross domestic product, in constant dollars, is less today than in 1980) combined with the collapse of traditional ways of settling disputes among the elites had finally brought about the breakdown of the system. It is true that the political indicators of the discontent generated by economic stagnation are ambivalent: the population voted for continuity and the PRI, theoretically disproving the existence of widespread anger. But we have already pointed to the peculiar optical refraction that came between the people's intended vote and the actual results. One of the exit polls—that of Warren Mitofsky, contracted by the Industrial Chamber of Radio and Television—illustrates that distortion: 65 percent of Zedillo's voters stated that they wanted a change in economic and social policy. Furthermore, one must not confuse relief—at leaving behind years of inflation and sudden variations in the exchange rate, as was the case until December of 1994—with well-being or real improvements in living standards. When he actually marks his ballot, the voter might confuse the two; but the government official can do so only at the risk of his job. In any event, the second condition for stability in Mexico—material progress, albeit slow and unequal—has not been met since 1981.

The same is obviously true of the first condition as well. From the perspective of a division among elites, it is immaterial whether the intended victim of assassination at the Guadalajara airport on May 24, 1993, was a drug trafficker known as "Chapo Guzmán" or Cardinal Posadas, or the papal nuncio Girolamo Prigione. Those who killed the cardinal fully intended to murder somebody—presumably not a chewing-gum vendor in the airport parking lot. Church officials have been members of the elite in this country since the first days of the conquest; and so have drug traffickers, at least since they joined the ranks of the most efficient, wealthy, and powerful businessmen in several important regions of Mexico.

Likewise, it is immaterial whether Colosio was assassinated by Tijuana drug traffickers, disillusioned local PRI militants, or PRI dinosaurs at the national level. The central point is that, whatever the identities of the parties in conflict and the reasons for their quarrel, they preferred to use guns over old-style negotiation or arm twisting. Finally, it is largely irrelevant whether Manuel Muñoz Rocha and Abraham Rubio Canales had Ruiz Massieu killed (if indeed they were involved in his murder) on behalf of drug traffickers, out of personal resentment, because they were ordered to do so by Raúl Salinas de Gortari or because they opposed the supposedly bold democratic reforms that the former governor of Guerrero was presumably going to carry out within the PRI (in a version believed only by foreign correspondents). In any of these accounts, the old mechanisms for settling problems among the elites —narco-businessmen, politicians from different groups, the various ideological factions within the ruling party—simply ceased to function.

The mess left behind by Carlos Salinas de Gortari consists mainly of this. For various reasons, his government dismantled or discarded many of the traditional means to settle disputes among elites. Corruption did not abate, of course; it was merely rechanneled toward a few privileged beneficiaries. In PRI jargon, it stopped splashing the way it did before. The distribution of privileges, posts, sinecures, jobs, seats in the Chamber of Deputies, governorships, scholarships, and embassy posts, and all the Mexican political system's scaffolding of cooptation, corruption, and consolation started shrinking. There are fewer state-owned companies, and those still there are handed over to groups that are ever more closed. At the same time, the consequences of settling disputes differently—that is, violently—have diminished: countless murderers are at large. In the absence of rewards for good conduct and punishments for bad, one doesn't need to be a rocket scientist to decide what to do if one wants to settle accounts with some enemy, rival, or competitor.

But even as Carlos Salinas set about destroying what was already there, he neglected to set up something new. He abdicated from the responsibility of putting in place the only structure viable in a country like Mexico, at the end of the twentieth century: a structure of representative democracy, as genuine as possible, and a lawful state that would render justice and ensure security. Manuel Muñoz Rocha might not have ordered the murder of Ruiz Massieu just because Muñoz was not named governor of his state or senator of Tamaulipas, if he had any hope of obtaining some other post by any means other than the "magic finger" of the PRI. The country was stripped of its old system, which, with all its defects and infamy, gave Mexican society half a century of stability. Today it is completely adrift, without a new system based on rules that, even if stricter, would at least be acceptable to everyone. No one with any vocation for democracy can possibly miss the old days; but only a sorcerer's apprentice dismantles and pulls things down without replacing them. We are currently paying the price for that abdication.

One such consequence, of lesser importance, is the proliferation of possible explanations for the chain of events of 1994. The lack of reliable data turns everything into speculation. However, some fantasies are more plausible than others; any one of them, like that which follows, is neither more nor less likely to be true than any other at this time. It parts from the Colombian precedent and follows a relatively classic script.

In Colombia, the drug traffickers' war against the state began with the execution of Justice Minister Rodrigo Lara Bonilla by a hired assassin on April 30, 1984. The reason for the murder, and for the conflict as a whole, was the drug cartels' fear that the extradition treaty signed by Colombia and the United States in 1982 would actually begin to be enforced. In 1983, extradition had been authorized but not implemented. From 1984 until the treaty was repealed by a constitutional amendment on July 4, 1991, the successive narco-ringleaders—the so-called *extraditables*—waged an all-out war against the Colombian state. Not so much to protect their business, which was flourishing, as to reverse a step that in their view violated the traditional understandings between drug traffickers and government in their country and thus threatened their survival. The Colombian government had been forced to negotiate and ratify the treaty, especially because of pressure from the United States. After dozens of assassinations and enormous damage and injury had been suffered, a Colombian president who was pro-U.S. (but also sensible) decided that it was better to negotiate with the drug traffickers than to fight them. When the Colombian congress modified the constitution—at the behest of President César Gaviria—Pablo Escobar surrendered, the Medellín cartel collapsed, and the Cali cartel triumphed with its better manners, its Harvard-educated offspring, and its wealth regained.

It is not inconceivable that the regime of Carlos Salinas should have reached an agreement with Mexico's drug traffickers at the beginning of his term, assuring three goals indispensable to both sides and of benefit both to them and (why not say it?) the country as a whole. The first goal of this speculative agreement was to encourage the drug lords to bring at least part of their money to Mexico, so as to ease the balance of payments. It is worth recalling that Colombia was the only country in Latin America that did not become overly indebted during the lost decade of the eighties, thanks in part to the so-called sinister window of Colombia's central bank. In Mexico, from the beginning of Salinas's term, there were rumors about the participation of drug money in the privatization of banks and regional money-centers.

The second goal would have consisted in ensuring that drug-related activities stop interfering with U.S.-Mexico relations. The profile of the trafficking, its methods and effects, would be subject to U.S. criteria and, would not expose or embarrass either the Mexican government (as did, for instance, the murder of DEA agent Enrique Camarena in 1985) or that of the United States. Discretion, tact, and the recasting of routes, rhythms, and partners (for instance, sacrificing the relationship with the Medellín cartel, in favor of the Cali group) would all have been part of the supposed agenda.

The third objective of this hypothetical tacit (or perhaps not even tacit) agreement would have been to allow the traffickers—or at least their most modern factions—to proceed with their activities if the first two objectives were met. The appointments in 1988 of Enrique Alvarez del Castillo, former governor of Jalisco (cradle of one of the cartels) as attorney general, of Javier Coello Trejo, former chief of staff to the governor of Chiapas, as drug tsar, and of other brand-new officials of similar character, and perhaps similarly well known to the drug lords, may well have been made in connection with this requirement. A series of articles, published in 1994 in the weekly magazine *Proceso*, about corruption and arrangements between the drug traffickers and Coello, were revealing in this regard. Tolerance toward one group of drug traffickers did not mean passivity toward all: one could repress and circumscribe one sector while giving the other free rein.

By mid-1991, the drug lords might have concluded that the Salinas administration had chosen to violate the agreements or tacit arrangements previously negotiated. Not that the authorities had decided to put a stop to drug trafficking: any Mexican knows that the force, presence, consumption, export, and trafficking of drugs are now greater than ever in Mexico. But the government might have broken certain agreements by allowing the United States a larger role in the war against drugs, or by concentrating its offensive on one sector and thus favoring another. In late 1990, P-3 airplanes of the U.S. government began flying over Mexican territory; radar and balloon stations were set up along Mexico's northern and southern borders. The widely publicized kidnapping of Humberto Alvarez Machain was the equivalent of an extradition without trial. Perhaps the number of DEA agents in Mexico was increased; perhaps investigations into money laundering in U.S. banks were stepped up.

There was a reason for both governments to move away from the *status quo ante*: it was called the North American Free Trade Agreement. On the U.S. side, while neither the Bush nor Clinton administrations ever acknowledged that the accord would stimulate drug trafficking, they both knew perfectly well that it would. The DEA and the U.S. Customs Service confided as much to anybody curious enough to ask. The growth in licit trade and vehicle traffic across the border, without a comparable increase in the budget for customs inspections, implied a growing illicit trade: drugs from Mexico to the U.S., arms and precursor chemicals from the U.S. to Mexico. Without stepping up the war in order to force the sources of drug trafficking to other latitudes, NAFTA could become a powerful instrument for record drug imports and consumption in the United States.

The Mexican government also had good reasons to bow to U.S. pressure: its imperative need for approval of the trade agreement. Having come so far, the Salinas administration was fully aware that the worst of all possible worlds would be a rejection of NAFTA. To prevent that, no cost was too high. But Salinas also knew the terrible risks of a futile war against the drug lords. Thus, possibly, his decision: to accept U.S. conditions, but only if Washington did the dirty work. Instead of Mexico handing over corpses, the U.S. would hand over money. As it turned out, we ended up supplying the corpses, anyway.

The drug lords probably understood for the first time what was happening with the incidents of Llano de la Víbora, in Tlalixcoyan, Veracruz, on November 7, 1991, when a U.S. Customs plane filmed a shoot-out involving the Mexican Army, the Judicial Police, and drug traffickers, with everyone shooting at everyone else and no one knowing who was who. At that point, the traffickers might have decided to send a series of signals in code, which the Mexican government understood perfectly, while others were confused by them—which was precisely the point. Thus began an escalation of violence—not generalized, but consisting of selective, well-planned, and destabilizing assassinations that could be interpreted in many ways but in fact conveyed one message: either we return to our previous agreements or the murders will continue. Thus, Cardinal Posadas, Colosio, and Ruiz Massieu might have been warnings that the government, for various reasons, chose not to heed. If this was indeed the case, the infernal dynamics of 1994 will continue, either with more murders or other types of criminal acts: bombs, plane crashes, kidnappings, and so on. Of course, drug traffickers in Mexico are no cleaner than anywhere else: they buy, use, join, and manipulate political, business, and other sectors to achieve their ends. It is not impossible that resentful PRI groups were used in these attacks. Nor is it inconceivable that at the top levels of drug trafficking, the distinction between politicians turned drug lords and drug lords turned politicians is a slight one indeed.

The collapse of traditional ways to settle disputes among Mexican elites, persistent economic sluggishness, corruption, and violence, all derived from the new and stronger presence of drug trafficking in Mexico, were powerful incentives to undertake a herculean effort of renewal. It would have been better—indeed, ideal—if that effort had been undertaken before the elections and had moved toward a transition, in accordance with the guidelines described earlier. It was not possible. But that didn't change the essential point: the task of rebuilding a viable country still lies ahead and requires the appropriate tools. It is the great task now confronting all those citizens who no longer believe that Mexico's basic problems can be solved within the scope of the existing political system, no matter how updated or modernized.

This will require forging a broad front, unifying affinities and points of agreement among the three principal political parties, civil society, and other sectors. Its banner would be the pursuit of democratic reform, an aspiration shared by a majority of citizens, according to one reading of the election results. The configuration of this front cannot be limited to the left of the political spectrum, though it will necessarily spring from it in part. It is thus important that we give some thought to the tribulations and perspectives of the Mexican left.

The original intent of the Party of the Democratic Revolution (PRD)—though not shared by many of those close to Cuauhtémoc Cárdenas, including the author—had a certain logic to it. It sought to join in one party all the fractions, shades, and sensitivities of the Mexican left, from Trotskyism, Maoism, and Castroism to the revolutionary nationalism of PRIista descent. Its common denominators were to be the struggle for democracy and the leadership of Cárdenas himself. The free play of ideas and the eventual dismantling of previous groups would allow for a gradual merging of all into a new whole, distinct from and better than its parts. The extreme left, the revolutionary or "hard" left, would coexist with a "light" left, essentially social-democratic, given that both currents derive from profound tendencies within Mexican society.

This did not materialize, though it might have under different circumstances. In any case, several new factors have come into play since 1994, and the design of the reformist opposition to the existing political system must be revised. First, there is now a radical and highly visible left outside the PRD: the Zapatista Army, Marcos, and the other more or less armed and active groups, in other parts of the country. The second factor is the disappearance of a previous element of unity: it is hard to imagine a third attempt by Cárdenas to reach the presidency, or to imagine any candidacy whose chances for victory would, in themselves, be enough to unite very different groups. In the third place, the defeat of 1994 has perhaps increased awareness of a central fact: to beat the system, the opposition must be united and the PRI divided. But to accomplish both things at once, a herculean task to begin with, is almost impossible with the constant frictions among factions of the PRD and the presence of a more radical left outside it, which for a number of reasons—good and bad—alienates many sympathizers (not to mention skeptical PRI or PAN supporters contemplating a break).

In addition, the overwhelming inequalities and endemic violence in Mexico virtually guarantee that the country will have a "hard" left for a long time. At the same time, the presence of a working class and a middle class of significant proportions bodes well for the emergence of social-democratic reformism in the medium term. Both groups in this portion of Mexico's political spectrum must be allowed to survive and grow, but it is not clear that they can do so within the same party. The most radical sector of the PRD will have to connect with the rest of the country's militant left; the more reformist sector might seek its natural allies or partners in other ideological quarters.

Within both the PRI and the PAN there are members who, if they can overcome their fear of reprisals by government (in the first case) and old quarrels (in the second), should forsake their old loves and begin building a new approach. So far, the system's enormous strength—and a great obstacle to democracy—has been the cost and difficulty of leaving it for those members who, for one reason or another, cease to agree with the regime's policies at a given moment. This was dramatically clear during the term of Salinas, though hardly restricted to his presidency. During those six years, important reforms were carried out that transformed the economy, the status of the church, land tenure, and sovereignty—all of which evoke the logical principle of the excluded middle: an honest person cannot agree with something and its opposite at the same time. Yet none of these reforms caused any breaks or separations. Everybody fell into step, nobody revolted.

If the new government really wanted to promote democratization, this might be its contribution: to allow dissenters to leave, without having their departure signify treason, a declaration of war, or perpetual banishment. If that were possible, many current PRIistas would undertake the crossing of the desert: old dinosaurs and young democrats; resentful ex-officials; former dignitaries who have fulfilled all their personal ambitions and would like to give something back to their country; the supporters of Colosio, Camacho, and other figures, now relegated to a silent diaspora of political discontent; businessmen, intellectuals, and artists who cannot or dàre not build something alone but would respond to a call from those who can—the politicians. Along their path, they would be joined by many PANistas, especially those with social-Christian or social-democratic leanings and those no longer willing to accept their leaders' complicity with the authoritarian modernization of the system.

A coalition such as this would attract many Mexicans, especially those who in recent years have joined together at various times for various causes. The coalition could build a position somewhere between the PRD and the PRI which would not necessarily be either leftist or social-democratic but would focus on democratic reform. In its initial phase, such an approach could only posit precise, yet important, objectives. The transition toward democracy and the rule of law, citizen safety, and morality in government, would doubtless be a starting point. This position would identify violence and instability with the system and not with the opposition, as was done in the 1994 elections in such a perverse and damaging way.

A second major objective would be a gradual and moderate redistribution of wealth and income through growth, social spending, investment in infrastructure, and an in-depth tax reform that would ensure greater revenues and an effective decentralization of both collection and expenditure. A third, indispensable focus would be the struggle against corruption. Few problems in the system have become so important in recent years or have caused such outrage among the citizenry. Another goal and point of agreement would be the defense of national sovereignty under NAFTA, while negotiating the noneconomic aspects of integration with the United States, such as the legalization and regulation of migratory flows toward the U.S., the drug trade, the development of a new Mexican industrial structure, and the democratization of the supranational institutions arising from economic integration.

This current would obviously have to include members and forces of the PRI, PRD, and PAN, including at least one possible presidential candidate from each party for the year 2000, so that no one figure would stand out prematurely. These would be, as things stand now, of course, Manuel Camacho, Porfirio Muñoz Ledo, and Vicente Fox. But the new current would mainly have to attract the gigantic party of all those who are now without a party: the huge number of activists, social organizers, members of the academic and business communities, and those citizens in general who in recent years have become involved in politics and the struggle for democracy. All of them should be able to choose with greater freedom where they wish to go: some will choose the more combative organizations, imbued with the militant spirit that sometimes fires a given region or generation; others will join more flexible organizations that are more open to negotiation.

It is not easy to build a front like this, as was shown by the contradictory experience of the San Angel Group. The experience of June, July, and August 1994 showed that within the academic, social, and political left on the one hand and the official sphere removed from government decision-making on the other, there is now a certain tolerance, a wish for joint action and an obvious maturity. It was much harder to find these attributes in center-right and business circles. Aside from a few honorable exceptions, such as Enrique Krauze and Julieta Campos in the cultural sphere, Vicente Fox, Javier Livas, and the Clouthier family within the PAN (or rather, within the PAN dissidence), and a few atypical business leaders who have served as public officials, such as Francisco Cano Escalante, recruitment within that segment of the ideological spectrum has always been very difficult. But aside from this deficiency, the San Angel Group proved it possible to join dissimilar forces into a single structure when the situation demands it and a common, important cause emerges.

It also became apparent, however, that groupings like the San Angel Group are transitory and circumscribed to narrowly defined causes. If the group effectively ceased to function on August 21, 1994, and survived thanks only to the artificial life support it received, this was because the obstacles to consensus became insurmountable. There was no agreement on the presidential election, or the future, or the minimal rules for coexistence. Ambiguity and the willingness to let time pass, undeniable virtues in the group, became untenable and even harmful in the process of building a new current. The attributes necessary for the group to function and appropriate to that moment did not suit the new times. These factors, and a certain intellectual honesty, explain why the San Angel Group could not give birth to another grouping, much less to a current able to compete at the polls with the party in power.

But that current can be built, especially if the dwindling of the state, the youthfulness of the four administrations preceding Zedillo's, and the limited opening of the political system lead to another split from the PRI and the system, which would come to complement the dissenting group of 1987-88, without necessarily joining it. That current would inevitably be in the opposition. Its first goal would be to push the existing political system toward a representative democracy, as yet unknown in Mexico. The coalition might negotiate and make arrangements with the system, but should take care not to be confused with it while it still survives. Perhaps the best precedent would be the so-called Agreement for Democracy in Chile, based on the 1985 National Accord for the Transition to Democracy signed by Christian and social democrats and members of the Party for Democracy (PPD), the Radical Party, and many others. This alliance already counts among its achievements the defeat of Pinochet in the referendum of 1988, the election of two presidents (Patricio Alwyn in 1989 and Eduardo Frei in 1993), the formation of two successive coalition governments under a presidential system, and the transition—slower than hoped for, but continuous and certain—from a military dictatorship toward the reestablishment of Chile's traditional democracy—and all of this within a context of sustained economic expansion. It is not the best nor the most glorious of all possible worlds, but, given this world, it is not at all bad.

CHAPTER 10

The December Debacle

THE LAST SURPRISE OF 1994 WAS NOT REALLY A SURPRISE. THE devaluation of December 20 and subsequent economic collapse were anything but unexpected. They were repeatedly announced by the countless observers who since 1989 had criticized the economic policy of the Salinas administration, and had foretold of a debacle time and again were that course to be maintained. Nonetheless, the devaluation was a surprise to the millions of Mexicans who had bought into the fond dream of entering the First World, into the countless delights of imported goods—whether the grandee's Mercedes or the household appliances—and into the bargain-basement dollars, good for trips to Orlando and condos on Padre Island, for medical and life insurance policies in Houston, and for restful cruises in the Caribbean. It was also a surprise to those businessmen who had become indebted in dollars—the only alternative to the outrageous cost of credit in pesos—or had switched from their domestic suppliers to foreign inputs (better quality at a lower price....until the devaluation).

In the wake of the shipwreck, three broad currents of explanation arose with their respective recipes for getting out of the latest devaluation swamp. The first, still dominant outside of Mexico and within official circles, was premised upon continuity and success. Accordingly, the exchange-rate adjustment, beyond its momentary vicissitudes, did not invalidate the model based on trade liberalization, privatization, and deregulation of the economy. The only thing missing was time and perseverance. For the purveyors of this interpretation, after a brief recessive phase, the fruits of the effort undertaken since 1985 would become apparent in a not-faraway future.

For the more experienced and cosmopolitan among these analysts, the relevant analogy was Chile. Between 1975 and 1981 Chile underwent a structural transformation not unlike Mexico's, also distorted by an overvalued rate of exchange. The collapse of 1982 came about when the currency was devalued, major companies failed, banks had to be renationalized, the most notorious speculators were thrown into jail, and gross domestic product (GDP) plummeted 14 percent in one year. Arturo Fontaine Talavera has narrated the Chilean catastrophe and the atmosphere that preceded it in his splendid novel, *Oír su voz*. For the supporters of this school of thought, the solution to the Mexican crisis was obvious. It consisted not only in more of the same, but in a deeper and quicker continuation of economic reform: greater liberalization in those sectors still protected (banks, pharmaceuticals, and the automobile industry), more privatization (Pemex, the Federal Electricity Commission, railroads), greater cutbacks in spending, less taxes, further deregulation. This was more or less the path followed by the government of Ernesto Zedillo. The emergency plan presented in early January 1995 and implemented with ongoing corrections during subsequent weeks and months accurately reflected its Chilean "origins": with time and a little luck, the country would return to growth and prosperity. That Chile changed its course beginning in 1982, that the definitive results of Chile's experience are still uncertain, and that Chile's population is six times smaller than that of Mexico did not detract from the virtues of the model.

This interpretative effort tends to highlight the contingent nature of the December 1994 gaffe, blaming the outgoing administration of Carlos Salinas for its delay in adjusting the exchange rate. Emphasis is placed on the idea of an accident: if Salinas and his finance minister, Pedro Aspe, had devalued the peso in time or had accelerated its rate of slippage, the worst could have been avoided. An adjustment was inevitable anyway, as the Mexican peso was indeed overvalued, but if not for certain political or personal factors in the outgoing team, the situation would have been manageable. Thus, it would be relatively easy to remedy the crisis: it would suffice to ensure that capital flows from abroad did not dry up entirely; to keep salary and price hikes from unleashing an inflationary spiral annulling the benefits of the devaluation (so as to achieve a "real" devaluation); and to continue relying on healthy public finances to recover growth in the medium term, perhaps with a few rectifications.

There is a second, far more critical way of looking at all this, which centers on the model's failure and its complete irrelevance to a country like Mexico. From this perspective, the governments of Salinas and Miguel de la Madrid before him conceived and implemented a whole "neoliberal" strategy for economic development —in part out of conviction, in part due to pressure from the United States. The model they followed, as did almost all the nations of Latin America, favored certain sectors—exporters, large monopolies, particular types of consumers—but is not viable in a country like Mexico. It was thus doomed to failure. The only question was how long it would take.

A series of proposals can be derived from this analysis, and the former presidential candidate Cuauhtémoc Cárdenas outlined several in his statement of January 6, 1995: salary increases, a moratorium on and renegotiation of the foreign debt, and renegotiation of the North America Free Trade Agreement with the United States and Canada. These steps—putting aside questions about the feasibility and implications of each—constitute a comprehensive strategy of another kind, also global and orderly, but of a different sign. The rationality of the response rests upon the opposite rationality of the starting point. On both sides we have a totalizing vision. If the general direction outlined by Cárdenas is logical—salaries must not bear the full weight of the crisis; we should seek better terms for the foreign debt; new chapters should be added to NAFTA—the idea of replacing one hypothetically complete strategy with another can only lead to dogmatic and reckless extremes.

Aside from these two interpretations, however, arose a third. It parted from a series of analyses carried out by economists, academics, and consultants in recent years. This approach took into account the specific crises and critiques as they unfolded under changing circumstances. It showed that the government of Carlos Salinas did not have an original, complete, and orderly strategy; that it resorted instead to ad hoc decisions that were almost always improvised and poorly conceived, with ever more frequent and irresponsible flights forward in order to face changing combinations of political and economic factors. Just as this interpretation emphasizes a certain Salinista impulsiveness in its explanation, it gives great importance to pragmatism as a solution. The Salinista model was not a strategy but a sum of pragmatic reactions, bound up with the efforts undertaken by international agencies based in Washington, D.C., as well as by U.S. authorities, to transform those decisions into a package that could be sold in other latitudes. The remedy to the Salinista fiasco should be strategic in nature, but not dogmatic. Nobody is advocating a return to the past. Proposals to make liberalization selective and gradual, to design and implement an industrial policy, to renegotiate the foreign debt, to carry out a tax reform, and to depend less upon speculative capital flows do not signify a return to the past—but they do not mean persisting blindly in the failed Salinista course, either.

Observers who advocated this view and deserve special mention include: Macario Schettino, whose Sunday articles in the daily *El Financiero* highlighted the links between the different facets of economic policy; Enrique Quintana, who in his columns in *El Financiero* and later *Reforma*, as in his essays and radio programs, showed the weaknesses inherent in the model from the start; José Luis Calva, who detected the devastating effects of liberalization in the countryside; Jaime Ros, who from his economics chair at the University of Notre Dame sounded the alarm at the absence of growth; Carlos Heredia, who in Washington, D.C., fought the battle of NAFTA and criticized the model; and, finally, former finance minister David Ibarra, who in many discussions emphasized that the exchange rate could not be sustained in the medium term and always insisted on the critical need for an industrial policy so as not to leave Mexico's trade balance entirely up to the market.

Fairness requires that we also mention three foreigners: Christopher Whalen and Andrew Reding, who, despite their strident tone, pointed to the link between political authoritarianism, an overvalued exchange rate, and the inevitable financial crash at the end of the road, and Guillermo Calvo, a former official at the International Monetary Fund (IMF), who warned in a seminal 1992 article that the capital flows going into Latin America were highly speculative, that they arose from low interest rates in the rest of the world, and that they masked persistently insufficient rates of internal savings and investment throughout the entire continent, with the exception of Chile.

BY EARLY 1989 IT WAS OBVIOUS TO MANY THAT THE ELECTORAL fraud perpetrated in the July 1988 election had sealed the fate of the new regime. This was especially true in one regard: the Salinas administration was extremely vulnerable to the pressures and demands of those who had helped it win the postelectoral conflict, and the Salinistas had to reconquer the sympathies of decisive portions of the electorate through measures that were politically defensible but economically questionable. This weakness in the government became especially apparent in two policies, born earlier (in November 1987, to be exact) but maintained and intensified by the administration. First of all, there was the sudden, indiscriminate, and excessive trade liberalization, or opening of the border to imports. The conceptual break with protectionism and industrialization through import substitution dated back to the end of 1985, when Mexico entered the General Agreement on Tariffs and Trade (GATT). For some time, particularly since 1985, the United States had called for a clear and significant liberalization of the most protected Latin American markets. For the U.S. economy, which was becoming less and less competitive, countries like Mexico, Brazil, and Argentina represented a unique chance to conquer new markets in a relatively easy and painless way. Through a series of restructurings of the foreign debt and interminable negotiations on structural adjustment with the World Bank, Mexico bowed more and more to U.S. demands.

The implementation of this policy was revealed in all its splendor in November 1987, when it became necessary to apply an anti-inflationary pact in order to avoid a major rout in the presidential elections set for the following July. But it was not until early 1989 that liberalization showed its true colors: not as an instrument of trade or industrial policy meant to promote the Mexican economy's competitiveness, but as a means to combat inflation, as a price ceiling for products made in Mexico. Together with a real and continuous appreciation of the exchange rate (beginning in 1989, the peso's slippage vis-à-vis the dollar was much smaller than the differential between inflation rates in the U.S. and Mexico), trade liberalization had three advantages from the viewpoint of the authorities. First, it put a damper on domestic inflation. Second, it made imports increasingly available to Mexico's middle classes at reasonable prices. Third, it obtained the blessings of the United States, whose exporters came to fulfill 80 percent of Mexico's astonishing thirst for imported gadgets. But liberalization also led to an accounting abyss: accompanied by a strong peso, liberalization would inevitably open a trade gap, especially if the Mexican economy were to grow, even in moderation. If to this were added the persistent burden of foreign debt service, the country would be doomed to an ever-growing deficit in the current account of the balance of payments.

This aspect of the crisis has received less attention that it deserves. Though in recent times the government and many commentators have used and abused the term *current-account deficit*, many people tend to identify it with balance of trade. They forget or ignore that an essential component of the current account (and, for Mexico, an essential component of its imbalance) is the interest due on the country's foreign debt, whether public or private. When the Salinista authorities threw themselves into liberalization and virtually froze the exchange rate, they doubtless believed that they could allow themselves the luxury of a large trade deficit, if only they could renegotiate the foreign debt so as to reduce its service. And indeed, a good renegotiation was an indispensable condition for stability in prices and the economy as a whole. If the exchange rate was fixed due to a precarious legitimacy that was barely being salvaged, and if liberalization was neither reversible nor subject to restraint due to the demands of Washington and the import frenzy of the middle classes, then the only category in the current account capable of being modified was indeed the interest on the debt. Thus the enormous importance of the July 1989 agreement reached with the international private banks and the final formulation, in February 1990, of the so-called menu of options in that agreement.

In *Proceso's* memorable cartoon depicting Salinas on television singing Mozart's *Requiem* instead of the national anthem, while dragging the shackles of the foreign debt beyond the limits of the screen, the cartoonist Naranjo illustrated the real tragedy of the regime: the failed renegotiation of the foreign debt. As much as the government tried to disguise a bad settlement as a definitive solution, the ordeal of the negotiations produced meager results. The net reduction in capital and annual service due was estimated at slightly over 15 percent by various analysts. The authorities' response to this and other observations was indignant, arrogant, and false. It might not have been possible to achieve easier terms in any other way, either; but the actual results did not match the country's needs or the government's exuberance. The regime threatened a moratorium and threw its best cadres and persuasive talents into the breach, but was finally unable to obtain the respite it needed. Above all, it did not compensate through the interest account the widening gap in the trade balance. When the net balance between debt and interest reduction and fresh available capital became known in the first quarter of 1990, it appeared obvious that betting on debt reduction to lessen the current-account deficit had not worked.

There were two alternatives left. One was to straighten out the trade account by reversing liberalization, allowing the currency to slide more quickly, and adopting a policy to promote exports through subsidies, selective protection, incentives, identification of market niches, and so on—in a nutshell, a long-term, Asian-style policy. The other option was to solve the problems in the current account through the capital account, attracting resources by other means and leaving the deficit to the market's free play. The final decision was never in doubt, due to the trade agreements with the United States, the middle classes' demand for low inflation and cheap dollars, and the free-market convictions held by the small circle of President Salinas's advisers. They chose to incorporate into Mexican economic thinking the famous thesis held by Nigel Lawson, Margaret Thatcher's former chancellor of the exchequer: "The only [current-account] deficit too big is that which cannot be financed."

Just as the solution to the financial collapse of November 1987 was a brutal liberalization and the response to the ensuing trade deficit was an attempt to renegotiate the foreign debt, the ad hoc response to the insufficient arrangement with the banks was also tactical and improvised. The government decided to sell assets in order to attract capital, preferably foreign but in any case the capital expatriated from Mexico, and undertook to negotiate NAFTA in order to ensure a large and lasting flow of direct investment. Regardless of the possible merits attached to these various options, the government's final decision had nothing to do with those merits, but rather its need to scrape through a difficult moment. It is worth recalling that, as late as mid-1989, Carlos Salinas enumerated in *Newsweek* all the excellent reasons for which he opposed a free-trade agreement with the United States.

Thus transpired the years 1990 and 1991: the secret beginning of negotiations on NAFTA was disclosed in January of 1990, and the banks' privatization was announced during the pope's visit in May, while the current account and trade balance begin to deteriorate. By 1989, the trade imbalance had already reached $664 million and that of the current account, $3.9 billion. The following year, the imbalance became even more pronounced: $4.5 billion in the trade deficit, $7 billion in the current account. And interest on the debt remained the same: $9.2 billion in both 1989 and 1990. The government had entered a race against time. If it wanted to recover minimal levels of economic growth before the federal elections of 1991 and to finance the growing deficits without devaluing the currency, it would have to sell assets and negotiate the treaty as quickly as possible.

It was in those months that many skeptical citizens began to say that the government was selling off the family jewels in order to pay the debts of spendthrift parents and offspring. Although some state-owned companies were sold more advantageously than others, and in some cases the divestitures seemed to provide huge revenues (the banks, and, to a lesser degree Telmex), the procedure had two inherent flaws. First of all, when one sells in great haste, one does not know for sure who the buyer is. Secondly, any attempt to bolster the current account by selling assets is eventually doomed to failure, because expenses continue while assets run out. Now we know the consequences of those two original sins, evident in the recent bank failures and financial scandals and in the shortage of funds to face persistent deficits.

As for NAFTA, three concluding comments are in order. First, the delay in negotiations—which made it impossible for the treaty to enter into force before January 1, 1994—was predictable, but had serious effects on the country. Among other things, it precipitated the recession of 1992-93, which was provoked by rising domestic interest rates, which were caused in turn by the need to attract capital in order to finance a current-account deficit that was still growing. By 1992, the price of the course chosen in 1987-89 was obvious: the trade deficit reached $16 billion and interest payments $9.6 billion; the current-account deficit approached $25 billion, or more than 6 percent of GDP.[17]

A developing country must incur current-account deficits; otherwise, it becomes a net exporter of capital, as happened to Mexico during the eighties. But the key is the size of the deficit: the rule of thumb is that the growth rate of GDP should at least be twice the current-account deficit as a percentage of GDP. Mexico's case was exactly the opposite: in 1992, the economy grew by 2.8 percent; the deficit surpassed 5 percent of GDP. As the free-trade treaty negotiations dragged on, the only means to solve the problem drew further and further away—and the red emergency lights were already flashing.[18]

Secondly, NAFTA was postponed at the worst possible moment —during two election years in Mexico—and for the worst possible reason—the election year in the United States. Mexico's election and succession timetables are extremely strict. In 1991, there were federal elections for Congress, which the PRI could not lose and which thus precluded any preventive adjustments in the rate of exchange. The following year, there would be elections in numerous states, including Michoacán, the cradle of the Cardenista movement; Guerrero, always tense; and Chihuahua, a PAN stronghold; and a special election in San Luis Potosí, which had caused such problems the previous year. Of all possible years, 1992 was perhaps the least bad for a devaluation. But it wasn't that urgent and it would have a high economic and political price—though less than at other times—and so the window of opportunity for a devaluation was allowed to slip by. The following year, 1993, would see the presidential succession—a terrible time for devaluation, first of all because it would cancel the chances of one possible nominee, the minister of finance. That year would also see the debate on ratification of NAFTA in the United States.

The forced postponement of NAFTA further delayed the goal most awaited by all Mexicans—economic growth—and the continuing absence of economic expansion was the worst legacy of the Salinas administration. Insufficient foreign resources, in tandem with a growing deficit, obliged the government to cool down the economy and raise interest rates, leading to the acute recession Mexico suffered from the second semester of 1992 to the first semester of 1994.

The third point about NAFTA has perhaps not been sufficiently emphasized. Those who followed closely the debate in the United

States between supporters and detractors of the free trade agreement will recall that the best, and to some extent the only, argument used by spokesmen from both governments was that concerning the treaty's benefits for the U.S. economy. Liberalization of the Mexican market, they said, would stimulate U.S. exports and create tens of thousands of jobs in U.S. industry. It is enough to recall the televised encounter between Vice President Al Gore and former presidential candidate Ross Perot. Gore repeatedly insisted on the advantages for the United States, which, thanks to NAFTA, would be able to sell countless new products to Mexico. But this depended on one factor: that the peso-dollar ratio remain favorable to the United States, ensuring that U.S. exports would continue to get cheaper and Mexican goods and services more expensive. A peso devaluation would destroy that prospect. Thus the opponents of NAFTA, like John Lafalce, chairman of the Committee on Small Business in the House, held hearings on the parity of the peso and systematically accused the Mexican government of keeping a devaluation up its sleeve until just after the treaty's passage. Any exchange adjustment was thus inconceivable before, during, or just after ratification.

The rest is history. The agreement with the United States did not help the country escape the blows to its political system in 1994. The efforts made by Mexico's government and monetary authorities to keep the economic and political spheres completely separate did not succeed. And politics returned with a vengeance in December to wrest its preeminence away from the economy. The surprises of 1994—the Chiapas uprising, the struggles between Manuel Camacho and Luis Donaldo Colosio, the latter's assassination, the presidential debate of May 12 and the meteoric rise of Diego Fernández de Cevallos in the polls, the assassination of José Franciso Ruiz Massieu—would have justified a devaluation, but they also made it impossible. Amid the tragedy and shock of that spring, it was neither feasible nor sensible to add to the accumulation of problems one more, the most serious: a collapse of the currency and a new outbreak of inflation. Nor was a devaluation viable in the summer of 1994, just before the election: since 1990, the keystone of the PRI's electoral strategy was to reconquer the middle classes through exchange-rate and price stability. Precisely because sustaining the parity and continuing to finance the current-account deficit was an essential part of that strategy, the government resorted to deplorable and dangerous maneuvers whose exorbitant price we are now paying.

When the stock market stopped growing at the stratospheric rates of 1991 and part of 1992, the interest paid on Treasury certificates (CETES) was raised in order to ensure that capital flows shifted from variable- to fixed-interest instruments, thus staying in Mexico. This strategy, however, began the transformation of foreign investors into creditors (the foreign owner of stock in a Mexican company is a foreign investor; the foreign holder of a Mexican bond, even one denominated in pesos, is a foreign creditor). The fear of devaluation among fund managers holding Mexican instruments during the first months of 1994—a fear caused by the Chiapas uprising and the assassination of Colosio—led to the proliferation of Treasury bonds (Tesobonos): short-term bonds denominated in pesos but indexed to the dollar.

When the crisis of December 1994 exploded and the Tesobonos became unpayable, the government simply converted them into medium-term dollar bonds, backed by the U.S. government, which was itself apparently backed, in turn, by future Pemex revenues. Zedillo argued that the conversion of Tesobonos into medium-term dollar bonds did not imply an increase in the foreign debt. But he never clarified when the previous—or current—administration had finally recognized that peso bonds held by foreigners were the equivalent of foreign debt and should thus be considered. The Mexican Congress never approved the contracting of billions of dollars more in debt, nor was it ever asked to.

By guaranteeing in dollars, through Tesobonos, the investment and returns of foreign financiers, the government was in effect adding to the country's dollar debt once again. Thus the bubble phenomenon we are witnessing today: if the government's foreign debt previously denominated in dollars is still about $80 billion, total foreign obligations exceed $160 billion when we include Tesobonos and the debt of the private sector and commercial banks. In addition, high interest rates in Mexico had another perverse effect. Thanks to deficient regulation, Mexican companies were able to obtain funds abroad at much lower interest rates. This caused the private sector's foreign debt to reach stratospheric heights. The country must now pay the interest on that debt.

THE OVERVALUATION OF THE PESO WENT HAND IN HAND WITH the economic policy followed since 1989. At least from early 1993 to November 1994, devaluation was simply out of the question: its political or international price would have been altogether excessive. It is important that we be consistent in our ideas and preferences; if we want the ends, we must also want the means to attain them. Those who believed in the virtues of NAFTA, and considered it crucial to keep the PANista or Cardenista opposition from winning the August 21 elections, also had to support Salinas's monetary policy: the three goals were inseparably linked.

Two doubts remain: why didn't the government increase the peso-dollar rate of slippage, so as to achieve gradually and imperceptibly the same goal, the peso's depreciation? Why wasn't the currency devalued in November 1994, when it would have been possible? Regarding the first question, one might argue that the first ten months of 1994 saw a de facto devaluation of over 10 percent without anything happening. The answer lies in the reality itself: the discreet and covert devaluation of the peso during the first eleven months of 1994 was not enough to reduce the current-account deficit or to bring down interest rates, but it did lower peso returns on foreign investment. If the slippage is too small, it has no effect at all. If it is very pronounced, it causes a tidal wave of inflation and other effects similar to those of a sudden devaluation.

As for the second question, it is true that a window of opportunity for devaluation was opened in early November, after Ernesto Zedillo was proclaimed president-elect. Everything suggests that Zedillo himself did indeed ask President Salinas to devalue the currency, supposedly on November 20 (the anniversary of the Mexican Revolution). According to some accounts, Salinas agreed but faced the categorical opposition of his secretary of the treasury. Pedro Aspe threatened to resign rather than devalue the peso and predicted a massive influx of foreign capital following the inauguration of Ernesto Zedillo; thus, there would be no need for a devaluation. Perhaps Salinas agreed because he knew Aspe would refuse; perhaps another obstacle would have appeared if the treasury secretary had agreed. In any case, time passed and, between one thing and another, Inauguration Day arrived on December 1 with the parity still in place.

Zedillo inherited an untenable situation, but for reasons that go far beyond a technical overvaluation of the peso or a simple correction of the current-account deficit. The figures for 1994 were appalling: the trade deficit totaled $18 billion, interest payments approximately $12 billion, and the ensuing imbalance in the current account $28 billion, or more than 7 percent of GDP. The economy had grown barely 3 percent. The country's total foreign debt surpassed 160 billion dollars and, as a former U.S. official explained to me, its renegotiation would be far more difficult than those of 1982 and 1986. This time, Mexico's creditors were not hundreds of banks represented by an advisory committee of fifteen or twenty members. They were thousands and thousands of foreign holders of Mexican paper, both government and private: pension funds, insurance companies, investment banks, and individual investors. They had no representatives, they were very numerous, and, since December 20, they were very angry. To restructure a debt of this nature is almost impossible. The only alternative to repayment would have to be along the lines of the railroad bonds issued by the tsarist government of Russia: the descendants of the little old

French ladies who bought them at the turn of the century are still waiting for them to mature.

The reluctance of Mexico's new government team to face reality and choose between incompatible goals was fully revealed in the design of its economic program for 1995. According to the new authorities, it would be possible to grow, control inflation, and finance the current-account deficit, all at the same time: nothing was incompatible. Thus the budget that President Zedillo presented to the Chamber of Deputies ten days after taking office, and ten days before the world collapsed around him. Zedillo's budget contemplated a growth rate of 4 percent, inflation of 4 percent, and a current-account deficit of $31 billion, almost 9 percent of GDP, which would presumably be easy to finance.

There was no reason to choose between goals that were all desirable and feasible, or to give priority to some while sacrificing others. To some extent, the proof that Ernesto Zedillo was still not convinced of the need for an adjustment, or that he thought he could postpone it or implement it very gradually, is to be found in the figures he sent the Chamber; in their incongruity, they completely sidestepped the real options facing the country. Nor did Zedillo choose to announce the inevitable devaluation on the day he took office, taking advantage of his predecessor's presence either to secure his support or else to blame him for it.

Six years of parity populism and an economic policy made of impulsive, improvised, and thoughtless decisions were compounded by indecision and simple wishful thinking after December 1. To this explosive problem was added the reappearance, with a vengeance, of the nation's other great pending problem, on December 19: Marcos and the Chiapas uprising. When international markets faltered at the spectacle of masked Indians taking villages in Chiapas, Mexico's monetary authorities were panic-stricken and the house of cards so carefully built since 1988 came crashing down.

SHOULD CARLOS SALINAS HAVE DEVALUED THE PESO BETWEEN early November and his definitive departure from Los Pinos? It was not possible before that, and not likely afterward. Carlos Salinas was caught in the abiding dynamics of the Mexican presidency and fell prey to that dread of devaluation shared by all previous presidents. As José López Portillo said in 1982, "The president who devalues [the peso] is himself devalued." He was right. As long as he could avoid it, Salinas was not going to take that step. His place in history depended on it, as did his candidacy to head the World Trade Organization and the possibility for him and his children to walk the streets of Mexico without being insulted. Those who supported and applauded his energetic, authoritarian, but apparently effective leadership for six years could hardly ask him now to demonstrate qualities that he had never shown: modesty, selflessness, the capacity to consult with others, and a sense of statesmanship going beyond the Bourbon-style identification of the State with himself. Some observers believe that Luis Echeverría and López Portillo devalued the peso in 1976 and 1982, respectively, because they ran out of time and money; others, that they sacrificed themselves for the sake of the system that carried them to power and glory. It is all the same. Miguel de la Madrid devalued the peso so many times that one more recurrence, at the very end, didn't make any difference. But Carlos Salinas had not devalued the currency and had struck so many blows against the system that it seems absurd to reproach him with not having sacrificed himself to save something he had helped destroy.

Was Salinas responsible for Mexico's debacle? There are three facets to this question. Is he responsible for having led the country into a dead end whose only issue was a devaluation with its all-too-familiar sequels? Yes, he is. But so are all those who sang the praises of the economic model that is the true culprit responsible for today's chaos. The blame rests with the model, the scheme that opened the border, appreciated the currency, and left the debt intact —and all this from one day to the next, with the United States as a neighbor, and following a series of flights forward devoid of any long-term strategy. As for the issue of deceitfulness, Salinas is doubtless also guilty of having woven the yarn of Mexico's entry into the First World. But we must not forget the Arab proverb: "The perpetrator of a first deception is he who deceives, but the perpetrator of a second deception is its victim." Salinas did not deceive Mexicans just once; he pulled the wool over their eyes dozens of times, and the responsibility for that must be shared. Finally, if the issue is the moral choice of having jeopardized the country's financial health just for the sake of winning the elections and ensuring his own succession, then obviously there can only be one verdict: guilty. But it is absurd to ask pears of the orange tree or Capablanca openings and elegant Sicilian defenses from an inveterate poker player. The man who governed Mexico for six years with certain priorities and a very idiosyncratic style of making decisions—in a selfish, shortsighted, and improvised way—was not suddenly about to display vision, altruism, and strategy. There can be no deception with forewarning. At the end of his term, Salinas behaved exactly as his entire performance suggested he would.

It would be absurd for those who systematically criticized the previous regime for its authoritarianism, its regressive economic policy, its pro-U.S. foreign policy, and the atmosphere of waste and corruption it generated, to suddenly defend the outgoing president. But even I, with my primary and persistent anti-Salinism, am shaken when I see the betrayals, the somersaults, and duplicities that are following the Salinas administration on its disgraceful way out. In the last six years, there were countless opportunities to criticize, dissent from, renounce, and oppose the policies that led the country into this abyss. Of course, there was a price to pay for being critical; some of us paid it, others decided not to. Very few people who did not already belong to critical or opposition circles chose to take advantage of those opportunities. All the others must now share the responsibility for disaster with Carlos Salinas —and they must share his fate, whatever it is. To make firewood from a fallen tree, one must have woodcutter's credentials. Those who now want to join in must show theirs.

IF ERNESTO ZEDILLO WAS LEFT TO DANCE WITH THE UGLIEST girl at the party, it is also true that he danced with very little grace or rhythm during those days of December 1994, days we would all rather forget. Beginning on the night of December 19, it seemed as if the new government had drawn up a list of blunders and mistakes and had then proceeded to check them off one by one. It is worth pointing to three of them, before going on to outline a few ideas for getting Mexico out of the abyss.

The first mistake was international. Intervention by the U.S. government was not prepared as it should have been or, more importantly, in the best way. The details are not public, but it is obvious that the emergency and its magnitude took Washington completely by surprise. Doubtless, this was partly due to the recent resignation of Lloyd Bentsen as secretary of the treasury, in November 1994; he had been Mexico's principal interlocutor in Washington. His successor, Robert Rubin, had not yet been confirmed by Congress. Clearly, the Clinton administration was not prepared for the crisis; nor was it able to take immediate and effective emergency measures like those it began to implement as late as January 10, when President Clinton expressed his support for Mexico.

According to many sources, a first run against the peso on December 16 cut the reserves by $2.5 or $3 billion. If this account is true, then the Mexican government had a full weekend to organize its defenses for Monday the nineteenth. It did not do so. Even on the night of the 19th, the Bank of Mexico still had $11 billion in its coffers. At the very least, the government could have waited until it had organized a devaluation package, immediate financial support mechanisms, press relations, and announcements to world markets to be readied in close consultation with Washington before changing the parity. It could have used that entire weekend and Monday, so that by Tuesday, December 20, all the actors would have been in place, waiting in the wings with their scripts carefully written and memorized. That was the bare minimum, and it was absolutely essential—especially after having paid such a high price for Mexico's "special relationship" with the United States.

A second error of improvisation: the measures taken by the government, and their timing, were deficient. First the authorities suggested a peso float, in an unequivocal display of desperation. Then they "widened" the flotation band to a margin that would prove untenable within a few hours, precisely because the private sector, whose wish to avoid a float or a devaluation was heeded even as it was told the urgency of the situation, proceeded to take out its money post haste, thrown into a panic precisely by its talks with the government. Then the peso was allowed to float when there were almost no reserves left, creating further uncertainty. Only afterward were interest rates increased, followed by a recovery program that should have been ready from the outset. Finally, weeks later, the government obtained sufficient support from the United States—but at a very high price and under intense pressure to maintain the peso's parity, if only for a while.

Even worse, to proceed as the Mexican authorities did was a waste of the opportunities offered by NAFTA, given the high price the country had paid for it. Instead of obtaining financial support from the United States and the world financial community in the old-fashioned way, through conditional loans and more or less compulsory austerity programs, it was time to go on to a new monetary relationship with the United States and Canada. As various government officials and analysts said in the first days of January, the moment was ripe to try something new, from the outset, in an orderly and determined way.

This would have resembled what was actually undertaken in a makeshift and miserly way on Monday, January 9, and was later abandoned in favor of a gigantic traditional rescue package. The strategy was to make the U.S. Federal Reserve responsible for the defense of the peso by buying the Mexican currency on the market, just as it does to sustain other currencies (the pound sterling and the French franc, always; the yen and the German mark when necessary; and, under certain conditions, the Italian lira and the Canadian dollar). At some point, the country that has received this assistance must buy back its currency and possibly pay interest; but this burden is lighter, and its consequences less serious, than the increased debt Mexico is incurring with the rescue package as it now stands.

Mexico is clearly not a member of the exclusive club of countries mentioned above; nor is the peso a reserve currency, which is a requisite for it to be bought and sold on the world market. But the health of the Mexican economy is certainly a matter of national security for the United States, and Washington would have to intervene anyway to avoid a total collapse of the country and its institutions. The U.S. executive and its allies were finally forced to extend guarantees and backing for Mexican credits exceeding $50 billion—an extraordinary amount, revealing the depth of the abyss and how much Mexico's supposed salvation is going to cost. Rather than subject the country once more to the merciless credit conditions imposed by the U.S. Congress and the IMF, the Mexican government could have used NAFTA as a membership pass into the exclusive club mentioned above. The proof: the Fed did intervene on January 9, 1995, buying the equivalent in pesos of over half a billion dollars.

Obviously, there could be no long-term agreement with U.S. monetary authorities without previously negotiating a detailed recovery program. And sharing the responsibility for sustaining a currency does indeed imply some abdication of monetary sovereignty. But this sovereignty has faded anyway in recent years, in Mexico and other parts of the world. If the Mexican government had acted this way from the beginning, it might have avoided the panic, the uncertainty, and the terrible hemorrhage of money, as well as some of the conditions subsequently imposed by Washington. The technical differences between a swap with the Fed, without declared limits or deadlines, and loans from the U.S. government, the IMF, and the International Bank of Settlements (IBS) in Basel for more than $50 billion might seem minor. But the psychological effect of an announcement by the Federal Reserve that it would sustain the peso's parity at 4.5 or 5 to the dollar would have blocked the speculators' attacks on the Mexican currency. It is one thing for a Mexican president to say, as López Portillo did in 1982, that he will defend the peso "like a dog"; it is quite another for the Fed to say it. Of course, the line of $20 billion to stabilize the currency might not have been enough, despite such an announcement. We will never know that, or what other options might have arisen from such a circumstance.

The Mexican government should have explained to Washington from the outset, with patience and anticipation, just how serious the situation was. It should have expressed Mexico's willingness to negotiate, with the Fed's support, a package for economic recovery geared toward growth, not recession, and regulating the migratory effects of the latest Mexican crisis. Everyone might not have understood it immediately; but there is no doubt that we would shortly have entered a new, post-NAFTA phase in U.S.-Mexico relations. Of course, this would have required that the crisis be confronted calmly and swiftly, with imagination and daring—attributes that did not exactly abound in Mexico during the interminable weeks following December 19, 1994.

An agreement of this sort with the United States—a watered-down version of which the Mexican government finally adopted, but late, inadequately, and under debatable conditions—would also have paved the way for two additional negotiations, under better conditions, without in any way dismissing the delicacy and complexity of their content. First of all, a monetary mechanism of this nature—like that used by the states of the European Union, financed by their virtual central bank, the German Bundesbank—lessens the effects of an excessive inflation differential between the two countries. The key to a true devaluation is to keep inflation from soaring out of control. If it does, the hypothetical competitive advantages offered by devaluation are lost and the country soon finds itself in the same situation as before. In the long term, inflation in Mexico cannot be significantly higher than in the United States. But had the new fixed parity been backed by the Federal Reserve, and had the markets known it, a high inflation differential would not have been too serious—at least, not for a time.

That margin would also have opened the possibility (not the certainty) of negotiating with the United States (not the IMF) an economic program for Mexico based on recovery and growth (not recession), a program both countries desperately needed. Mexico needed it because, after thirteen years of low or zero economic growth (in constant dollars, Mexican per capita GDP is lower than in 1980), the population could not take any more austerity and unemployment. The United States also needed such a program because another recession in Mexico, plus the free fall of Mexican salaries in dollar terms, would lead to a new wave of migration that U.S. society might not tolerate. Conditions today are exactly the same as in the eighties: recession and devaluation in Mexico, a sturdy U.S. economy, and a skyrocketing demand for unskilled labor.

A program for recovery with growth would necessarily have corrected the previous administration's major mistake, which dated back to its beginnings in 1988 or even the transition period stretching from October of 1987 to December 1, 1988: it would have forced the government to stop acting only upon the capital account of the balance of payments, leaving the current account to the vicissitudes of the market, creditors, and Mexican consumers' insatiable demand for imported goods and services. A change of course was necessary, correcting the imbalances in the current account by focusing on it alone and leaving the capital account to the market. The authorities should have let in the capital that wanted to come and was able to, but without bending over backward to attract it through discounted assets, stratospheric returns, and gimmicks such as Tesobonos. All such gimmicks have a price, and it is always the

Mexican taxpayer who has to foot the bill—not the novice New York investor who got strong.

Focusing on the current account meant three things. First of all, it implied reducing imports even more than the devaluation itself would. Had Mexico recognized that trade liberalization—no matter how necessary or urgent—was too broad, abrupt, and improvised, it could then have revised it. This would have required using all the safeguard and tariff mechanisms allowed by GATT and NAFTA itself to reduce imports, especially those that contribute absolutely nothing to Mexico. Then we should have drawn upon the fullest possible range of ploys, maneuvers, loopholes, and administrative red tape to stop the flood of imported goods. This strategy began to be implemented in 1994, but without the necessary zeal. It would have given Mexico the time to decide calmly which sectors of our economy we wanted to protect and which should indeed be exposed to the full rigors of international competition.

In the second place, Mexico needed a policy to promote exports, without simply allowing the market to choose those areas and niches of the economy to be pursued and conquered. A great deal had been written about the compelling need for an industrial policy based on "export substitution" in Mexico. Suffice it to recall that no country—not England or Germany in the nineteenth century, nor Japan, Korea, Brazil, or even Chile in the twentieth—became a world-class exporter without deliberate policies for promotion, protection, subsidies, and planning, without a coordinated effort to seize foreign markets.

Thirdly and finally, focusing on the current account meant reducing interest payments on the foreign debt—this time, one hoped, for real. By 1995, as already noted, these payments would exceed $14 billion—twice the value of Mexico's oil exports. Renegotiating the debt did not mean fooling Mexicans or even markets with intelligent but untenable subterfuges. There were two options. One was to include a chapter for debt reduction and compensatory financing in the North American Free Trade Agreement, taking advantage of Mexico's exceptional place in the universe of debtor countries. The other was to seek alliances with those countries, especially Brazil and Venezuela, to negotiate jointly a definitive solution with the creditors (and especially the governments of wealthy countries). This was more plausible than ever, simply because the sovereign liabilities of banks represented a much smaller proportion than they did in the eighties.

Giving priority to the capital account and leaving current-account corrections solely to devaluation already led to NAFTA, sky-rocketing interest rates, and the Tesobonos. To persist in doing so would eventually force us to sell our last jewel, which we had carefully set aside precisely because we all draw sustenance from it and its glory—the nation's oil. Mexicans must not fall prey to the new ruses and deceptions of those government officials still trying to deceive the public. The issue is not the privatization of Pemex; in all probability, nobody would want to buy its old scrap iron. In the oil business, too, there are real jewels and mere trinkets: the gem in the crown is crude oil, with its extraction and marketing. The temptation for the government—which will prove irresistible, if the current course is pursued—will not be to make Pemex into a common carrier or to allow foreign investment in petrochemicals or refining.

What really titillates the financiers is something else: to sell licenses for oil exploration and extraction in the Sound of Campeche or Chicontepec through risk contracts. Thus, the Bank of Mexico would fill its coffers twice: once, with revenues from selling the licenses; and again, with the royalties that Exxon or Chevron (the latter is apparently the oil authorities' favorite) would pay for every barrel of oil it discovered and extracted. The logic is impeccable: Mexico does not have the money to increase its exports, yet it needs the revenue from selling more barrels. The oil companies finance exploration, investment in rigs, pipelines, buoys, and so on. Mexico gets something for every barrel—less than if it were to extract the crude on its own, but more than if it did not extract it at all. The reason for not selling licenses is also impeccable, and implacable: if we do this, we will be selling today, at bargain-basement prices, something that we might need tomorrow—and that we might sell more dearly.

THE SUPPORT OF THE U.S. FEDERAL RESERVE SHOULD HAVE BEEN linked with the negotiation of a growth-oriented recovery program. The latter would not have been easy to sell in the United States without a component that the Republican Congress was already beginning to demand (with racist and xenophobic overtones) in the person of various senators and representatives: that the issue of immigration be addressed. It is true that any negotiation of migration issues poses complicated problems for Mexico. This includes deciding the degree of responsibility its authorities want to assume for those migratory flows beyond any possible agreement on seasonal or sectoral legalization. But this dilemma exists anyway, and must be faced anyway, with or without the devaluation crisis or the economic debacle. By linking migration negotiations with all the rest, Mexico might have obtained the support it needed in exchange for the very painful concessions it will have to make someday, anyway.

In reality, it would have been far better to follow the opposite sequence. Once the Federal Reserve had agreed to support a given, fixed parity—say, 4.50 pesos per dollar, or else a more realistic level of 5.20 to 5.50—interest rates should have been raised so that, *together with* the U.S. Federal Reserve Board's commitment to intervene in the markets, the announcement of the new parity would be received by all as a definitive change. There would have been no extension of the band, no flotation, no later recovery or exchange panic, simply a new exchange rate, backed for an indefinite period by the Fed and in the short term by high interest rates to keep the money in Mexico. The basic difference between this process and the ad hoc, improvised, and always belated responses of the Mexican government from January through March 1995 lay precisely in its conceptual design and the subsequent evolution of things. The details (or the trees) may, in some cases, be the same; the focus (or the forest) was quite different. In one case, the first step would have been an agreement with the United States designed by Mexico; the parity would be adjusted in an orderly way; and a growth-oriented recovery program would have been designed to weigh less heavily on salaries and allowed more inflation. Instead of getting the country into massive debt in order to reimburse Wall Street investors who took a risk, received extraordinary returns, and now protested, the package would have included a new debt renegotiation to reduce its service. Finally, this would begin to repair the errors of the past, in order to prevent Mexico from finding itself in the same situation a few years later—with an unmanageable deficit in the current account, insufficient or exorbitantly expensive financial flows, and, finally, the devil's alternative: devaluation or continuing economic stagnation.

In the other scenario—which actually happened—we resigned ourselves to a rescue package of almost inconceivable dimensions, geared toward correcting debatable causes and accompanied by intolerable conditions. As U.S. Treasury Secretary Robert Rubin admitted, it was designed in Washington, D.C., to protect U.S. interests and especially the earnings and mental health of Wall Street investors. Yet the fund managers and stock brokers of New York knew what they were doing when they invested in Mexican stocks and received colossal returns: they were taking a risk. Now, thanks to the package, the cost of that risk (which produced lavish returns for two or three years) has been transferred completely to the Mexican taxpayer. The American investors made the mistake. Mexicans are left to pay, becoming more indebted and dooming our economy and that of our children to indefinite stagnation.

The third and final mistake of Ernesto Zedillo's spanking-new regime was failing to understand that, if a devaluation and in-depth economic adjustment were necessary early in the term, it was better to effect those changes with all the opposition and the country's social and cultural forces inside the government, not outside. A long time has passed since that July 1994 meeting between Ernesto Zedillo and the San Angel Group, when the PRI candidate categorically refused to form a coalition cabinet. Many had already subscribed to that idea, beginning with Carlos Fuentes and most members of the San Angel Group. Others did so later, including Cuauhtémoc Cárdenas when he called for a government of "national salvation" and the PAN, which actually took a first step in that direction by allowing one of its leaders to serve as attorney general. The idea has obviously gained ground and, though Zedillo did not implement it in his first cabinet, it is not too late for him to do so.

Only a step of this magnitude would pave the way for the great democratic reform the country requires. This at bottom means shaping a new political system out of the ashes and debris of the system created in 1929, now archaic and ineffectual. It includes electoral and judicial reforms and resolving the conflicts of Chiapas and Tabasco; but it is not limited to any one of these critical but partial areas. It also signifies building a genuine freedom of the press and of unions, a vigorous and diverse civil society, a reform of the state, and the beginnings of an accountability that does not yet exist in Mexico's vocabulary, let alone its politics. Unless everybody participates in this task, it will be extremely difficult to carry out. And it will be very easy to block, torpedo, and finally suppress.

The reason to form such a government is not so much "to call upon the best Mexicans." It may well be that a cabinet including members of the business and academic communities, opposition and social leaders is not the best possible team, either in terms of the individuals involved or their sum. The main reason to pursue this course is to prevent certain interest groups from taking advantage of the situation while others make sacrifices, and to commit all sectors to make the efforts and pay the costs that will be incurred. Certain conditions must be met for such an undertaking to succeed; they include firm and convinced leadership on the part of the cabinet's head, the president. Plurality works only if there is a guiding principle behind it; otherwise, it only generates division and paralysis. But it is worth noting that the cabinet in place since Zedillo took office, bland and perplexing from the outset, has not exactly proved a paragon of effectiveness or cohesiveness, either. There is no need to belabor this point: many are convinced that Zedillo will eventually form a government of national unity, coalition, salvation, concord or whatever. He will do so because he will have no choice and because it will be best for the country. I only wish to reiterate that in this, as in many other areas, it is better to do sooner what will have to be done later anyway.

Finally, a plural government would represent a definitive, but also tacit and indirect, break with the previous regime. Tireless dialogue with the opposition—even at the risk of overdoing it and having nothing more to say—is a refreshing change from the Salinas barricade. However, opening the door to all social and political forces, especially those least liked by the president, would mark a much deeper, yet relatively painless break with the outgoing government. It would be a more elegant, and less drastic, separation than others that have been proposed and promoted.

The agreement signed by the political parties on January 17, 1995, somewhat pretentiously called the Pact of Los Pinos, was a step in that direction. But it was only a step. Such an agreement had great potential to transcend itself and become a substantive national accord leading to plural government, but it also contained serious contradictions.

The first consisted in the privileged negotiating position granted political parties by the government, and their undeniable lack of representativity. Of course, the parties must be addressed, especially the PRD: six years of ostracism demand it. But the relevance or scope of a dialogue, or even substantive agreements with the parties, must not be overestimated: an enormous majority of Mexicans and the country's political, ideological, and social forces are outside the parties. Mexico needs a strong party system; it does not yet have one.

A second potential contradiction: a reverse Salinism. Ernesto Zedillo might be tempted to maintain his predecessor's leitmotif, but inverted: to maintain a separation between politics and the economy, making changes in the political system while leaving the economic model intact. Salinas attempted the exact opposite, and failed when political issues undermined economic stability. If Zedillo insists on opening the political system without allowing that to "contaminate" economic policy, he will merely subvert the political process and probably soon be forced to negotiate the course of his economic policy. As he will have to do anyway, and sooner rather than later.

WHEN THE ANTICLIMACTIC ELECTIONS OF AUGUST 1994 produced the outcome we now all know, a number of explanations sprang up like mushrooms. One was that the Mexican electorate had, in its wisdom, understood that things were going well enough to keep the same team and party in office and that the opposition had failed to convince public opinion that continuity was more dangerous than change. The nation was not in crisis, Mexicans did not want any great upheavals, and there was no need for enlightened, messianic, or inexperienced leaders. Everything suggests that this interpretation was the basis for Ernesto Zedillo's plan of government, his choice of governing team and inaugural speech, with its focus on calming things down, persevering, and making necessary changes without touching the essence.

Another reading of the August elections and the situation today can be summed up by a historical metaphor. In 1918, the France of Georges Clemenceau ("the Tiger"), after four years of war, one million dead, the holocaust of Verdun, and the near-fall of Paris in the Battle of the Marne, was yet able to defeat the Kaiser and German-Prussian war machine. The national effort made by the French people and elites alike was heroic and truly extraordinary. But it turned out that the cost of victory was too high. The Third Republic was exhausted and drained of its lifeblood. The consequences would become apparent during the thirties, when French society proved incapable of seeing through the reforms of the Popular Front in 1936, and in the tragic spring of 1940, when France's political, business, military, and intellectual classes surrendered readily and shamelessly before the Nazi offensive. For four years, Paris and half of *la France éternelle* lived the worst possible humiliation for a country: foreign occupation.

Mexico's political system, mortally threatened many times during 1994, made a supreme effort of unity and concentration and managed to survive against all expectations. After the Chiapas uprising, the murders of Colosio and Ruiz Massieu, the divisions, kidnappings, and uncertainty of the first semester, and the forecasts and foibles of the weeks before the election; the state apparatus, PRI, and government were able to join together and overcome a critical situation that had seemed hopeless up to the last moment. But the price of having triumphed over probabilities, years, and circumstances was excessive, as in France: the system was left drained, exhausted, paralyzed. This gave rise to divisions and quarrels—some settled by gunfire, others through accusations and recriminations.

Then came the devaluation crisis and the subsequent resigned acceptance of the U.S. rescue package. Left without chips or credit, strength or spirit, Mexico's elites surrendered to the understandable, almost irresistible temptation of a short-term and very costly salvation, for which the country will be paying for years to come. Inertia triumphed, and the terrible crisis that swept over the country overwhelmed Mexico's political system, the PRI, and its members. After the system's victory in August came an internal collapse: the vigor that had sustained the system and its men ran dry, dragging all of Mexico with it into the abyss.

It may seem foolhardy to say, these days, that countries do not just disintegrate. Quite a few of them have, in recent times, one way or another, and perhaps we should not trust in our awareness of our own destiny. With the U.S. bailout of early 1995, Mexico reached the end of a year that lasted almost fourteen months—a year that began, like these pages, with a hope anchored in the United States: the free trade agreement. Neither the rescue nor the hope are the right path, though they may help to build it. Mexico must change course, and rely instead on imagination and daring, agility and calm, patience and open-mindedness. A package of agreements with the United States, designed in Mexico and negotiated on an equal footing; a recovery program with growth, correcting the substantive errors of the last ten years; a government of national emergency, with room for everybody, beginning with the real opposition: here are ideas to escape the bloody trenches of Verdun, the springtime fall of France, and the winter of our discontent in this land of surprises.

PART III

MEXICO IN LATIN AMERICA

CHAPTER 11

Democracy and Inequality in Latin America:
A Tension of the Times

DEMOCRATIZATION IN LATIN AMERICA HAS BEEN THE OBJECT of a great deal of study, introspection, and doubt over the years. Every wave of democratic institution building has been accompanied by analysis and speculation about its origins, duration, and inevitability; every rush of dictatorships has generated endless reflection about its motivations, contingent nature, or fatal rooting in the political culture, history, and social configuration of the hemisphere. When in the 1950s it seemed that a recently created middle class had finally laid the ground for the emergence of democratic rule, great emphasis was placed on this social determinism as an explanatory factor. In the 1960s, the Alliance for Progress and the Venezuelan and Colombian paradigms were rapidly explained by economic and social change, as well as by international considerations. Together with the ideological justification of two-party systems, they were quickly prescribed as the best antidote to the spread of the Cuban Revolution. More recently and with a great deal more sophistication, the transitions from authoritarian rule that began in the early 1980s and came mostly to fruition in the course of that decade were analyzed with much detail and substance. Many authors attributed the new wave of democracy to the application this time around of the well-learned lessons of the past. The transitions would be successful and lasting on this occasion, it was hoped, because the factors that contributed to democracy's ephemeral nature in previous eras were neutralized by maturing leaders, a fortified civil society, and more responsible international partners.

Whatever the nuances—and they were not unimportant—one of the central points stressed by the transition theorists as well as by the politicians in charge of or involved in the transitions themselves was that the just-born democracies not be "overloaded" by political, but mainly economic and social demands. The concern of nearly all observers and participants was that emerging, fragile, and "thin-skinned" political systems not be suddenly and immediately submitted to overwhelming demands of an economic and social nature that would strain them to the breaking point. These demands, if presented and insisted upon, it was thought, would lead to a breakdown of the infant democracies and entail, however unwittingly, serious prejudice to the very sectors of society intended to benefit most from the satisfaction of these demands. Whether the demands involved retribution for past human rights abuses, a rapid repayment of the social debt, or a more general redistributive economic policy, it was believed—not unreasonably—that by insisting upon these demands and not allowing the new regimes a breathing spell—something like a honeymoon—they simply would not last.

Largely because many of these conditions for successful transitions were met in nations like Chile, Argentina, Brazil, and, to a lesser extent, Uruguay, the new democracies did endure, or, more specifically, the transitions from authoritarian rule were consummated. And despite sporadic or localized setbacks—Peru after April 1992, Venezuela during that same year, Chile, for as long as Augusto Pinochet remained in place—Latin America was by and large considered, quite rightly, to have begun to consolidate its democratic regimes and credentials. One after another, elected presidents were succeeded by other elected administrations, human rights were to a large extent respected, a free press flourished, basic freedoms were safeguarded, and most of the trappings of representative democracy were preserved. But three preoccupations rapidly surfaced both in the literature and in real life, all pointing to the same dilemma.

Firstly, many naysayers and pessimists wondered whether the virtuous identity established between the consolidation of democratic regimes and the implementation of economic reforms along radical free-market lines (which came to be known in Latin America as "the neo-liberal program") would not be sundered by a populist backlash. Would not demagogues and those nostalgic for bygone times take advantage of the short-term discontent provided by unpopular economic policies and of the democratic openings guaranteed by the liberalization dynamic to jeopardize the entire process by pressuring for redistributive policies or running on populist programs? What, they asked, could be done to retain the economic reforms on the one hand and democracy on the other, given that some were using the latter to fight the former? Many doubted that the current reforms and marvels of free-market Latin America would last, given the region's penchant for doing the wrong things and its proverbial incapacity to stay the right course.

Secondly, others more knowledgeable and sophisticated and less enchanted by the market for the market's sake, expressed doubts about the depth of the democratization process in light of what appeared to constitute the indispensable conditions of its success. It seemed that the only way the nascent democratic regimes could last was if they guaranteed the permanence of the economic and social policies that had been carried out by the dictatorships that preceded them. The example of Pinochet's Chile was often waved by these skeptics: the necessary (and indeed sufficient) condition for a return to more or less democratic rule in Chile lay in the absolute maintenance of the free-market, free-trade policies pursued for more than fifteen years by the military regime. Democracy was fine, as long as it did not make too much of a difference insofar as economic and social matters were concerned. But how long could this sort of arrangement last, given the pent-up social demands that had accumulated and the economic biases that had built up during the long period of authoritarian domination?

Thirdly, and perhaps most crucially, many observers of the current democratic interlude in Latin America asked a harder question. Was the region's ancestral, abysmal inequality no longer the apparently insurmountable obstacle to democratic rule that it had been in the past? Inequality has been a permanent fixture of Latin American reality since independence. Alexander von Humboldt had made the point as early as 1802. The bishop of Michoacán, Fray Antonio de

San Miguel, had written at the same time: "On the one hand we see the effects of envy and discord, of skill, theft, and the penchant for hurting the rich in their interests; on the other, we see the arrogance, the hardness, and the wish to abuse always the weakness of the Indians. I do not doubt that these ills are born everywhere from great inequalities. But in America they are even more horrendous because there is no intermediate point; one is rich or miserable, noble or infamous, in law and in deed." Was this inequality not the cause of the absence of democratic rule, had the situation improved, or was the interminable inequality of Latin America no longer the obstacle to democracy it always had been?

After some soul-searching and much hand-wringing, a certain consensus began to emerge among students of the region's politics in relation to the type of question that needed to be asked, even if broad disagreements remained over the answer that the question called for. How compatible, it was asked, could democracy and widespread inequality and injustice be? Could representative democracy coexist with poverty of one sort or another affecting between half and two-thirds of the population? Could democratic rule survive under conditions of growing and acute inequality? And if not, wherein could the right answer to an ultimately perverse question be found?

The current debate in Latin America about the nature of the region's new democracies and the possible tensions between the latter and the type of economic and social structures presently in place is not totally new. Nor is it limited to present-day discussions regarding the compatibility—or lack of it—between free-market programs and democratization processes. Indeed, what is perhaps most interesting about contemporary worries over the precarious nature of the region's institutions and advances is that they reproduce previous debates and doubts. And they reflect an underlying communality: somewhere in the abstract thinking about and the everyday politics of Latin America, there is a tension between the region's social configuration and its political aspirations. It is nonetheless important to warn that a significant dose of today's tensions between these two trends is novel. The problem no longer is exactly what it was in the 1950s, when the identity between an emerging middle class and the possibility of two-party alternation was posited by numerous students of the region. The tension is greater than ever before because, on the one hand, the numbers are worse, yet on the other, the aspirations for and the roots of democracy are deeper.

There is a great deal of current debate in Latin America and in the multilateral agencies that deal with the region, over exactly what occurred in the hemisphere during the 1980s vis-à-vis inequality. The debate persists in part because of the undeniable problems in finding reliable data. In some countries the data is sufficient and illustrative, such as in Mexico and Brazil, and it is distressing. In 1960 the poorest 50 percent of the Brazilian population received 17.7 percent of national income; in 1970 its share dropped to 15 percent; by 1980 that share had dwindled to 14.2 percent; and in 1990 it dropped to 10.4 percent. In Mexico, a similar process took place. In 1984 the poorest 50 percent of the population received 20.7 percent of national income; by 1989 the proportion had fallen to 18.7 percent, and by 1992, to 18.4 percent. Conversely, the richest 10 percent saw its share rise from 32.7 percent in 1984 to 37.9 percent in 1989 and 38.1 percent in 1992. According to the World Bank, in eight of the twelve countries of Latin America for which comparative figures exist, "the income distribution—measured by the Gini coefficient—deteriorated in the 1980s." According to a review of other studies and sources of information regarding income distribution in Latin America before and after the "lost decade," "while most groups during the adjustment process saw their share in total income falling . . . the top 10 percent—the richest to begin with—improved their relative position (with the exception of Colombia)."

If data were available in relation to distribution of wealth rather than income, the early 1990s would almost surely show the same process of concentration—or one even worse. This is particularly true in countries that carried out significant privatization of state-owned sectors of the economy in the first years of this decade. Regardless of the merits and motivations of these privatizations (given virtually all of them were effected by sales to existing private-sector conglomerates, without any of the share dispersion that at least nominally took place in Britain, for example) there is little doubt that they further concentrated assets in nations where small numbers already controlled huge chunks of the national patrimony. Suffice it to say that the thirteen Mexican billionaires on the Forbes list of the world's richest individuals own upward of 10 percent of the nation's annual gross domestic product.

There is not only more inequality in Latin America; it is of a different nature. There is a new inequality—and a new poverty—in the hemisphere: that produced by the conjunction of the rush to the cities and the disappearance of the high economic-growth rates most of Latin America became accustomed to between 1940 and 1980. The large majority of the poor and excluded are now in the cities, even if a greater proportion of the total number of each nation's rural inhabitants are poor. The new urban poor labor in the informal economy, on the streets and corners of the sprawling metropolises of a now overwhelmingly urban hemisphere. They live in the shantytowns beyond city limits, and in the increasingly segregated "poor" neighborhoods of the cities themselves. They are, more recently, the laid-off or half-time employees of shut-down plants or streamlined bureaucracies that perhaps did not need them and, so left them indigent in the streets.

But these urban poor are no longer the first generation to have left the countryside. In many cases, they are the sons and daughters of the rural exodus of previous decades; they have gone at least to grade school; they read and write and watch television, and they are directly exposed to the trappings and opulence of middle-class and wealthy urban life. They do not live in another world; they live in the metaphorical cellars and tenements of the same high rise the penthouse occupants dwell in.

Yet, at the same time the deterioration in income distribution was occurring, the democratization processes of Latin America were coming to fruition. Democracy did come to Brazil during this period, if by democracy we understand at least the prevalence of basic freedoms, alternation of power by different parties, competition for power exclusively through electoral means, the rule of law, and so on. Democracy did not come to Mexico, although the demands for it were building up rapidly. In both cases, the pressure being built up by the increasing inequitable distribution of income—as good an indicator of inequality as any other—was rapidly growing. While rights and choices were being granted to broader sectors of the population, the inequality that breeds growing demands and tensions was also increasing. Little wonder that the democratic transition was being resisted by Mexican officials or that the fiscal crises of the Brazilian federal government and of virtually every state government reached astronomical dimensions.

Another innovation consists in the fact that the democratic institutions of Latin American *are* more firmly rooted than in the past. The national security dictatorships of the seventies and early eighties, the dirty wars and torture chambers, did teach a chilling lesson that was mostly well learned: it is better to build strong institutions that protect democracy than to do without them. Civil society is stronger, the middle class larger, respect for human rights more widespread.

Additionally, the international context is different. It is far from certain that the United States has, after the Cold War, truly become a force for democracy in Latin America. But Washington has probably ceased to be a force *against* democracy, no longer combating it when it threatens American economic or, more importantly, geopolitical interests, as it did during the fifties, sixties, and seventies in much of the region. Finally, the ramshackle Latin American welfare states of the past are being dismantled today and are often being replaced with radical free-market policies that tend to aggravate existing inequalities, at least in the short run. Thus the entire inequality/democracy debate, which was not just born in Latin America but is, rather, an unquestionable part of the region's political and ideological tradition, is cast in a new light today.

Simply stated, the dilemma is this: the kind of representative democracy that Latin America has sporadically enjoyed and that it seems to be consolidating today is not compatible with the region's social structures, particularly the enormous gaps between rich and poor, black and brown and white, town and country, industrial powerhouses and rural backwaters. Whatever stance one may take regarding the relationship between the emergence of a broad middle-class constituting a majority of the population and the viability of representative democracy, a certain simultaneity must prevail for the latter to endure. Because there is more inequality in Latin America today than before, and because Latin America was already more unequal than any other part of the world, the fragile democracies whose births or resurrections it has witnessed in the past decade are likely to be superficial or short-lived.

Before proceeding any further, it is crucial to distinguish between the analytical statement that in principle there is a tension between poverty and inequality, on the one hand, and democracy, on the other, and the political statement that democractization must be postponed until the continent's economic and social lags are surmounted. One statement is strictly analytical in nature and has no prescriptive value in itself, other than to imply, as we shall see, that without progress in the attempt to reduce inequalities, democratic rule is at risk. The other statement—that democracy must wait until poverty is eradicated, as has been so often argued, implicitly or explicitly, by authoritarian regimes in Latin America of all ideological inclinations, but mainly by those on the right—is politically motivated. It can mean that democracy should be suspended until inequality is reduced, or it can imply that, given inequality and poverty, certain shortcomings in the organization and functioning of democratic rule in Latin America are more or less inevitable. But it is essential to acknowledge that the political statement and the analytical statement are logically distinct. One could both detect the tension between inequality and democracy and be a firm supporter of democracy; and one could be a committed opponent of democratic rule in Latin America, for whatever reasons, and at the same time not believe there is any incompatibility between inequality and democracy. In fact, the political statement subsumes and implies the analytical judgment, but not the other way around.

The reasons for the presumed incompatibility mentioned above are clear. Democracy means giving free rein to the expression of pent-up demands of downtrodden or even marginalized sectors of society and then finding and implementing solutions or giving satisfaction to at least parts of those demands, soon, if not immediately. The demands cannot be forestalled: they are too pressing. And satisfaction cannot be indefinitely postponed, because those who do so proceed at their own peril, given they can be voted from office in the next election. The gradualism and various virtuous cycles that made democracy and capitalism compatible in Europe and North America since late last century do not operate in Latin America today, at least from this perspective.

There is every reason to believe that the problem thus stated does exist, and in order for democracy and existing inequalities to cohabit in Latin America, it is the second term that must be addressed in order for the first one to survive. "Something special" —that is, changes beyond what inertia and "natural" mechanisms will provide—must take place in order for the tension between both terms not to become unmanageable. But it is worth stressing that this incompatibility is not impervious to time and circumstance; it is so abstract a statement that its verification in practice can be a drawn-out matter. The dilemma must be formulated as a general principle or premise, that will materialize only if a certain number of circumstances coincide. Conversely, if certain conditions of a different nature are all present, the consequences of the incompatibility can be avoided, though generally only for a set period of time.

Recent empirical work carried out by economists -and even by the World Bank—shows that there is a clear link between democracy, equality, and economic growth. The traditional Kaldorian or Kuznetsian approach—whereby it was believed that inequality fostered growth, since the rich save more than the poor and a greater concentration of wealth leads to a higher rate of investment—has fallen into disfavor. A different and contrary correlation is currently posited, and some empirical evidence seems to indicate it is more accurate. According to this view, most recently researched by Alesina and Perotti for the National Bureau of Economic Research, great inequality correlates with political instability, and political instability correlates with low investment rates. Working with data from seventy countries for the period between 1960 and 1985, Alesina and Perotti found that "income inequality increases sociopolitical instability, which in turn decreases investment," obviously leading to lower growth. They add that more acute inequalities also make for stronger pressures in favor of fiscal redistribution, which can act as a deterrent to investment.

In Latin America, the recurrent cycle of democracy, overwhelming social and economic demands, public spending, inflation, devaluation, and disenchantement of the middle-class and the power elite, followed by a tragic outcome, is well known. The reasons for this cycle, regardless of whether on occasion they are identified with a simplistic assessment of mere economic-policy mistakes, are quite evident. The inequities in Latin American society, the information available to broad sectors of the population about how matters could be different, and the obvious injustice prevailing throughout the region are all such that most lasting democratic experiences eventually bring to office governments or leaders that try to satisfy these aspirations. But given the scarcity of resources and the overall economic obstacles existing throughout the region, it is impossible to satisfy virtually any demand in a significant manner without engaging in some sort of redistributive exercise. This implies alienating or ostracizing the powerful sectors of society from which the resources to be redistributed must be obtained.

In most Latin American nations this amounts to turning these sectors against the democratic process that brought up the redistributive issue in the first place. Given this dynamic, which has appeared repeatedly in Latin America, some have reached the conclusion—self-serving or sincere—that until the gaps between rich and poor are reduced, thus defusing the intensity of the poor's demands, democracy will simply not work. It is not so much a question of the *desirability* of having inequalities and democracy coexist, but of the *impossibility* of that coexistence. Thus the political statement previously made explicit encloses this substantive premise: democracy must be suspended until inequality is reduced, because otherwise democracy simply will not work.

This dilemma is specific to the region and to the contemporary era. It is, in a sense, a strictly historical problem, and largely located in Latin America, the "middle class" of world societies as Alain Touraine has often said. It is a historical problem because of the compressed evolution of modern Latin America, and it is a localized problem because of the specific traits of Latin America.

First, it is a localized problem. In the world's industrialized nations, although inequalities do subsist and are probably widening, they are sufficiently narrow to be manageable. A large enough majority of the population is equal unto itself, and democratic institutions are sufficiently old and well-rooted, that the undeniable contradiction that does persist between the basic premise of equality in principle before the law and the market, and the inequality that in reality prevails in much of modern society (between poor and rich, black and white, foreign and national, men and women, adults and children) remains within the bounds of what democracy will countenance. In the wealthy nations, the tension between democracy and inequality is just that: a tension that can be adequately managed, or has been from the end of the last century until now.

Latin America has always been the most unequal of the world's poorer regions. Even in 1978, for example, just as the period of the continent's sustained economic expansion came to a close, the share of total income received by the poorest fifth of the population was lower than in any other region: 2.9 percent compared with 5 percent for southern Europe, 6.2 percent for East Asia, 5.3 percent for the Middle East and North Africa, and 6.2 percent for sub-Saharan Africa. If in many Latin American countries the richest 10 percent of the population today obtains between 40 percent and 50 percent of national income, in East Asia, the average is approximately 35 percent.

In the utterly destitute regions of the world—Africa, most of Asia—either inequality is far less dramatic than in Latin America, though poverty may be much more acute, or, more commonly, democratic governance is a relatively new phenomenon whose vicissitudes are understandable, given its youth and the awesome challenges of economic development. Most of the nations of Asia and Africa did not exist as independent entities as recently as forty years ago; the others either have democratic governance and a high standard of living (Japan, for example), or low levels of inequality, even though they have not enjoyed democratic rule (China and Korea), or levels of inequality below those of Latin America and something like electoral democracy at work (India, for instance). It is useful to recall that India, despite its abject poverty, has a ratio of income shares of the richest 20 percent of the population and poorest 20 percent far better at around 10 percent, than countries such as Mexico (15 to 17 percent), Colombia and Venezuela (20 percent) or Brazil and Ecuador (25 percent and 45 percent respectively). One could surmise that one of the reasons behind this difference lies in the Indian political system, and in the redistribution wrought by the lasting existence of even as skewed a system of representative democracy as India.

Only in Latin America are the degree of inequality, the size and existence of a middle class, the level of economic development, and the sufficiently consummated process of nation-building all far enough along to explain the number of failed attempts to establish democratic rule over the past century and a half. And only in Latin America have those attempts proved so frequently unfruitful that the issue is truly a burning one. In a nutshell, only in Latin America is there both enough democracy for it to be at risk and so much inequality for it to be a problem.

But the tension we are dealing with is also a historical phenomenon. It did not really occur elsewhere at other points in time, although conceivably it could have. In principle, the immensely poor and unjust Western European societies or the United States in the nineteenth century could have been forced to simultaneously live with emerging democratic rule and forms of social organization and economic development that excluded vast sectors of the population from the benefits of the market, employment, consumption, and so on. What difference is there truly between Dicken's England and the ABC suburbs of São Paulo?

The answer lies in the different historical rhythms involved. The fact is that democratic rule expanded only at a slow pace, social sector by social sector, in most of western Europe until after World War I. The franchise itself was extended gradually; in England, for example, the vote was only granted to all males (and only to males) late in the century. For practical purposes, democracy and incorporation into the modern market economy went hand in hand, and while early attempts did emerge to push democratic rule further ahead than the economic and social situation of the "dangerous masses" warranted (the Chartist movement, the revolutions of 1848 on the continent, even the Paris Commune of 1871), the little they temporarily achieved was swiftly rolled back. A certain contemporaneity prevailed: no idea or reform was truly "ahead of its time."

But in Latin America, of course, matters were quite different, from the very caricatured outset. Just after independence, nations that barely existed adopted sophisticated, enlightened liberal constitutions inspired by French philosophers and the American Founding

Fathers. And this continued through the first hundred, then hundred and fifty years of independence, although certain formulae were often employed to alleviate the pressures diacronicity generated. Thus elections were scheduled now and then, and in some countries at some moments in time, power was formally contended for at the ballot box; in fact, extraordinarily few people voted.

In Brazil, for example, even as late as 1960, there were only sixteen million registered voters, of which barely eight million actually voted in federal elections—this in a country of eighty million inhabitants at the time. In the 1940s, the situation was, of course, much worse, not only in Brazil, but throughout Latin America: where elections were held, few voted. Still, the franchise was extended to everyone, and as democratic regimes consolidated in the early eighties, they awoke to a paradox illustrated, again, by the Brazilian example. At the time of Brazil's presidential elections in 1989 there were seventy-five million registered voters, a large majority of which went to the polls. But only seven and a half million Brazilians paid taxes; that is, only a tenth of the electorate was actually incorporated into one of the basic aspects of citizenship and modernity. Throughout Latin America the same paradox surfaced: on the one hand, the hemisphere had adopted nearly across the board—and, from a historical perspective, virtually overnight—the political structures of the industrial democracies for governance and the transfer of power; but the social structure of those nations was nowhere to be found in Latin America.

The gradual extension of the market economy, the construction of a social safety net, and the move toward universal suffrage could not all occur in Latin America little by little and more or less simultaneously. In the late twentieth century, no one can be easily denied the right to vote because they cannot read or write, or because they do not own property, or because they are black, or because they are women. In a sense, the right to vote is either denied to everybody by authoritarian rule or afforded to everyone thanks to the ongoing democratic transitions. But nothing could be done as rapidly on the social front: the 60 to 70 percent of the Latin American population that is poor, lacking employment, decent education, health care and housing, that does not pay taxes, and whose level of consumption is just above the minimum for survival, cannot be transformed overnight into a European or Canadian middle class.

Hence the *historical* nature of the problem. The gradualism of the nineteenth century and parts of this one is not applicable to Latin America. Indeed, the immediacy of the situation is even worse than just described, if one factors in another contemporary ingredient absent in previous eras. The impoverished Latin American masses who can now vote, organize, demonstrate, and demand are part of a more informed world than that of their nineteenth-century predecessors. Television, urbanization, literacy, and the global flow of information all enhance the tension between democracy and inequality today. The demands generated by the perception of widening social gaps are greater and more intensely felt, because there is far more information available today to the destitute and excluded about how desperate their fate actually is.

The "overload syndrome" that characterizes Latin American economic, social, and political life today is thus specific and historical. This entails that the solution to the problem, once accurately assessed, must also be solidly anchored in the region's traits. An additional effort to circumscribe the issue with greater precision is consequently in order. We must address the exceptions, lags, and alternatives that the problem presents.

One apparent exception to the hypothesis that Latin American democracy only barely survives under conditions of severe and worsening (or in any case not improving) inequality lies in the periods following either hyperinflation or authoritarian rule. In both cases, it would seem that, despite growing inequality, poverty, and injustice and the implementation of economic policies that severely concentrate wealth and income, democratic institutions and regimes tend to thrive, enjoy broad popular support and acquire an enhanced capacity to pursue their agenda. Among the best known examples of this are Argentina under Carlos Menem, vis-à-vis hyperinflation; Chile under Patricio Alwyn, vis-à-vis a return to democracy; and, likewise, Bolivia since Victor Paz Estenssoro's stabilization experiment began in the early 1980s. Some might conclude, in light of these examples, that by resorting to the market and establishing democratic rule, a virtuous cycle was set in motion in these countries whereby the two pillars of enlightened societies—democracy and the market—mutually reinforce themselves and render irrelevant matters such as inequality of outcomes, since equality of opportunities is extended to all.

On the other hand, it can be argued that, in the case of a victory over hyperinflation, the honeymoon that some democratic regimes enjoy despite widespread, standing injustice can be explained by the fact that runaway inflation is the inequality generator *par excellence*, and thus its elimination provides a respite, and in some cases an improvement, in overall inequality. The poor and the harassed middle class often perceive that an easing of inflation improves their lot not only in absolute terms but even in relation to other sectors of society.

This is particularly true when price stabilization is linked with trade liberalization and local currency appreciation, as was the case in Mexico between 1989 and 1994, in Chile from 1977 through 1981, and in Argentina from 1990 onward. Access to imported goods generally identified with up-scale consumption, the possibility of traveling abroad, and the feasibility of saving in dollars are all contributing factors to this sentiment. The popularity of regimes that implement draconian adjustment programs right after serious bouts with hyperinflation does not negate the tension between inequality and democracy. If anything, it reaffirms this tension by showing how a perceived, if only temporary, bettering of the affliction of inequality reinforces democracy. It also does not demonstrate that the success in fighting inflation will forever discourage the tensions to which this essay is devoted. It is reasonable to expect, that after time weakens the memory of high inflation, reality weighs in and unsatisfied demands for other forms of reducing inequality—higher salaries, increased social spending, job creation—kick in, the enthusiasm for democratic institutions and their elected stewards will begin to wane.

A return to democratic rule is also a motivation for a honeymoon. Often, after lengthy periods of dictatorship and repression, electorates and varying social movements are willing to grant newly installed democratic governments a breathing spell. They do not press all their pent-up demands immediately; they do not "overload" the system overnight, particularly if there is a widespread belief that such overloads led to authoritarian rule in the first place. This is clearly relevant to the Chilean case today, where after sixteen years of military dictatorship and sweeping inequalities, the people of Chile did not insist on the prompt satisfaction of their aspirations for justice, higher salaries, and more social spending. The return of democratic rule in Uruguay in 1983 under Julio Maria Sanguinetti can also be interpreted in this fashion.

But again, appearances can be somewhat deceiving. In fact, the government of Patricio Alwyn in Chile did raise social spending (and taxes to finance it), and did reduce part of the poverty generated in Chilean society by a decade and a half of radical free-market policies. And as time went by, the honeymoon wore off, with the traditional militancy of the Chilean labor and popular movements resurfacing, albeit under new forms. This led to a greater emphasis on social spending with the inauguration of the new administration headed by Eduardo Frei. If anything, the social honeymoon in Chile and the relatively rapid, though still incomplete, restoration of Chilean democracy owe part of their existence to the modest but undeniable redistributive policies of the Alwyn-led center-left coalition.

A third explanation for certain apparent exceptions to the democracy-inequality tension revolves around the type of country under consideration. It can be surmised that there is a certain threshold of inequality: below it, tensions are almost always present; above it, they can be avoided or postponed. It may be no coincidence that three of the countries mentioned above as exceptions—Argentina, Uruguay, and Chile—are, together with Costa Rica, the least unequal nations of Latin America (despite degrees of injustice that are far greater than those of the industrialized world) and those that suffer the least ethnic, regional, racial, and social disparities. It is true that in relative terms, the deterioration in at least two of these nations—Chile and Argentina—has been as marked as elsewhere, if not more so, and that it is small consolation to the poor of metropolitan Buenos Aires or Santiago that they are "less unequal" than their counterparts in Recife or Mexico City. But there may well be a question of an absolute level here: the starting point for any decline in these nations is clearly higher than in the rest of Latin America, and thus the capacity to absorb broader inequality without "overloading" a newly reestablished democratic system is also greater.

Finally, there is the question of time. On many occasions in Latin America, particularly in the nations with a strong pre-Columbian heritage, time moves differently—some would say more slowly—than in other regions and countries. Immediate reactions, quick responses, rapid cause-and-effect relationships are rarely the case. Time lags, delayed reactions, an often incomprehensible patience tend to be much more common. The famous Mexican saying "In Mexico nothing ever happens until it happens" is a symptom of this: the quick pace of causes is not always matched by an equally fast rhythm of effects. Where a given cause—say, growing inequality—should (but in fact does not) produce a determined effect rather quickly (the absence of which suggests that there may not have been much of a cause in the first place) the explanation for the apparent mismatch is time, not the lack of causality.

The exceptions, then, are explainable. Nothing in these examples vitiates the substantive contradiction between democracy and a given threshold of inequality, or a given evolution of it. This last point is essential: if Albert O. Hirschman is right in positing a "tunnel effect" whereby it is more important for matters to be moving in the optimal direction and for there to be a perception among those affected that things are improving, then the opposite is also true. If there is a reverse "tunnel effect" and people sense that their lot is deteriorating (and in reality it probably is), the "overload syndrome" will almost certainly come into play at some stage. The main thrust of this line of reasoning is that other than under exceptional circumstances, such as those outlined above, and in the absence of a "tunnel effect," democracy and the levels of inequality prevalent in Latin America are not compatible and the tension between the two will inevitably become exacerbated. At some point, the elastic band will be stretched too far.

The fundamental difficulty in untying this knot lies in another Latin American dilemma, which touches on the heart of the matter: the question of redistributing wealth. There are two indisputable premises for reducing inequality in Latin America: producing new wealth and distributing it more equitably than before. Without growth, no redistribution is possible. But distributing new growth the same way as before will only insure that existing disparities are maintained: there is no automatic way of reducing inequality just by generating new wealth. To reduce injustice in Latin America, given growth, implies a redistributive imperative.

There is a growing body of literature suggesting that there are sound economic and political reasons for redistribution in highly unequal societies, in addition to the obvious ethical justifications. The first, mentioned in the previously quoted work by Alesina and Perotti, stresses the countervailing pressures exerted by redistribution. The old approach emphasizes the discouraging effects on investment generated by high taxation, which is still the most efficient instrument of redistribution. But these authors point out that redistribution through taxation, if effective, makes for less unequal societies, which in turn makes for more stable political systems that generate certainty, guarantee property rights, and so on, which finally encourages higher levels of investment and thus of growth. Another twist to this same argument is that more just societies permit sounder and more accountable governance, because it is more democratic. Any comparison or counterfactual exercise involving higher or lower levels of taxation and redistribution has to take into account the deterrent effect on savings, investment, and growth generated by high degrees of social inequality and the political instability that generally accompanies it. The fundamental question is how to set in motion the trends toward redistribution and lesser inequality in a context from which these two trends have been mostly absent.

Here is where the issue of democracy comes into play. In principle, there are several ways of redistributing wealth, income, opportunities, achievement, and ultimately capability, to use Amartya Sen's enumeration. Universal suffrage is not the only one: revolution, command capitalism along Korean lines, or outside intervention —the American factor in Japan, Taiwan, and also Korea in the late forties and fifties—are among them. Unfortunately, none of these other ways is quite suitable or viable for Latin America. Revolution has certainly worked from a redistributive perspective: Cuba is the least unequal country in Latin America by any definition, and, until a few years ago, this was not simply equality of the destitute. But that road does not seem to remain transitable in the post–Cold War world, and few in the region today would find it attractive.

Command capitalism, with a strong authoritarian state, an honest civil service, and an agreeable private sector has been tried too, also with some success as far as growth and the reduction of poverty are concerned, but with much less to show for itself in terms of reducing inequality. The Brazilian model from 1964 onward, and even the Mexican example, are cases in point, up to a point. But here again, given current aspirations for democracy and the bittersweet taste left by those experiences, it seems unlikely that redistribution from above can truly function in Latin America today. Nor does redistribution from abroad appear to be functional: it has never worked well in the past—the precedent set by the Alliance for

Progress is ambiguous at best—and it is difficult to conceive of conditions under which the United States could actually take charge of land reform or other distributive mechanisms in Latin America, as it did in Japan under the occupation after World War II.

Indeed, there is every reason to believe not just that the only path conducive to some sort of redistribution today is democratic governance, but also that the absence of democracy explains a fair share of the inequality prevailing in the region today, or even a decade ago, after what Hirschman has called *"les trente glorieuses."* We now know that even high levels of economic expansion—such as those Mexico and Brazil enjoyed from the forties through the early eighties—in the context of undemocratic governance do not necessarily improve distribution and may even worsen it. Conservative economists or commentators have argued that the explanation for the paradox of high growth and poor distribution lies in the *type* of economic growth that countries like Mexico and Brazil experienced: protected, subsidized, with an overpowerful state-owned sector of the economy which encouraged rent seeking and concentration of assets and income. While there is no doubt that the type of growth in question was clearly of that nature, it is less evident that therein lies the cause of the inequality. The best counterexample is Chile from the mid-seventies through the late eighties—a sufficiently extended period to warrant comparison with other cases. Chile did achieve high growth during this period, particularly after 1984 and before 1982; and the type of growth it enjoyed was precisely the kind radical free-market advocates advocate: nonsubsidized, unprotected, private-sector-driven. Yet by every indication and source, Chile was a far more unequal nation and society in 1990 than in 1970, or 1975, when the Pinochet experiment truly got underway.

Unfortunately—for Chileans and for the perspective suggested in this essay—Chile is not a much more equalitarian society today, after five years of democratic rule, than it was before. Without democracy in Latin America today, it seems nearly impossible to achieve the aim of alleviating widening disparities; yet one must not exaggerate the extent to which democracy alone can accomplish this task. This thesis should be posited only with caution and wide-open eyes.

Since 1988, Chile has negotiated a treacherous transition to democratic rule. It has done so successfully, although serious handicaps and restrictions endure. The former military rulers are still in command of the armed forces and several institutions still not subject to any type of democratic accountability; in fact, a significant share of the national budget remains automatically and unmovably allocated to the military. Nonetheless, by just about any standard that is relevant to Latin America, Chile no longer suffers from one of the most atrocious episodes of authoritarian rule the region has ever known. Largely as a consequence of this transformation, the social policies of the dictatorship have been overhauled. Spending on education, health, housing, and the poor has increased. In order to finance this "repayment of the social debt," as it is known in Chile, taxes have been raised, if not as much as they should be; but Alejandro Foxley, Alwyn's finance minister, was the only Latin American technocrat in favor of higher taxes, not lower. Chile was, until 1995, for practical purposes, the only country in the hemisphere pursuing some sort of redistributive effort, chiefly as a result of the drastic shift from authoritarian rule to representative democracy.

The emphasis on social spending has partly paid off. The number of officially poor Chileans dropped between 1990 and 1993, from five million to three million. But income distribution has not budged: it remains stuck at the same levels as in 1988, in turn far worse than in the early seventies. In other words, a significant four-year effort—in a country enjoying high rates of economic growth and an undeniable democratization process—has left virtually no trace in terms of redistributing income and thus in reducing inequality. There are, of course, plausible explanations. One is time: four years is simply not enough, perhaps. Another is the locked-in nature of the economic policies of the dictatorship. Despite the social effort, wages remain low and must continue to do so to attract investment; trade liberalization and the absence of subsidies make it difficult to transfer resources from the rich to the poor. Furthermore, so much ground was lost in this realm during the previous fifteen years that simply arresting the decline is an accomplishment; reversing trends is a much more difficult task. Finally, the tax system, given trade policies, capital mobility, and political restraints, has not really been stretched very far. The increase in revenues remains low. Yet the Chilean case cannot but make one wonder: Is any sort of redistribution possible, even under favorable political conditions?

The Chilean case also opens another line of discussion. Is the main impediment to democratic rule inequality or poverty? Or, conversely, may it be possible to consolidate democracy if extreme poverty is significantly alleviated, even if inequality stays the same (that is, if the bottom deciles of the income scale improve their lot in absolute terms, even if in relative terms they do not)? This is a central question in Latin America today, precisely because it does seem possible to reduce absolute levels of poverty, at least among the most destitute sectors of society, but it is much more difficult to redistribute wealth and income.

Indeed, many students of the region are suggesting that the new forms of combating poverty—highly targeted programs, nongovernmental organizations' efforts, philanthropic sectors' work, and so on—are the modern equivalent of previous, now obsolete efforts at Keynesian redistribution. It is important to distinguish two issues here. One is that combating extreme poverty does not necessarily alter the income-distribution structure of a nation, or, in any case, it mostly affects the bottom decile in the scale by subtracting from the share of the lower-middle-class deciles. This is basically what occurred in Chile from the late seventies through the late eighties. Poverty and inequality are not the same thing. As we already saw, India may be poorer than any country in Latin America, but it is less unequal.

A different issue is whether combating poverty can be an adequate and effective substitute for reducing inequality, as far as its effects on democracy are concerned. If the key issue is poverty, not inequality, then the current democratization boom in Latin America might be consolidated simply by following well-planned anti-poverty programs, even while income and wealth remain highly concentrated.

The benefit of this alternative is that it does not alienate the wealthier and more powerful sectors of society, alienation which is, after all, the single most prejudicial and counterproductive by-product of traditional redistributive schemes. The problem in Latin America has always been that any attempt at reducing the wealth, power, and impunity of elites, be this attempt democratic or authoritarian, conservative or revolutionary, has inevitably provoked their wrath and reaction. And the ire of the elites has in turn unleashed a series of uncontrolled forces that have either done away with democratic institutions or clamped down on them, leading to exile, plotting, and the *contra* syndrome. Whether the redistributive exercise was accomplished with moderation (Guatemala, 1951-54) or excess (Cuba, 1959-61), democratically (Chile 1971-73) or by the military (Peru, 1968-74), it has systematically brought a negative, antidemocratic and visceral counterattack by those affected by it. Were it possible to simply reduce poverty without diminishing inequality in the short term, and were the antipoverty effort to have virtually no redistributive effect, there would be a painless, effective, and democracy-stabilizing solution to the age-old dilemma. No wonder that, in theory, this silver bullet has received the blessing of all the powers that be, from the Washington Consensus to the Chicago Boys in Santiago.

There is little empirical evidence yet available (in either direction) in this regard. The new microtargeted antipoverty programs in Mexico, Chile, and Argentina are either too recent or insufficiently quantified to permit any evaluation either of their actual, lasting effects on reducing poverty or of their impact on the stability of the democratic (or not-so-democratic) institutions of the countries in question. It may well be the case, however, that it is not necessary to redistribute income from the rich to the middle-class and to nudge the poor gradually into a widening middle class in order to stabilize democratic institutions, that it is enough to shift the extreme poor into the next-higher category—just poor, period—in order for the virtuous cycle of democracy and justice to be set in motion.

While this possibility cannot be discarded, it seems safer to believe that a democracy that fails to reduce economic inequality can only endure under great stress and under exceptional conditions; at the same time, only democracy can reduce the disparities that make it untenable. It seems safer to say that the only way to consolidate democratic rule in Latin America today is by redistributing wealth and income by combining economic growth—virtually of any type (the variable is not the nature of the growth but its existence and the context in which it takes place)—with a sufficiently democratic political system that allows those sectors of society who have traditionally been excluded from the fruits of previous growth to fight for and achieve a larger share of the pie.

Federal, state, and municipal elections, tax reform to finance higher expenditures on education, health, and housing, labor rights, a more vigorous civil society, land reform in those regions where it is still relevant, urban reform in other areas: all of these are, among other things, redistributive factors operating through democratic channels. Workers do obtain higher wages if they are allowed to negotiate collectively, to organize unions and when useful, to strike. Citizens can vote for parties and measures that raise taxes to finance greater social spending; for municipal authorities that do not steal, that do redistribute wealth to society in general.

There is little disagreement here. That democracy can redistribute, even in Latin America, seems a truism. Any sustained alternation in power through elections, with the broader trappings of democratic rule, will, in Latin America, generate almost unavoidably a redistributive effect. The mechanics of how to proceed are also well-known: between investment in human capital (that is, education, training, and health care) and other forms of social spending (housing, child care, and so on) and investment in job creation and the development of infrastructure to promote growth, there is no great mystery as to what must be done. The problem has always lain in finding the money to achieve these goals, not in the exact nature of the goals. The fact that the fiscal option—as opposed to direct public-sector involvement in the real economy—is today the preferred option does not alter matters greatly, nor does it imply that the taxation avenue does not lead to a certain state presence in the economy in the middle term. Nor does this imply that ideological and policy fads will not shift again, sometime.

The main point is that the trick is political, not technical. The problem lies in the consequences both for democratic rule and redistribution of "going too far" and in the difficulty of defining "too far." The scope of the latter phrase is by definition in the eyes of the victim: what is "too far" for a landed oligarch may be acceptable for an ECLA-born industrialist, whose definition may in turn be narrower than that of the telecommunications magnate who got rich during the sobering years of the debt crisis. And all of their estimates of the acceptable breadth of reform may be far narrower than that implicitly or explicitly held by the presumed beneficiaries of the reforms themselves. Normally, that is what elections, debate, congressional accountability over the budget, and collective bargaining are for: to determine in a democratic, universally accepted fashion, what is "too far" and what is not. In Latin America, this has not even been the case, really, anywhere, with the possible exception of Costa Rica since 1947.

But there are some grounds for being optimistic in this regard. The persistence in time—as opposed to the actual rooting—of democratic institutions makes it more difficult for them to be overthrown; a return to military rule in countries like Brazil, Chile, or even Venezuela (a more complicated case) seems improbable. There is a virtuous gradualism in this. The discredit of the military, the attachment of broad sectors of society to the democratic paradigm, and the international context make a simple destruction of democratic institutions à la Chile or Guatemala more unlikely than ever.

The new international context is also a deterrent to the refusal of the powerful sectors of society to accept some form of redistribution. Short of conspiring and succeeding in overthrowing the institutions of representative democracy, the privileged instruments of resistance to redistribution are capital flight and and refusal to invest. Greater capital mobility in today's globalized economy would seem to make this a more potent weapon, and one nearly impossible to defend against. At the same time, to the extent that there are signs of a shift in world attitudes regarding the need to reduce inequalities in certain regions, and because there are growing possibilities of achieving new forms of international cooperation—on taxation of assets abroad, for example—that weapon may begin to lose its effectiveness.

Moreover, if other conditions in the world, the region, and a given country are favorable to investment, the exact behavior of certain domestic elites may no longer be as relevant as before. In the same way that speculative capital has flowed in nearly identical proportions to "best students" (such as Mexico, Chile, and Argentina) as it has to macroeconomic basket cases such as Brazil, it is quite possible that if the overall fundamentals are kept sound, foreign investment would continue to flow to nations that pursued a serious redistributive effort, even if domestic investment were to dry up for a time as a form of resistance to that effort.

Finally, there is the "greater evil, lesser evil" dynamic. Important sectors of Latin American elites still believe they have no need to countenance any redistributive intent. Either through ideological windmills such as what is currently called neo-liberalism, and good old-fashioned cynicism, these elites continue to sustain that under no conditions will they accept any reduction in their wealth, income, privilege, and power. But other elite sectors are beginning today, as they did in some nations in aftermath of the Cuban Revolution in the early 1960s, to understand two facts, one of convenience, the other of indifference.

Certain segments of the rich and powerful today realize that their profits are so huge, that the difference between the rates of return on their investments in Latin America and elsewhere are so great, and that the gap between their situation and that of the vast majority of the region's inhabitants is so broad, that there is much room for painless concessions. Accepting higher taxes, paying higher wages, tolerating lower profits is not the end of the world; it might even be a way of making the world somewhat more livable. Other sectors are beginning, once again, to be frightened by the specter of violence, armed uprisings, crime and drug trafficking, and the gaping inequalities from which all of these blights utlimately stem. They are starting—just barely—to acknowledge that, while a revolution along Bolshevik, Chinese, or Cuban lines is no longer a realistic threat, armed chaos and popular fundamentalism is, and whatever the final result of such outbursts might be, in the meantime the current way of life of the wealthy and powerful in Latin America would become untenable.

The vicious cycle of democratization, social pressures, reforms, and the counterreaction to end democracy is precisely what has made democratic rule such a sporadic and unlikely feature of Latin American life. The only way to break the cycle is, of course, to simultaneously attack all its links: make democracy deeper and broader, so that it is more firmly rooted and more difficult to destroy; reduce inequalities as quickly and decisively as possible, so as to defuse social pressures to go "too far"; encourage and implement reforms bold and substantive enough to reduce inequalities and give satisfaction to social demands, yet moderate enough to bring at least part of the business and foreign elite along, all the while neutralizing the military so they do not act on behalf of those who do not go along; at the same time, bring to bear sufficient international cooperation to forestall capital flight or at least obtain some benefit from it, while welcoming foreign investment with tax rates that are higher than before but still lower, given overall rates of return, than in the wealthier and poorer nations.

The increments in leeway or breathing space one obtains through each of these changes and cautious steps enhances maneuverability in the next stage of the cycle: more democracy, in order to channel greater social pressures into more redistribution, thus defusing additional pressures and enabling the continuation of a moderate pace of reforms, consequently allowing the process to maintain allies in the business and international communities. Until the effort is undertaken in this or a similar manner, with a sustained political will to proceed in this direction and with the broad support and skills needed to stick to such a course, we will not know if it is simply a naive aspiration or a realistic blueprint for change.

In this way the vicious cycle can become the beginning of a virtuous dynamic that can make the two terms of our tension self-reinforcing instead of antagonistic. If democracy lasts long enough and is accompanied by at least moderate but sustained economic growth, it can be a fulcrum for redistribution. If so, the institutions and mechanisms that bring about a reduction in inequality will be credited with this success and will enjoy the popularity and backing that comes not only from their intrinsic merits and from the memory of the evils of authoritarian rule, but from a specific improvement in the lives of millions. If democracy and growth coincide, and the former redistributes the fruits of the latter, democratic rule and inequality can be compatible, for a while. If democracy does not coincide with growth and with redistribution, in all likelihood it will not last in Latin America during these last years of our century.

EPILOGUE

AS MEXICO STUMBLED INTO 1995 AND ARGUABLY ITS MOST trying economic, social, and political straits in many decades, three broad interpretations were offered to explain and lighten the nation's travails. The magnitude of the economic contraction that hit the country after the December 1994 devaluation, the concessions President Zedillo made to Washington to ensure the viability of the winter mega-bailout, the social impact of the recession (unemployment, bankruptcies, cuts in public spending), and the relevations of widespread corruption and abuse within the previous administration (ranging from the former president's brother's involvement in the Ruiz Massieu assassination to the mysterious links between the drug cartels and key government officials) all contributed to the need for an overarching analysis of Mexico's dilemmas.

The first explanation emphasized the transitory nature of the critical juncture Mexico was passing through, as well as the inevitably painful nature of any such crossing from authoritarian rule and a closed, presumably quasi-socialist economy to a democratic political system and free markets. The second explanation of Mexico's problems—the "bump-in-the-road" theory—highlighted the word *crisis*: thanks to the economic reforms implemented by former president Carlos Salinas de Gortari, the nation had already negotiated its transition but had hit a series of technical obstacles, which, thanks to a painful but quick adjustment, would be rapidly overcome. The third view, voiced most clearly by the Harvard historian John Womack at a conference on Mexico held at Dartmouth College in the spring of 1995, questioned whether the adrift character of Mexican politics, economic performance, and social limbo had not, in fact, become a status quo of sorts: neither a crisis nor a transition, but a standing state of affairs.

The view that Mexico finds itself in awkward transition from one stage of economic and political development to another is based on the volume and intensity of changes that have occurred in Mexico over the past decade. The liberalization of the country's trade and the reduction of the breadth and scope of the state-owned sector of the economy, the growth of Mexican civil society together with the emergence of the right-of-center PAN as a virtual coparticipant in and viable contender for power, along with the radicalization of the Mexican left associated with the Zapatista rebellion in Chiapas, all point toward change with direction. This theory is also buttressed by the fact that the social pressure for democratization, for a return to economic growth, and for the reduction of inequality cannot be resisted forever.

Whether this transformation is consummated peacefully, promptly, and successfully is a different matter. The pacific character of this hypothetical transition is not quite apparent, given the assassinations of 1994 and the uprising in the Lacandón jungle. Its immediacy remains doubtful, given the decade that has transpired since the economic changes began, and since the 1985 earthquake that many identify as the birth of the new era of Mexican civil society. More doubtful still is the success of the endeavor, in view of the persistent stagnation of the economy, the resistance to change in the political system, and the ongoing passivity of most mainstream Mexican social movements. Lastly, Mexico's transition does seem to lack an agent: the social or political force that can set the course and lead the way.

For a transition to exist, it must at some point come to fruition, whatever its pace or purpose. And for an explanation to have a minimal degree of sense and efficacy, it must provide some criterion by which to judge its adequacy—in this case, whether the transition is actually underway or not. The best face this theory can assume is to insist that while Mexico has not yet found the path to renewed economic growth nor to a political system that allows power to be competed for peacefully and democratically by

political forces representative of most if not all of the nation's inhabitants, and its civil society has yet to achieve the balance between the
"shake-up" the country needs and the social stability it demands,
all of these goals will soon be attained.

The interpretation by crisis—the preferred theory in the United
States—holds that the fundamental modifications of Mexico's economic and political structures have already been achieved. The
fruits of the sacrifices and effort of the past decade can be clearly
discerned above the horizon. This explanation draws a sharp distinction between past Mexican collapses (attributable to the old,
now-dysfunctional economic and political structures) and the
current breakdown, the responsibility for which lies in personal
weaknesses and unforeseeable accidents in an otherwise healthy
environment. From this perspective, the modernization of the
Mexican economy undertaken by Salinas unavoidably entailed an
overhaul of the political system. That restructuring, admittedly slow
and turbulent on occasion, has now evolved toward a relatively
democratic two-party arrangement, with essentially fair elections,
a free press, and the beginnings of the rule of the law.

Proof of these assertions presumably lies in the events of 1995: the
arrest of the former president's brother on charges of murder, the
arrest of the former deputy-attorney general Mario Ruiz Massieu
in the U.S. on charges of corruption and covering up *his* own
brother's assassination, and the PAN's electoral victories in the
Jalisco and Guanajuato gubernatorial elections. Once the economic adjustment is over (probably by early 1996), the economy
will begin to grow briskly and the encouraging signs already visible
today (booming exports, sound public finances, rapid restoration
of confidence) will enable Mexico to return to the high, sustained
rates of economic expansion the country experienced in the 1950s
and 1960s, but on a more solid, lasting foundation. This analytical framework has the intellectual advantage of setting its own
time frame and standards of verification: the economy will or will
not recover soon, alternation at all levels of office will or will not

occur in the near future, Mexican society will or will not achieve a new equilibrium between the apathy of the recent past and the eruptions of more distant years.

But this explanation enormously simplifies Mexico's intractable problems. Moreover, it has been invoked too often in the past. Many, including this author, believe that it will take far more than a trade opening and a few privatizations to return to 6 percent annual growth rates. The evolution of the political system is at best superficial, at worst a perpetuation of the exclusionary nature of Mexican politics, with the PAN and the technocrats taking over where the PRI and the politicians left off. Finally, the challenge of bridging the class, regional, and ethnic gaps in Mexico seems too daunting to simply hope that the market will handle it. Finally, the ticking time bombs of Chiapas, the Colossio, Ruiz Massieu, and Cardinal Posadas murders, and the former government's ties to the drug trade are too unpredictable for such a fragile economy. They can go off at any moment and derail an incipient economic recovery occurring in a precarious international setting.

Conversely, the third theory—that Mexico's current state is neither a transition nor a crisis but rather a period in and of itself, with its own logic and laws, and devoid of a purpose or a foreseeable conclusion—while highly pessimistic or even despairing, is well rooted in the country's history. To begin with, it may well be that after the long cycle of economic growth that began in the 1940s and endured through 1981, Mexico has entered a lasting phase in which its economy faces successive obstacles to expansion. Since 1981, the economy has performed poorly, on occasion suffering through terrible years (1983 and 1995), sporadically enjoying a degree of acceptable, though not spectacular growth (1984 and 1990). But since 1981, Mexico has proved thoroughly unable to string together several years of expansion at the pace it had experienced before, or that Chile, Brazil, and even Argentina had enjoyed in recent years. There is no guarantee that an era of economic stagnation doesn't still lie ahead of us today, just as between the beginning of the revolution in 1910 and the renewal of growth in the early 1940s a full three decades passed before the economy improved.

If one attempts to establish a periodization of Mexican political history, it appears that both intermissions and long stages of continuity were quite prolonged: the instability extending from independence to the advent of the Porfirio Díaz, regime, or Porfiriato, in 1876; the stability of the Porfiriato lasting until the revolution of 1910; the birth of the PRI-inspired political system in 1929, or perhaps more correctly, in 1934, and lasting through the present. There is no basis a priori to expect that the current interregnum—if that is what it truly is—will be particularly short-lived. If it is a stage in itself, there are many reasons for anticipating that it will enjoy a long life of its own.

Lastly, and perhaps most importantly, this third conception rests on the premise that not much will actually happen in Mexico: there will neither be a dramatic improvement in economic, social, or political affairs nor an explosion or breakdown. Things might get worse at certain junctures or in certain areas of the nation, but a predetermined threshold will not be crossed: matters will not spin fully out of control. This is indeed a likely scenario. The country seems reticent about upheaval and drastic change, yet the impediments to improvement are overwhelming. Thus the status quo becomes a state of equilibrium. More precisely, a slowly deteriorating balance is achieved where state power does diminish, but without entirely evaporating into chaos.

The deterioration of state power would be attributed to the one factor this interpretation does not fully address: the collapse of law enforcement and the continuing rise of the drug trade and its barons. Those two processes have gone hand in hand since the mid-1980s, when the infamous Directorate of Federal Security was disbanded. Its multiple successors have proved no more able or willing to succeed in their drug enforcement mission. As the very idea of a federal police was delegitimized, and as local authorities were overcome by corruption and discredited, the lack of effective law enforcement spread well beyond the drug business and into nearly every aspect of daily life. When the economic crisis of 1995 began to bite, its most visible effect on all sectors of Mexican society was the exponential rise in crime. Former policemen, the unemployed, and people in debt all at once began to take advantage of one unquestionable reality: the risk of getting caught in the commission of petty (or not so petty, but unprofessional) felonies was virtually nil.

At the same time, the drug lords were becoming . . . businessmen. As a greater share of U.S. cocaine imports passed through Mexico—a consequence of shutting down other routes, and of more trade between Mexico and the United States, which made the Mexican route safer and more expeditious—and as power passed from the more primitive and violent cartels in Colombia and Bolivia to more business-minded groups, the Mexican drug trade boomed. The need for capital during the Salinas years and the "no-questions-asked" approach to privatization led to the surfacing of purchasers of regional banks—or regional affiliates of national banks—and other enterprises with overnight fortunes. Some were caught, detected, or accused of other misdeeds (the case of Carlos Cabal Peniche, who bought Del Monte Fresh Produce, two banks, and huge spreads of banana and tropical-fruit acreage in Tabasco), but most were not. Whether some form of accommodation between the Salinas administration and the new drug magnates was reached, or whether this will have to occur in the future, is not yet evident. In either case, the Mexican state does not have the power to wage war on the drug cartels, and Mexican society does not have the stomach for it. A tendency toward the unraveling of law enforcement and the sliding under the counter of greater chunks of the Mexican economy are two caveats to the theory that sees the current mess as a lasting phenomenon.

If we set aside the second interpretation—the crisis as accident —hoping it is true but knowing it isn't, several conclusions can be drawn from the other two disquisitions. A protracted transition can abort, and a prolongation of the status quo can feed on itself. Political vacuums are filled everywhere, and in countries like Mexico, with weak political institutions outside the state and huge concentrations of power that arise from unabashed concentrations of wealth, voids are rapidly occupied by the powers that be, by existing political forces. These, needless to say, have little stake in change: they tend to perpetuate their own standing and the situation that has allowed them to conserve their power for decades. So unless the second interpretation described above holds true, and the present difficulties are nothing more than a minor liquidity crisis that has almost already resolved itself, Mexico faces a difficult future due essentially to one fundamental feature of today's imbroglio: the absence of agency for change.

If the first explanation—the crisis as transition—is accurate, it follows that, for an across-the-board transition to be consummated, a constituency for it has to exist and a driving force has to lead it. Neither are truly present in Mexico, although support for the existing political system is thin. Pressure from abroad—an important component in other latitudes—has been limited to economic reform; the demands of an aggrieved opposition have been reduced to electoral reform—a central aspect of any transition, but far from its totality. There has not been a powerful, national figure who has placed himself at the head of any movement for change from above (the Gorbachev formula) nor has an overpowering movement for change from below emerged from the grass roots. What's more, the different factors favoring change in Mexico differ in their motivations for desiring it. The United States and the business community want economic reform along free-market lines, but have expressed little enthusiasm for the profound modifications the Mexican labor movement requires. The PAN undeniably supports democratic change and more honest and accountable government, but devotes scant time to pushing for labor emancipation and democratizing peasant organizations and indigenous communities. The Left wants democracy in most areas of Mexican life, together with redistributive policies, but lacks the strength and the imagination to achieve these goals.

If the third and final theory—the permanent crisis—is deemed valid, it follows that, in order for Mexico to emerge from the doldrums of the status quo, overpowering political force would have to be brought to bear. This is nowhere in sight. The government of Ernesto Zedillo, however decent its intentions, and whatever justifications of passivity it may brandish, does not seem to have the strength to break out of the prison of the present. The opposition similarly lacks the authority, the leadership, and the support for providing the necessary direction. There is no Mandela in Mexico today. And the other forces through society—the church, the military, the business community, the old political elite, the United States—while all indispensable components of any long-term solution, are too fragmented and weak to shoulder the burden individually. As so often in Mexican history, the question of who is the agent of change reigns practically supreme. The surprise answers of the past are nowhere to be seen today. Then again, before they appeared on the scene in the past, they were equally invisible.

What we can do is speculate on who those agents would be, in either of the two hypotheses in question. The nature of the change, or the platform to be implemented, is not dissimilar in both cases. What varies is the driving force behind the hoped-for transformation. The nature of this transformation can be summed up in four broad planks, each one inseparable from the others but autonomous in its conception. I borrow heavily from conversations with Roberto Mangabeira Unger for this summary, as well as from his writings and from the last section of my *Utopia Unarmed.*

The first plank involves the implementation of a productivist economic policy, resting on a long-term alliance between business and government. Instead of seeking either to produce for a protected domestic market (via import-substitution industrialization, or ISI) or for export from a narrow, technologically advanced and competitive sector subject to trade liberalization, this alliance would attempt both to conquer export markets and produce for the "excluded sector" of society. It emphasizes industrialization and high value-added economic activity, but subject to market imperatives and globalization. State intervention in this scheme is unabashed, productivist (not purely redistributive or focused on infrastructure and education, although it emphasizes this), and lasting. Yet it shifts constantly, concentrating on one sector or task and subsequently on others.

The premise behind this approach is that Mexican society, like virtually all societies in Latin America, is divided into two: the modern, middle- and upper-class segment, which has access to markets, employment, capital, and technology and a vast "underclass" of sorts, often equal to more than half the total population, which is deprived of that access. The neoliberal road to development focuses on producing and importing for the advanced sector, on transferring resources, when possible, to the poorest sectors of the underclass, and hoping that time, the market, emigration (in the case of Mexico and a few other countries) and demographics (in other cases) will allow one sector to absorb the other. The productivist intervention approach, based on strategic alliances between business and government, is a quasi-Fordist stance in one specific sense (only superficially paradoxical in a presumably post-Fordist era): it seeks to absorb the underclass through employment, not merely transfers, striving to create jobs by producing goods and services at least partly for the very people employed in their manufacture. This contrasts sharply with the current trend, whereby the consumers for the goods produced by Mexican workers in the modern, often U.S.-, German- or Japanese-owned export plants are U.S., German, or Japanese workers, not Mexicans.

At the same time, the productivist policy is squarely anchored in the export sphere, thus ensuring that domestic manufacturers do not end up producing shoddy wares at exorbitant prices thanks to tariff protection. In opposition to import substitution industrialization, the export market keeps domestic producers honest. In contrast to the neoliberal model, the domestic market plays a central role, and the state conserves and even enhances its place in the economy and in production itself. In this sense, and in this sense only, it is an "East Asian" state.

The fluidity between the two sectors of society and the economy is developed and consolidated by the second plank of this platform, that is, the reform of civil society (see the pages in chapter 5), or what Unger calls the decorporativization of civil society. In Mexico this means, for starters, a complete overhaul of the labor movement. It entails the emergence of democratic unions in industry and agriculture that will defend existing workers' rights as well as the possibility for others to join their ranks, rather than confining the unions' role to protecting acquired advantages at the expense of the rest of society. This also implies a major reform of the media, beyond simply breaking up the existing monopolies, by allowing and encouraging the sectoral and regional media to surface and flourish. It implies government policies and resources to promote the emergence and development of other forms of organization of civil society, including, specifically in Mexico, given the basic features of the country, students, women, and indigenous communities. Finally, this involves a significant process of decentralization, but without ignoring the fact that reducing social, ethnic, and regional inequalities necessarily means redistribution of wealth through a strong central state.

This takes us to the third plank, what Unger would call a democratically sanctioned "hard state," that is, one that can carry out the tasks outlined above, that is sufficiently autonomous from different interests in society to do so freely (like the East Asian states), but that is also (unlike East Asia) democratically accountable and legitimized, in an era and an area where the democratic imperative cannot be dodged. There are precedents, from the French and

German *dirigismes* to the Scandinavia regulatory states. There is also a wide range of instruments available for these purposes, ranging from decentralization of state functions and accountability to users, workers, consumers, local government, and markets to oversight and regulatory mechanisms. Abuse can be avoided by a "hard state"; authoritarian drift can be impeded by reform of civil society and of the state, and by the emphasis on accountability.

The fourth and final plank outlines how all this is going to be financed, and parts from two basic premises. First, without a dramatically higher rate of aggregate savings in Mexico (the 1994 figures, atypical as they may have been, were nonetheless dismal; 15 percent of GDP), the economy will never grow at the pace it needs to reduce the gap between the two sectors and absorb the million odd Mexicans who will arrive on the job market each year. Foreign savings alone, while an indispensable component of the overall effort, cannot make up the difference. But raising private domestic savings, while necessary and feasible within limits, is constrained by extremely low incomes in Mexico (nearly 60 percent of all households receive less than $500 U.S. per month, according to recent market surveys published in the *Miami Herald*). Different strategies, from raising low incomes to enhancing the efficiency of savings schemes (pensions, tax incentives, and so on) are useful, but insufficient.

Thus public savings will have to carry much of the weight; given that there is little leeway left on the spending side, that means, fundamentally, increasing Mexico's abysmally low "tax take," particularly disappointing when one discounts receipts from Pemex, the national oil company. This can be accomplished by means of indirect taxes (more effective, but also more regressive) or by imposing a wealth tax and increasing the income tax on the affluent (more progressive, but more difficult to collect and more prone to evasion). It can also be partly achieved by further tax treaty negotiations with the United States and other countries, whereby Mexican-held assets abroad would be taxed by host countries and the receipts would be shared with Mexico. The exact dose of each remedy—and of many other possible measures—is open to discussion. What seems unquestionable is that the necessary steep rise in domestic savings will have to depend largely on public savings, and these on increasing the overall tax burden.

Who could enact this platform for reform? It depends largely on which explanatory theory of the current debacle one subscribes to. If one accepts the transition perspective and believes that, with sufficient movement from below and from within, Mexico will soon arrive at a final destination of democratic governance, reasonable economic growth, and the initiation of at least a modest redistributive effort, then the logical support for that driving force would be a bold, modern, semicentrist, opposition that was strong enough to bring the entire process to fruition. Since neither the PRI nor the Zedillo administration can become their own opposition, since the PAN is strong but unwilling to fulfill such a task and lacks the social base to attempt it, and since the PRD is too weak and divided among different constituencies to play such a role, it would follow that a new and different opposition force must be constructed. It would have to be made up of nonparty politicians, regional leaders, intellectuals, social activists, and even businessmen, who would join with the disaffected of the PRI and the PRD, along with any unhappy *Panistas.*

This new opposition force would distinguish itself from the government and the PRI in various ways. On economic grounds, the difference would lie in the platform outlined above, instead of the current austerity program and the traditional neoliberal plank; in the political sphere; by the call for broad political reform, as opposed to exclusively electoral improvements. Other important differences would be the emphases on honest government, in contrast to the cover-up (in the best of cases) of the previous administration's misdeeds, on national sovereignty (contrasting its stance with the Zedillo regime's subordination to Washington), and on a social policy that recognizes the need for reducing inequality in addition to combatting poverty. The new force would differentiate itself from the PAN through its accent on social policy, on a new economic approach, and on the overall transformation of the political system and its stance on cultural issues (separation between Church and State, birth control, women's rights, etc) and from the PRD by way of its moderation and its acceptance of a series of constraints on economic and foreign policy (NAFTA, WTO, an open economy, the nonreversibility of the Salinas privatization, and so on).

Conversely, if the interpretation of the present as a new and lasting status quo is considered valid, then a totally distinct agency would seem to be in order. Instead of an opposition to navigate and fuel the transition, a very broad, nearly all-encompassing coalition would appear to be required to break out of a harness that is both tough and lasting. No one political party or movement would appear to be strong enough to achieve the changes necessary to escape such a predicament. President Zedillo himself would have to assemble this coalition, bring the opposition parties, the business community, the grass-roots NGOs, and the intellectuals into a government of national unity, or something to that effect. That government, once established, would subsequently set a timetable for the implementation of a program along the lines laid out above. Once this was accomplished, everyone could go their own way and compete for power under new rules, no longer in a critical context, but in a reinvigorated environment.

The crucial problem facing Mexico today and in the coming months and years may well be that, of the three theories alluded to, the interpretation whereby Mexico's present state is a lasting one is the most probable. Yet, of the two solutions—the construction of a new centrist opposition or the formation of a national unity coalition—suggested for Mexico's travails, the one most likely to surface is that of a new opposition force.

Thus Mexico faces a unique and tragicomic dilemma. It has a probable solution—a viable opposition—to a problem of an entirely different nature: the indefinite prolonging of the current state of chaos. Meanwhile, this terribly acute and pressing problem seems to have no solution at all, as the only agent Mexico has ever had for curing its ills—government, good or bad but always strong —disintegrates in the face of international naïveté and domestic indifference.

A YEAR HAS TRANSPIRED SINCE THE HARDBACK EDITION OF *The Mexican Shock* was published: both an eternity and a fleeting moment in recent Mexican history. Since September 1995, many things have happened in Mexico, but many others have not. The country went through its worst economic collapse since the 1930s, but Mexico's famed social and political stability remained intact. The most dramatic crime wave and onslaught of insecurity since the Revolution of 1910 hit the larger cities, but the calls for a crackdown and law and order went unheeded by those who could respond to them. A sixty-five-year-old political system suffered its most pronounced crisis and deterioration, but neither demands for reform nor warnings of institutional breakdown were satisfied or received widespread backing from the population.

Carlos Salinas de Gortari became the most unpopular ex-president on record, and his brother was accused of murdering their former brother-in-law, José Francisco Ruíz Massieu, and of stashing away upward of 100 million dollars in bank accounts around the world. Yet the former has not been prosecuted or even questioned for any of the myriad felonies for which Mexican public opinion holds him responsible, and the latter has yet to be sentenced for the crime with which he was charged in February of 1995. The three assassinations that rocked the nation in 1993–1994 (of Cardinal Juan José Posadas, Luis Donaldo Colosio, and Ruíz Massieu) are still unsolved in the eyes of most Mexicans. There is every indication that matters will stay as they are.

The opposition has achieved significant electoral victories in several important states such as Jalisco, but substantive political change and even a watered-down version of electoral reform is still pending, and may only take place in a very edulcorated fashion in time for the 1997 congressional elections. The negotiations in Chiapas with the Zapatista rebels are not unlike the ongoing talks in Mexico City on free and fair elections: everyone agrees the dialogue must be pursued, there is a broad consensus regarding the worthiness of the cause, but few are terribly excited either about the outcome itself or its urgency. As long as the process continues, there is little concern about its results, or absence thereof.

Relations with the United States, as President Ernesto Zedillo relies increasingly on the only constituency he has left—Washington, D.C.—are getting more and more difficult for both countries. Emigration from Mexico and the perception of the growth of drug-trafficking from the south have resurfaced as political problems in the United States. The American closing of the border and increasingly intrusive drug-enforcement policies toward Mexico are generating a great deal of unease in Mexico. Yet, in neither country have these issues come to the fore, dominating political or intellectual debate.

In a nutshell, a lot has occurred in Mexico over the past year, but as important are the things that did not happen: neither a significant improvement in the situation through economic recovery or major political change, nor an explosion or social and political meltdown, which in current circumstances might well have been warranted elsewhere or in Mexico at other times. This is why it seemed fitting to devote this postscript to a rapid, broad analysis of the long-term trends in Mexican life that may explain this double paradox, where nothing gets better, but nothing falls apart either. The following pages seek to understand and explain why it is unlikely for Mexico to rediscover the path toward sustained economic growth soon, while maintaining the essence of its stability and political system. By definition, this is a speculative effort; hopefully, it is a useful and accurate one.

WE MUST LOOK BEYOND SHORT-TERM CONCERNS REGARDING electoral reform, an economic upturn, or the credibility of the current government. Mexico's longer-term trends and dilemmas are far more challenging and relevant. One of the reasons Mexico has been stuck in place for nearly twenty years is the excessive concentration on short-term problems and solutions. In fact, the most reasonable prognosis regarding Mexico's mid-term and long-term future may well stem from an understanding of some of the more abstract trends and problems facing the country. These trends run counter to much of the conventional wisdom about Mexico today. They dispel notions both of an imminent social explosion or of an economy poised for growth as the political system is rapidly reformed. They may explain the most notable features of Mexico's likely evolution through the beginning of the next millennium: no breakdown or eruption, no take-off or renewal. It is worth examining two of these trends in some detail.

Perhaps the most worrisome drift in Mexico, for those convinced that its unfinished nation-building process is the root of all its tribulations, consists in a new cleavage that is rapidly cutting across Mexican society. For lack of a better metaphor, the increasingly decisive split separates those Mexicans "plugged in" one way or another to the United States from those who do not enjoy the benefits of that status. The cleavage has in fact existed for many years, but has acquired an impact and extension in recent times that would have been unthought of just a few years ago. While the gulf has existed in Mexico for many years in isolated or sporadic fashion—undoubtedly as far back as the last century—since the Salinas years and the subsequent unraveling of the Mexican miracle it has possibly become the single most significant rift in Mexico's economy, society, and class structure.

It divides Mexicans who are highly sensitive to government macroeconomic policy from those who are indifferent to it. It separates those who believe—rightly—that their destiny is still basically linked to politics and events in Mexico, from those who—just as correctly—understand that the most crucial decisions in their lives are made in Washington, D.C., and New York City, not in Mexico City. It distinguishes between those who are relatively impervious to devaluations of the peso, rises in interest rates and prices, and to austerity packages; and those for whom the price of tortillas, milk, and beans are the most important variables in their lives. It is a cleavage between Mexicans who, in many different ways, are being integrated into global flows of capital, goods and services, and people, and those who remain on the margins of those flows, even if they are not marginal to Mexican society as a whole.

The fracture is not regional, class based, or ideological. Despite a great deal of recent commentary about the North-South divide beginning to sunder Mexico, the cleavage referred to here is much more complex and broadly based. The fate and well-being of vast regions of the Mexican south and east are as directly connected to the United States as Tijuana and Monterrey. It is not a rich-poor cleft; there are myriad Mexican magnates whose wealth and power are totally devoid of any American connection, and there are millions of destitute Mexicans whose meager livelihood depends almost entirely on their association with "*el otro lado*." Finally, it is not a left-right fissure. Aside from the fact that the crack is emerging regardless of opinions in its favor or against it, many on the left see bonds with the United States as powerful levers to transform the country, while many free-market right-wingers in Mexico see American influence in the country as a deadly menace to the nation's mores and morality.

The line-up then is diverse, contradictory, and complex. It is difficult to gauge the relative weight and impact that each side of the cleavage brings to bear in today's Mexico. The first and most numerous contingent of Mexican citizens whose affiliation with the United States distinguishes them from their countrymen and women are, of course, the migrants. Millions of Mexicans, for a few months of the year or for an entire lifetime, work and send money back from the valleys and sweatshops of California and Florida and from the restaurants and flower shops of New York and Chicago.

Quantification is enormously complex; yet some indicators are available. We know, for example, yearly remittances from north to south amount to nearly four billion dollars and the official figures seriously underestimate the total. If the ballpark average of one hundred dollars per month per family is accurate, three-and-a-half to four million Mexican families receive income from abroad. Since most of the migrants are young and either single or just beginning to form their families, the generally used figure of five people per family does not apply. It is still safe to say that upward of ten million Mexicans live directly off remittances sent home by their sons, husbands, or fathers working north of the border. Given that their number has greatly increased since Mexico's economy ceased growing in 1982, the volume of Mexicans dependent on resources from abroad has similarly expanded. What was previously a small minority of people concentrated in the rural areas of central states such as Jalisco, Michoacán, Guanajuato, and Zacatecas, now includes homes from the Mexico City metropolitan area, the western Sierra of Puebla, Oaxaca, Morelos, and Guerrero. It is anyone's guess how the current U.S. crackdown on unauthorized migration will affect this, but it will doubtfully diminish the importance of the resource flow. If anything, the anti-immigrant scare in the United States will enhance the privileged status of those receiving checks and money orders, as departure becomes more strenuous and costly.

The second group that belongs to the "U.S.-side" of the division are the growing number of Mexicans (businessmen, workers, accountants, lawyers, families, etc.) involved in Mexico's rapidly swelling export sector. The numbers have been exaggerated. For example, manufactures represent a larger share of total foreign sales than fifteen years ago partly because the price of oil is less than half what it was in the early eighties. Moreover, the impact of foreign sales on employment is sadly restricted. They are also, and more decisively, increasingly split off from the rest of the country.

The most obvious example of this is the *maquiladora* industry, that is the 2500-odd plants along the border, employing upward of six hundred thousand people. As is well known, virtually all of the *maquiladoras'* inputs are imported, and 100 percent of their output is sold abroad. Practically no backward linkages have been constructed over the years. Though they are allowed to sell part of their wares domestically, they, in fact, ship everything back across the border. Their influence on employment and the local economy is thus modest. What's more, since wages are low—even by Mexican industrial standards—and many of the employees are women or young, single men, the spillovers are limited. Nonetheless, at least two million Mexicans live directly or indirectly off the *maquiladoras*. These are hooked up to the American economy as to a life support system; without the former, the *maquilas* would simply disappear.

But these plants are only a fraction of the booming Mexican export sector. The rest of the Mexican outward-oriented segment of the economy—the automobile industry, steel, the garment trade, cement, mining, glass—is also expanding its sales abroad, also increasing its imported content, and also delivering a growing share of output abroad. Cars provide an excellent example, since the automobile industry is the largest export activity in the country after oil and the *maquiladoras*. In 1995, domestic demand plummeted nearly 70 percent, but exports rose 30 percent; so total sales grew despite the meltdown of the internal market. As more and more vehicles are exported, the volume of imported components grows. The companies, their owners, and their workers are increasingly cut off from the performance of the Mexican economy and are largely indifferent to the fluctuations of the Mexican business cycle. And while overall employment in the industry has remained stagnant since 1989 at around 17,000, it still supports half a million Mexicans whose job security, wages, and benefits are considerably detached from economy policy and macroeconomic indicators in Mexico.

Of the country's largest export firms, a growing number sell more than half their output abroad. They range from General Motors de Mexico, the nation's largest private sector exporter, which even in a strong year such as 1994 sold 30 percent more vehicles abroad than domestically, to Mexico's chief cigarette manufacturers, three quarters of whose total sales are foreign, to multinationals such as IBM and Kodak, as well as to steel mills. Two particularly interesting cases are worth noting. The manufacturer of Corona beer, Mexico's twenty-eighth largest exporter, with foreign sales of more than 150 million dollars, the best network of outlets of virtually any institution in Mexico, now sells nearly one bottle of beer abroad for every one washed down by Mexicans. This is both an indication of its competitiveness and of the shift in its fortunes. The jobs and salaries of the nearly 40,000 workers of this domestic-based firm depend at least as much now on foreign profits as on domestic ones. A similar situation occurs with Cementos Mexicanos (CEMEX), one of the world's largest cement producers. In 1993, a year of virtually no growth in the Mexican economy and of a sharp contraction in the construction industry, CEMEX sold 90 percent of its output abroad, mostly in the United States—an outstanding achievement, but also a telltale sign of the transformations it is undergoing.

Then, of course, there is the tourist trade, practically impermeable to Mexican economy fluctuations, since its prices are almost entirely quoted in dollars. Broad areas of Mexico, such as Cancún, Baja California, Puerto Vallarta, and, to a lesser extent, Mazatlán, Manzanillo, and Ixtapa cater exclusively to foreign (meaning 80 percent American) tourists. They are, in a way, duty-free dollar zones. Most services are purchased through tour operators in the United States, most local stores and restaurants take dollars, and many of the inputs necessary for the tourist trade to function properly, from dish antennas to sparkling water, are imported. The hundred thousand odd inhabitants of Cancún, and the half million Mexicans employed in the tourist industry nationwide are notably insensitive to domestic macroeconomic indicators, and even to noneconomic factors, such as violence, inequality, and political strife. The tourist spots are isolated from the rest of the country, except for the jobs they generate. Sometimes, it is hard to tell if one is really in Mexico.

Finally, there are the countless Mexicans with links to the United States of a more unspecified nature, from the billionaire with apartments in Vail and Manhattan to the drug lords in Sinaloa, Ciudad Juárez, or Tamaulipas who also export all their wares, and import much of their raw goods (cocaine) from South America. They also end up serving time in the United States if they are apprehended. This category equally includes the hundreds of thousands of Mexicans with bank accounts, credit cards, insurance policies, and other assets in the United States, as well as the growing number of professionals who spend part of their time working or studying in the United States (teachers, doctors, dentists, engineers, etc.).

Of all these Mexicans whose lives are increasingly determined by their links with their neighbor to the north, few would want to cross the line permanently, supposing they could. They prefer to stay in Mexico, but they make their living in one way or another through the United States. Their status is not unlike that of the expanding group of Cubans with access to dollars, either through tourism, family in Miami, or sales to foreigners. Their lives are radically different from those of the rest of the island's dwellers, regardless of their awareness of that difference. With time, the interests of the Mexicans in the "U.S.-connected" sphere will displace their traditional affection and concern for Mexico. They are different from other Mexicans because they have a way out. Their income is in dollars; their credit is cheap, if hard to obtain; their inputs— intermediate goods or raw materials, cocaine or tourist revenues, foreign-learned expertise or dollar-denominated loans—come from abroad. They are the modern equivalent of an enclave-based plantation economy: more vast and democratic, with much more substantial trickle-down effects, and far more sustainable in the modern world than commodity production. But they are, unfortunately, a minority, and probably condemned forever to be one.

The key to understanding Mexico's future may well rest in correctly assessing the impact of this minority, which conceivably includes between a fifth and a quarter of the population today. It is numerous and accessible enough to serve as a ballast for the country as a whole. One can hardly imagine a nation-wide social explosion, such as the Mexican revolution of 1910–1917, while such a large and regionally well-distributed, broadly based segment of the population is thriving, and as long as a sizable portion of those outside this realm can rationally expect to attain its benefits in a foreseeable future. At the same time, the country is simply too populated for all those excluded from this cohort to be embraced by it in any reasonable timeframe.

The sheer size of the segment of Mexican society for whom job losses, a devaluation of the currency, a contraction of the domestic economy, or a sharp rise in mortgage, credit card, small business or car loan interest rates are devastating blows, makes this an intrinsically unstable situation. It also insures that the fruits of access to the global economy will be severely restricted. There are simply not enough export firms in Monterrey or low-skill jobs in California to go around. Given the present structure of Mexico's economy, society, and politics, there is no visible method by which to extend the process to a wider share of the nation's inhabitants, much less to all of them or even to a majority. Yet enough are enjoying the gains inherent in these ties to the rest of the world for the status quo to remain more or less indefinitely sustainable. There is no reason why high growth rates and improving wages and employment in the modern sector of the economy, coupled with stable remittances from abroad and adequate revenues from tourism, drugs, and other bilateral exchanges, cannot coexist with a stagnant, traditional, domestic economy. Sporadic and isolated outbursts of rage and despair from the inward-oriented sector of Mexico's society will inevitably continue, but as the Chiapas rebellion demonstrated, these can be contained and managed, as long as they do not occur in too many places at the same time.

The only way to avoid this future of precarious stability in a country divided between those with access to the United States and those deprived of it, would be to found a new political system, in which the fundamental trade-offs, sacrifices, and concessions that different factions of Mexican society would have to make could be carried out. The persistent inability to achieve this goal is the second trend worth analyzing. It explains why the chances of a significant upturn in Mexico's fortunes are not greater than those of a major collapse.

Herein may lie the secret of Mexico's demise over the past twenty years. Mexico has only prospered when the enormous domestic, foreign, historical, regional, and cultural obstacles in the way of its success are subdued by lasting political pacts among its elites that are equally accepted by a large fragment of its population. The political system created in the late 1920s and early 1930s, with all its drawbacks, allowed the country's elites and organized masses to reach partial consensus on economic, social, and foreign policy such that for more than four decades the economy grew at 6 percent yearly. When the time came to reconstruct the obsolete, underlying foundational agreements of the 1930s—obsolete, in part, because of Mexico's success in transforming its own society and economy— the old political system had become dysfunctional.

Pressure from abroad and the ideological abdication of the nation's political, intellectual, and business leaders allowed for formal reforms to take place: trade liberalization, privatizations, a haphazard dismantling of the existing narrow welfare state, the free-trade agreement with the United States. But the political bargains among competing social and regional factions, and the ideological retooling necessary to achieve companies in the country at large, remained elusive. The new pacts indispensable for a resumption of growth, a democratization of Mexican politics without jeopardizing governance, and even a moderate reduction in inequality could not be delivered by the old system. The latter regained a sufficient strength, though, to impede the birth of a new one.

Thus the trade-offs between savings and consumption, between taxes and public spending on the one hand and an efficient private sector on the other, between opening the borders to low-priced and attractive imports for exporters and the middle class and supporting national industry and agriculture in domestic and world markets, between a strong exchange rate encouraging low inflation and a competitive one to promote exports, between decentralizing federal expenditures and redistributing revenues among unequal states, between democratizing the union movement and insuring labor peace, between attracting foreign investment and maintaining a modicum of national autonomy in the design and implementation of economic policy, between proceeding rapidly with modernization and leaving throngs of Mexicans behind. All of these, and many more alternatives, had no political areas or institutional mechanisms in which to be fleshed out and resolved.

Tinkering with the existing political system, improving electoral fairness, curtailing human rights violations and corruption all constituted improvements, but they did not address the basic dilemmas confronting the country: the absence of a mechanism for debating and deciding the fundamental issues facing Mexico. Since new agreements could not be reached, the traditional obstacles to growth and welfare were not overcome, and the country entered a prolonged period of economic stagnation, political involution, and social regression. Every now and then, new ideas were introduced and hailed: free-market policies, a new relationship with the United States, electoral amendments, judicial reform, export growth, and raising domestic savings through pension fund privatizations. It is a symbol of the country's potential and the magnitude of its problems that none of these worked, and yet all were expected to deliver the country from its misery.

Fashioning an entirely new political system, in which new factions and actors can contend for power and solve their differences, is a task that has never come easily for Mexico. Sixty years elapsed from independence to the beginning of the Porfiriato in the nineteenth century. Twenty-five years went by from the coming of the revolution in 1910 to definite continuity in the mid-thirties. At least fifteen years have transpired since the emergence of the current interlude, if one chooses 1982 as its starting date. None of these transitions were negotiated painlessly; all of them entailed costs, though some were obviously less traumatic than others. It appears reasonable to hope that further excruciating passages can be avoided, but it is foolish to expect that the virtual foundation of a new republic can be achieved without turbulence.

Free elections are a keystone of a different political system, but they are just part of it. The rule of law is essential, but inconceivable without an independent judiciary, which in turn cannot be established without imposing an authentic separation of powers. This will be unattainable as long as Mexican civil society is not reinvigorated or liberated from its age-old shackles, allowing industrial workers, indigenous communities, the Church, women, peasants, students, intellectuals, and civic groups to fight for their rights on a level playing field. But, in the modern era, reforming civil society means granting and guaranteeing it access to the media, to the outside world, to every corner of Mexican politics, economic policy, and culture. While these are all procedural transformations which in themselves cannot solve Mexico's problems, they would create the framework where the substantive confrontations and bargains could begin to take place. Allowing this, let alone encouraging it to occur, requires a heightened tolerance of the unavoidable upheaval it entails, both on the part of Mexico's elite and of its neighbor across the river. It also calls for a degree of leadership that Mexico has been sorely missing for many years.

Mexico needs new leadership, from truly different walks of national life, and it will not blossom and flower as long as the old cliques and groups remain in place. This, in a sense, is the heart of Mexico's plight, and the passkey to its future. The creation of a new political system in Mexico calls for exceptional talents, statesmanship, and political skills of compromise and firmness. It demands a grade of sensitivity to the country's illusions and insecurities, and a commitment to honesty and service that those who have governed Mexico for years have sadly lacked. It must be democratic and consented to, but bold and imaginative at the same time. It must be strongly and individually rooted, yet broad enough to incorporate, for a time at least, representatives of all sectors of Mexican society. It would have been extraordinarily fortunate for the country to have discovered such leadership in accidental appointments, such as that of Ernesto Zedillo, or in the traditional ranks of the PRI, as would have been the case with Luis Donaldo Colosio. History, however, seldom grants such favors, and rarely spares societies the effort of seeking vision and direction outside traditional channels. Mexico might still be reprieved, but time, which has always obsessed its people, is not endless.

ENDNOTES

1. Mike Davis, *City of Quartz* (New York: Verso Books, 1991).

2. Ibid., p. 315.

3. Jackie Goldberg, *Comments at the Third Annual California Studies Conference,* California State University, Sacramento, 7 February 1991.

4. Kevin Phillips, *The Politics of Rich and Poor* (New York: Random House, 1990), p. 25.

5. Georges Vernez and David Ronfeldt, "The Current Situation in Mexican Immigration," *Science 251* (8 March 1991), p. 1191.

6. "Current Population Survey Voter Supplement File, 1988, Voter Registration, Voter Turnout and Citizenship by Race and Ethnicity."

7. Goldberg, *Comments at the Third Annual California Studies Conference.*

8. *Los Angeles Times* (10 November 1994), p. B2.

9. Thomas Byrne Edsall and Mary D. Edsall, "The Real Subject Is Race," *Atlantic Monthly* (May 1991), p. 84.

10. Vernez and Ronfeldt, "The Current Situation in Mexican Immigration," p. 1191.

11. Encuesta Nacional de Ingresos y Gastos de los Hogares INEGI, 1984, 1989, 1992; Phillips, *The Politics of Rich and Poor,* p. 17.

12. Carlos Montemayor, *La Jornada* (January 1994).

13. "Version de Propuesta del EZLN para que se inicie el dialogo," *La Jornada* (11 January 1994), p. 10.

14. Rudi Dornbusch and Alejandro Werner, *Mexico: Stabilization, Reform and No Growth* (Cambridge, Mass.: Massachusetts Institute of Technology Press, 1994).

16. *GEA Politico,* No. 103 (20 September 1994), p. 15.

17. *Informe Anual del Banco de mexico* (1993), p. 205.

18. Ibid., p. 13.